The
ILLUSTRATED
CATECHISM

Catholic Belief in Words and Pictures

A REDEMPTORIST PASTORAL PUBLICATION

LIGUORI
PUBLICATIONS

One Liguori Drive
Liguori, MO 63057-9999
(314) 464-2500

Text: Christopher Gaffney, C.SS.R., and
John Trenchard, C.SS.R.

Illustrations: Christopher Higham
Design: Roger Smith

First published in England by
REDEMPTORIST PUBLICATIONS
Alphonsus House, Chawton, Alton, Hants, England

Copyright © 1980 Redemptorist Publications

Nihil Obstat: Terence K. Walsh, S.T.D., D.C.L.
Censor Deputatus
Imprimatur: + Antonius Emery
Episcopus Portus Magni

Arranged by Christopher Farrell, C.SS.R., in accord with *Sharing the Light of Faith,* the National Catechetical Directory for Catholics of the United States.

Copyright © 1980, Liguori Publications
Imprimi Potest: Edmund T. Langton, C.SS.R.
Provincial, St. Louis Province
The Redemptorists
Imprimatur: + John N. Wurm, Ph.D., S.T.D.
Vicar General, Archdiocese of St. Louis

ISBN 0-89243-135-0
Library of Congress Catalog Card Number: 80-84312

FOREWORD

The Illustrated Catechism is the latest in a long line of catechisms which stretches back to the very first days of printing. In its 112 pages the influence of earlier catechisms, such as the Penny Catechism of Britain and the Baltimore Catechism of the United States, is clearly evident. This continuity with the past enables the Catholic readers to feel at home as they explore the great mysteries of the faith. But a modern catechism must not only open up new vistas to the older reader; it must also meet the needs of a new generation. The Illustrated Catechism represents an attempt to meet this challenge by a careful blending of three elements: the catechetical practice of the early Church, the structure of the traditional catechism, and the teaching methods of our own day.

The Early Years: "What we have seen and heard we are telling you so that you too may be in union with us, as we are in union with the Father and with his Son Jesus Christ" (1 John 1:3). In his first letter Saint John focuses our attention on the main concern of the catechesis of the primitive Church: the proclamation of the Word of God. The early catechists were spurred on in their work by the memory of Pentecost Day when people from every nation were filled with the Holy Spirit and began to speak of "the marvels of God" (Acts 2:11). In the first 500 years of the Church's life this same joyful faith was transmitted by an oral explanation of the Creed which, as the works of the Fathers show, was rooted firmly in the Scriptures and enlivened with examples taken from everyday life. By using the same methods adapted to the written Word,

The Illustrated Catechism seeks to hand on this same faith which proclaims Jesus Christ as Lord and rejoices in "the wonderful works of God."

The First Catechisms: Martin Luther was the first to use the invention of printing for religious instruction in the form of a catechism. Its appearance in 1529 did much to strengthen the Protestant movement and led in 1530 to a Catholic response in the form of the Augsburg Catechism. This was followed by a series of counter-reformation catechisms which proved a major factor in safeguarding the purity of doctrine. The Illustrated Catechism draws freely on this great heritage and is inspired by the same vision which led to the publication of the very first Catholic catechisms: namely, to lead those who use it to listen to the Word of God and celebrate that Word in their daily lives.

Modern Educational Techniques: The 20th century has seen great advances in the field of education. Gone are the days when we feel we have only learned well if we have learned painfully. The Illustrated Catechism uses the latest techniques so as to make learning a real pleasure.

All that is best in our catechetical heritage has been assembled in these pages in the fervent hope that all who read this book may, in the words of Saint Peter, "go on growing in the grace and in the knowledge of our Lord and Savior Jesus Christ" (2 Peter 3:18).

INTRODUCTION

A catechism presents the facts about Jesus Christ as witnessed by those who knew him. These facts were outlined by Peter, their leader, who told the crowds in Jerusalem: "It is the God of Abraham, Isaac and Jacob, the God of our ancestors, who has glorified his servant Jesus, the same Jesus you handed over and then disowned in the presence of Pilate after Pilate had decided to release him. It was you who accused the Holy One, the Just One, you who demanded the reprieve of a murderer while you killed the prince of life. God, however, raised him from the dead, and to that fact we are the witnesses" (Acts 3:13-15).

A catechism presents the reflections of the first witnesses and of those who followed them. These reflections, inspired by the Holy Spirit, are contained in the New Testament and in the tradition of the Church. These reflections begin with Saint Peter and, led by men like Saint Augustine, Saint Thomas Aquinas, Cardinal Newman in England, and Saint John Neumann in the United States, continue in every age of the Church to the present day.

The faith of a Catholic is built upon the preaching, the pondering, and the prayer of the Church. Through these activities, "as the centuries succeed one another, the Church constantly moves forward toward the fullness of divine truth until the words of God reach their complete fulfillment in her" (*Divine Revelation*, #8). Through preaching, through pondering, through prayer, the Body of Jesus Christ grows.

What is true of the Church is true of each member of the Church. The Church's first member was Mary. God's word was first preached to her. The angel announced: "Listen! You are to conceive and bear a son, and you must name him Jesus. . . ." Mary pondered this in her heart: "But how can this come about?" And after the preaching and the pondering came her perfect prayer: "Let what you have said be done to me."

Today's Church continues to grow in the same way, as indicated by the following story. That gray day in December 1967 started just like any other day for the workers on the sprawling building site in Brussels, Belgium. The men gathered in little groups around their foremen to hear the orders for the day. Egide van Broeckhoven, a young Jesuit worker-priest, stood with his gang and nodded silently as he and his fellow workers were told to guide some massive metal plates down a ramp and release the clamps holding them to the crane. Minutes later he was dead. One of the supports had given way and the 34-year-old priest was crushed under several tons of steel.

There is little one can say about this young priest's life from a career point of view. He never held any position of authority in the Society of Jesus, never founded anything, controlled anything, or wrote anything but a personal diary. His only desire was to work alongside the dechristianized workers, the "little guys," as he called them. "It is what God is doing in me that is important," he wrote in his diary, "and not what I am doing." When he died, hardly anyone noticed.

This is precisely why we have chosen this sentiment often expressed by Father van Broeckhoven in his diary to introduce this *Catechism*. The very ordinariness of the man reminds us that the deepening of our life and faith has nothing to do with great learning or high rank in the Church. The way of the greatest theologian and the way of the greatest saint must always be to follow in the footsteps of Mary, the humble virgin of Nazareth. We do well to remember that when God revealed himself to her she pondered over this startling event in her heart and immersed herself in a life of prayer.

Our God is a living, loving God who is constantly revealing himself to us as Father, Son, and Holy Spirit. And so, we have had no hesitation in basing the whole structure of this *Catechism* on the way Mary, the Church's first member, responded to God's invitation. Time and time again we will invite you first to consider the Word of God, then, to ponder and pray.

But let us return to Egide van Broeckhoven and his keen awareness of God's constant activity in his life. We ask you now to commit to memory that sentence from his diary: *"It is what God is doing in me that is important and not what I am doing."*

We all know how important it is to remember that God made us to know him, love him, and serve him. Perhaps we forget, however, that life itself springs from God's love and we can only live as we should if we first accept the love God continually offers us. Mary did and so did Father van Broeckhoven. That is why we have made acceptance of God's abiding love our starting point.

CONTENTS

Part I The Christian Vision

This section shows how Jesus Christ revealed himself as Redeemer
by offering us a share in his own life: the life of Father, Son, and Holy Spirit.

Part II The Church

This section shows how the Church is "a people made one with the unity of
the Father, the Son, and the Holy Spirit." The Church was established by Jesus Christ
as a structural community to be an infallible sign of his presence in the world.

Part III The Sacraments

This section presents the seven signs
of Christ's continuing activity in his Church.

BAPTISM

CONFIRMATION

THE EUCHARIST

ORDERS

39 What is a priest?
40 How does the priest act in the person of Christ?

41 How did Jesus Christ institute the sacrament of Orders?

MATRIMONY

42 How is marriage a sacrament?
43 What do we mean when we say that married love is fully human?
44 What do we mean when we say that married love is total?

45 What do we mean when we say that married love is faithful?
46 How is married love fruitful?
47 Is the family the foundation of society?

RECONCILIATION

48 What is the sacrament of Reconciliation?
49 What is meant by change of heart?
50 What is sin?
51 What is God's law?
52 What is the New Law?
53 How do we fulfill God's Law?
54 What Christian value is expressed by the first Beatitude?
55 What Christian value is expressed by the second Beatitude?
56 What Christian value is expressed by the third Beatitude?
57 What Christian value is expressed by the fourth Beatitude?
58 What Christian value is expressed by the fifth Beatitude?

59 What Christian value is expressed by the sixth Beatitude?
60 What Christian value is expressed by the seventh Beatitude?
61 What Christian value is expressed by the eighth Beatitude?
62 How do we use the Beatitudes to examine our conscience?
63 What is conscience?
64 What is confession?
65 How do we confess and what sins are to be confessed?
66 What is meant by satisfaction for sin?
67 What is absolution and what are its effects?
68 What do the words of absolution teach us?

ANOINTING OF THE SICK

69 What is the sacrament of Anointing?
70 What are the effects of the sacrament of Anointing?

71 How is the sacrament of Anointing celebrated?
72 Why must we suffer and die?

Part IV The Dignity of the Christian

This section shows how union with Christ, already perfectly fulfilled in the life of our Lady, inspires the Christian to work for the dignity of all people.

73 What is meant by the resurrection of the body?
74 What is judgment?
75 What is the kingdom of heaven?
76 What is meant by the communion of saints?
77 What is a saint?
78 Why do we honor Mary as the greatest of the saints?

79 How is Mary Mother of the Church the model for all Christians?
80 Are all people modeled in Christ's image?
81 How are Christians to work for the dignity of all people?
82 Do all Christians enjoy an equal dignity?
83 What other ways of life express the dignity of the Christian?

Part V Prayer

This section shows how the Holy Spirit leads the Christian to the Father through Jesus Christ, the center of our faith.

84 Why is prayer necessary?
85 What is prayer?
86 How do we pray?

87 What is the most effective prayer?
88 How does the liturgical year help us to pray?

Supplement

Section A The Church in History
Section B The Church at Prayer

Section C The Law of the Church

1 What is the meaning of life?

Everyone at some time in life asks the question posed in this opening lesson. It is the question asked by great thinkers like Aristotle and, a century later, by the Jewish sage, Ben Sira: "What is man, what purpose does he serve? What is the good in him, and what the bad?" (Ecclesiasticus [Sirach] 18:7)

In body, or flesh, we are at one with creation. But our deeper questionings set us apart from the material universe. The power within us by which we surpass the material universe is called the spirit or soul. In our soul we feel ourselves boundless and summoned to a higher life.

Jesus Christ claimed to answer our deepest questionings. By the Sea of Galilee he told his listeners: "It is the spirit that gives life, the flesh has nothing to offer. The words I have spoken to you are spirit and they are life" (John 6:63). This *Catechism* proclaims the words of Jesus which answer our deepest questionings.

Babies stare. They seem to have eyes only for the outside world, upon which they fix their gaze.

It is not long, of course, before babies are told that "it is rude to stare." But that is not really the reason why they stop staring. The truth is that as children begin to take in the outside world they become more aware, too, of themselves. Eyes which used to be wide open and blank become alive with personality. Their deepening consciousness of the world around them leads to deeper consciousness of self.

Our individual experiences vary a great deal. They are mirrored in our different interests and concerns. But the ultimate reflection remains the same: it is the reflection that we see written in every pair of eyes that are alive and seeing. It is the reflection that every one of us makes at some moment in life, although more intensely at some moments than others. It is the reflection: "Who am I?"

We want to know. The questions are almost instinctive: "Where did I come from? . . . What am I doing? . . . Where am I going? . . ." But although every sane person who ever lived has asked these questions in some form, the answers seem elusive. Still, we wonder!

All the great religions of the past grew out of these questions. Hinduism, for example, sees life as a search for salvation through "release" from the round of birth, death, and rebirth. Like Buddhism and many religions far more ancient than the Christian religion, it exalts the qualities of wisdom and kindness. It tries to answer our fundamental questions by looking at ourselves as persons.

But this was not the way of the Jewish faith. "The eyes of all creatures look to you, O Lord," was the cry of the Hebrew Psalmist. And indeed all the Psalms, which we still pray during every Mass, focus our attention on God. The life of every Jew, as was the life of the Jewish nation, was directed to God as the source and fulfillment of that life.

This, we might say, was the difference, in the ancient world, between the Jews and other peoples. Others tried to answer their deepest questionings by looking at themselves; the Jews were led to realize that they could only be answered by looking at God.

In the modern world this remains the difference between Christians and those around us. Many non-Christians achieve astonishing success in their search for answers to their questions. But most flounder! The multiplication of all kinds of strange beliefs proves the correctness of Chesterton's remark that "when people stop believing in God they don't believe in nothing; they believe in anything."

This *Catechism* will look at God. For we believe that it is only by looking at God as he has shown himself to us that we can begin to answer our deepest questions: Where did I come from? . . . What am I doing? . . . Where am I going? . . .

2 Who was Jesus Christ?

Jesus Christ was born of Mary, wife of Joseph, in Bethlehem about 4 B.C. and worked as a carpenter in Nazareth. About the age of 30 he began preaching in Galilee, building up a reputation as a "rabbi" — a teacher of the Scriptures.

About A.D. 30 Jesus journeyed with his followers down to Jerusalem for the greatest of Jewish feasts, the Passover. The Jewish leaders saw him as a threat to political stability; one of them even said it would be "better for one man to die for the people" (John 11:50). They considered that Jesus deserved to die because he made himself equal to God. And so, on the Cross, Jesus endured the taunts: "If you are the Son of God, save yourself."

Jesus Christ is barely mentioned outside the Gospels. Critics of our faith are quick to seize on this. "If Jesus did all that you claim," they object, "why was his life so little known and why did it end in such humiliation? Surely, an impartial observer must have written *something* about this extraordinary man!"

How, then, did Jesus appear to those who lived with him? If we could travel back in time to ask one of them, "Who is Jesus?" we might get the following information.

"Jesus began his life as a village carpenter. When he first began to preach he seemed to do quite well for himself. Gradually, his reputation spread and he began to be accepted as a man who was successfully trying to purify the old Jewish religion.

"But then he went too far! Priests and people knew that reforms were needed; but when they realized that this man was demanding more than the alteration of a few laws, they became impatient. Eventually, because he claimed to be God, they had him crucified."

Those are the facts! Not much to write about, is there? Unless, of course, the writer believed that Jesus really *was* God! The writers who really did believe this wrote down his life in the Gospels.

It should be clear that if we went back to ask someone who knew him, "Who is Jesus?" the reply would have to be more than "a few facts." We would probably get one of the following statements:

1. "They hanged Jesus of Nazareth on the eve of Passover because he practiced sorcery and was leading Israel astray."

2. "You can all be certain that God has made this Jesus whom you crucified both Lord and Christ."

With which of these statements do you agree? The first is by a Jewish historian who lived at the same time as Christ; the second is by Saint Peter on the day of Pentecost. You obviously cannot agree with both statements because they contradict one another. But you have to agree with one of them. Clearly, there can be no such thing as an "impartial observer" of Christ's life. We *have* to make a choice. As Jesus himself tells us: "He who is not with me is against me."

In other words, no one could just "observe" the life and teaching of Jesus. Everyone who saw him or his disciples was forced to make a judgment. Christ was a mirror to whom people looked and saw their true selves reflected. Some people did not like what they saw, and so they hated him. Jesus himself tells us that he performed works that no one else had ever done, but still "they hated me for no reason."

Others, on the other hand, realized that they were called by him. They realized how desperately they needed him. It was these who gathered around Jesus during his life on earth, and formed the foundation of the Church after his Resurrection.

Beginning on the third day after the crucifixion, and continuing for another 40 days, many of his disciples claimed to see him. The message went around: "The Lord has risen, as he said he would." Jesus, the "carpenter" and "rabbi" came to be recognized as the Son of God. His followers proclaimed: "Jesus Christ is alive."

3 Is Jesus Christ truly alive?

Our witnesses are those to whom God chose to reveal himself as recorded in the Old Testament. The Jews — God's chosen people — were unique among all people on earth. They alone possessed God's true word; they alone worshiped one, personal God. God revealed himself in action, by such events as delivering his people from slavery in Egypt; and in word, by speaking through the prophets, most notably John the Baptizer. God's actions and words in the Old Testament both point to Christ.

Our witnesses are those who knew Jesus and recorded his actions and words in the New Testament. These actions and words point to the truth that Jesus was everything that he claimed.

Our witnesses are those who continue the actions and words of Jesus since his bodily departure from this earth. Christ's actions and words are continued most especially in the sacraments and in the solemn teaching of the Church. Both deepen our realization that Christ did truly rise from the dead.

No one actually saw Jesus Christ rise from the dead. Only the soldiers who guarded the tomb were there at the time. But they were more preoccupied with preventing his followers from stealing the body away. And so, having made the tomb secure, they were looking the other way.

"If Christ has not been raised then our preaching is useless and your believing it is useless" (1 Corinthians 15:14). Saint Paul's blunt statement confronts us with the plain truth: if Christ did not rise from the dead we are wasting our time; worse, indeed, we are living a lie.

Can we be sure that we are not fooling ourselves? We claim to follow the risen Christ. More, we believe that we are living with the very same life with which Jesus now lives. But there are moments (which sometimes extend to several years) when he seems remote — even dead! And the thought must occur to us that we have never actually *seen* him. His only bodily appearances were to a few disciples in the days following his Resurrection until, as Saint Luke tells us, he was "carried up to heaven."

Jesus Christ no longer appears to us bodily and in his risen glory. Many Christians, of course, wish he would! They think it would solve all their problems, transforming a life of doubts into a life of certainty. They forget, of course, that even if they were to see the risen Lord, they would hardly believe the evidence of their eyes. Christ himself reminded the people that they would "not be convinced even if someone should rise from the dead" (Luke 16:31).

All Christians must find themselves asking, at some time or another, whether Jesus really *did* rise from the dead and now lives. The question penetrates to the core of our faith. Christ claimed to be the center of history, to have transformed the universe, to have the power, even, to change us; he claimed to answer our deepest questionings. But these claims all rest squarely on the truth that he rose from the dead: that he is *alive*.

How can we be sure that he *is* truly alive? How can we meet the Lord whom we cannot see?

The truth is that the risen Lord meets us at a far deeper level than our sight. Many of those who lived and worked with Jesus *saw* him, but they did not *recognize* him. We, like them, recognize Jesus and learn to know him, not with our eyes but with our minds and hearts. The Lord who answers our deepest questionings penetrates us at the deepest level. Our hearts and minds must be open to receive him.

We have already emphasized the supreme importance of an open *heart:* that acceptance of God's abiding love in prayer is our starting point in the faith. But we also need an open *mind.* The witnesses mentioned in the illustrations are for us sources of our knowledge of God and of his love for us. As we increase our knowledge of these sources, our minds can only be enlarged by God's very presence — Christ's risen life given that we, too, may truly live.

4 What did Jesus Christ reveal to us?

Jesus made three great claims. By listening to these statements about him we build up a full picture of Christ. And so we learn to understand the answers to our deepest questionings.

Jesus claimed that God was his Father. His first recorded words were in the Temple in Jerusalem to his parents who had spent three days looking for him: "Did you not know that I must be busy with my Father's affairs?" (Luke 2:49)

Jesus claimed to be the Son of God. In the Temple precincts he said: "The Father and I are one" (John 10:30). The people tried to stone him for blasphemy.

Jesus claimed that he came to make us children of God. At the Last Supper with his disciples we hear Jesus' final prayer to his Father: "I have made your name known to them and will continue to make it known, so that the love with which you loved me may be in them, and so that I may be in them" (John 17:26).

Saint Thomas Aquinas, echoing the Greek philosopher Aristotle, used to say that true happiness comes when the mind reaches truth. Now perhaps it sounds a little farfetched to say that we are all searching for truth, since few of us are tempted to bury ourselves in books or set out like a pilgrim on some amazing voyage of discovery.

But let's be clear in our minds from the outset about this. Everyday life brings with it all sorts of experiences which touch us in different ways. Some bring us happiness, some cause us pain; and yet, all of them force us gradually into making some concrete decision about the true meaning of life. There is something of the Pilate in all of us which longs for an answer to the question, "What is truth?"

The Church confidently tells the world that there is an answer to this eternal riddle. This is a very big claim indeed, and it is hardly surprising that many turn to the Church to hear what she has to say. Very often, however, they are disappointed. These are the people — and we are all tempted to join them — who are looking for a pat answer, an answer which can be written down in black and white and be immediately understood and digested.

But the Church will have none of this. She simply points to Jesus Christ and reminds the world that he said, "I am the Way, the Truth, and the Life." There is no beating about the bush on this point. The Church simply says in so many words, "If you want to grasp the truth, the meaning of life, then you must get to know Jesus Christ well!"

That is why we begin by focusing our attention on Christ. To date, we have made two statements about him.
1. That he really did exist. (Lesson 2)
2. That after his death he rose from the dead, and is still alive. (Lesson 3)
Now, we continue to build up a fuller picture of Jesus by introducing our readers to three great claims that he made about himself:
A. that God was his Father;
B. that he was the Son of God;
C. that he could make us children of God.

These are three quite amazing statements for anyone to make. But don't let us be too nervous or overwhelmed to go deeper into the matter. When Jesus revealed these things about himself he was talking to ordinary people like Peter and James. He was sowing the seeds of the truth and promised them that he would send the Holy Spirit to cause these seeds to blossom in people, like the tiny mustard seed that grows into a towering tree.

The promise still stands. Jesus continues to sow the seeds once more in our hearts. Now, with the help of the Holy Spirit, they will help us to grow in understanding and happiness.

The Father reveals himself in creation. Jesus told his disciples: "Think of the flowers growing in the fields; they never have to work or spin; yet I assure you that not even Solomon in all his regalia was robed like one of these. Now if that is how God clothes the grass in the field . . . will he not much more look after you, you men of little faith?" (Matthew 6:28-30)

"I have always been fascinated," writes Alan Watts in his book *The Wisdom of Insecurity,* "by the law of reversed effort. Sometimes I call it the backwards law. When you try to stay on the surface of the water, you sink; but when you try to sink you float."

When we come to consider the Christian vision of God, it is very important to remember this law of reversed effort. We have to learn to "let go" of our preconceived ideas of God. Those who first heard Jesus speak of a new vision of God found this very difficult indeed. In the end it was the closed minds of those who clung to their religious traditions, their old rocks and securities, who sent him to his death with hardly a hearing.

The three short years of his public ministry, however, were time enough for Jesus to coax his followers into a complete revolution in their customary ways of thinking about life and God. He encouraged them to open their minds and "let go." To those who were trying to understand the mystery of life by grasping and hanging on to it he said, "Anyone who finds his life will lose it; anyone who loses his life for my sake will find it" (Matthew 10:39). And to those who wanted to hold on to him as a triumphant Messiah: "Unless a wheat grain falls on the ground and dies, it remains only a single grain; but if it dies, it yields a rich harvest" (John 12:24).

It is important in our approach to God that we follow the directions indicated by Jesus.

This means there are two points we should always keep in mind:
1. We must put aside our preconceived notions of God and approach him with an open mind.
2. We must try hard to understand the paradox that to experience God one must not grasp him but, rather, let him go.

This does not mean, however, that our approach to God is mindless and irrational. One of the greatest achievements of the medieval theologians, particularly Saint Thomas Aquinas, was to construct a series of arguments from reason to demonstrate the existence of a superior Being. The kernel of the argument, which Saint Thomas built up in five different ways, was that the world needs a cause other than itself and that this cause must be self-sufficient.

Unfortunately, we can do no more in this *Catechism* than boldly state that from the standpoint of reason the conclusion that God exists is unavoidable. We are concerned here to look more closely through the eyes of faith at God as *Revealer.* This is the One whom Jesus called Father. This is our Father who reveals himself in creation and in the Old Testament — and fully in Jesus Christ.

And that is why it is so important that we approach this mystery in a particular frame of mind. It needs a mind that is open and ready to plunge into the unknown. It means taking a great risk. After all, Jesus did say, "Anyone who loses his life for my sake will find it."

The Father reveals himself through the men and women of the Old Testament. Other people depended on creation alone for their knowledge of God. This led to false ideas so that people often ended up in worshiping creation itself. But God led the Hebrew people to a unique intimacy. This special revelation began, it may be said, with the call of Moses (about 1250 B.C.) when God revealed his name: "I Am who I Am" (Exodus 3:14).

The Father reveals himself fully in Jesus Christ. The apostle Philip said to Jesus: "Lord, let us see the Father, and then we shall be satisfied." And Jesus replied: "To have seen me is to have seen the Father" (John 14:8-9).

God's work of creation is described in the first two chapters of Genesis.
This Old Testament book tells us that God created the world by the power of his word. Man was the summit of his creation: "God created man in the image of himself" (Genesis 1:27).

"4004 B.C." is not the title of a new science-fiction epic. It is the date worked out by Archbishop James Ussher for the beginning of the universe. He established the year (and, indeed, the month!) by working back from Christ's birth, using only the information given him in the Bible.

It would be wrong to ridicule the bishop's efforts. He worked at a time when the Bible was regarded as man's primary source of information in every field of knowledge from archaeology to zoology. But the Bible does not set out to reveal such information. The Bible has only one purpose, and one alone. It reveals God's love for man. In a word, it tells us about "salvation."

This truth is evident in the story of creation. It comes right at the beginning of the Old Testament, although it was certainly not the first part of the Bible written down. Every single word of the account is true. It is true because it tells us the truth about salvation. But it tells the truth in a way that belongs to an age and culture totally different to our own.

If we want a crystal-clear expression of creation in words adapted to our own mentality, we would undoubtedly prefer the statement of the Fourth Lateran Council (A.D. 1215) which tells us: "The one true God, from the very beginning of time, made from nothing creatures — both spiritual and corporeal — that is, angels and material things, and finally human creatures, a blend as it were of both spirit and flesh."

Compare that expression with the more familiar statement written two thousand years earlier in Genesis: "God fashioned man of dust from the soil. Then he breathed into his nostrils a breath of life, and thus man became a living being" (Genesis 2:7).

Does that statement from Genesis mean that God modeled man from clay and then gave it the "kiss of life"? No, the Church tells us, that was not the writer's intention — any more than it was his intention to suggest that the universe was created within the week.

His intention was to state that man received his life from God, indeed, shared his life with God. That tells us something about our "salvation" — and far more powerfully, surely, than the expression of the Fourth Lateran Council! Saint John was later to use the same image when he described how Jesus appeared to the apostles after his Resurrection and "breathed on them, saying: 'Receive the Holy Spirit.'" In this way, Christ gave us new life.

Every single word of the Bible is true. But of every single word of the Bible, in order to penetrate to the truth, the Church has to ask the question: *"What did the writer intend to convey to the people of his own day?"* That question is not always easily answered. But it is a question which the Church continues to try to answer, so that we can more fully understand the full story of God's creative love.

The Scriptures talk of God's work of creation in "a symbolical way, well suited to the understanding of a primitive people" (Pope Pius XII). They cannot be interpreted by modern standards of historical composition. The work of science, then, in no way contradicts the Scriptures: "for the same God gives revelation and reason; one truth cannot contradict the other" (Vatican I, 1870).

Genesis emphasizes certain truths. Inspired by God, the sacred writer teaches that all God's creation is good; that man was created in full friendship of God; and "was appointed by him as master of all earthly creatures that he might subdue them and use them to God's glory" (*The Church Today*, #12).

God did not create evil. Our first parents in their origins were created in a state of knowing God. But they freely chose evil. As a result, the state of "knowing God" was lost: our nature as created by God was disturbed. This fallen nature was transmitted by way of generation to all people. The first sin — original sin — is described in a symbolic way in Genesis 3.

The guilt and effects of this unique "original" sin remain as the initial reason for sin in the world. In personal sin, for which each individual is actually responsible (actual sin), we freely follow our inclinations toward evil. This sin is symbolically described in the story of the tower of Babel (Genesis 11).

The Scriptures and tradition tell us far more of restoration and redemption than of original integrity and original sin. "However great the number of sins committed, grace was even greater" (Romans 5:20). In the story of Noah, for example, the rainbow becomes a sign of God's promise of restoration (Genesis 9).

"Whatever else is true of man, man is not what he was meant to be." Chesterton's remark reflects our own experience. We seem to have all the ingredients for happiness. But the power of evil within us and outside us seems to triumph. Our hearts are restless, sometimes broken. "Our hearts were made for you, O God, and they will know no rest until they rest in you" was how Saint Augustine put it.

Unhappiness and evil in the world are definite problems. If the world was created by God who is infinitely good, how did evil come to reign so powerfully?

Our question was asked — and answered — under the inspiration of the Holy Spirit by the writer of Genesis. The story of Adam and Eve and how they fell from God's grace is familiar to us all. But as we have seen, the Church has to answer the question: "What did the writer of the story intend to convey to the people of his own day?" And the Church, of course, enjoys the assistance of the same Holy Spirit who inspired the writer.

The Church's answer is in the doctrine of "original sin," a term which was first used by one of her greatest teachers, Saint Augustine, in the fifth century. The outline of this teaching is given in the illustrations. The Church tells us that our first parents were made to know God but rebelled against him. By their own sin they became separated from God and from one another. All people, with the exception of Mary, share this sin when they are conceived and born into the world.

It would be foolish to pretend that the story of the Fall is fully understood. Pope Paul VI asked those who study the Scriptures to present the teaching of "original sin" in a more modern way which "answers the demands of faith as expressed by men of our day."

How, for example, is the Church to explain what life was like before original sin? The writer of Genesis shows Adam talking with God as "he walked in the garden in the cool of the day." Saint Augustine explained to his contemporaries that in the state of "original justice" the body was submissive to the soul. The findings of science do not demand that we abandon these explanations of our original condition in which God revealed himself and humankind was without sin.

The findings of science show, for example, our physical evolution as a gradual process. There is no reason why we should not also see our spiritual development as a gradual process; as our mind physically grew so also did its capacity to receive the all-powerful God. Our nature, which thus consisted of a body dominated by the soul, was destroyed by sin.

"O happy fault," the Church exults on Easter night, "O necessary sin of Adam, which gained for us so great a Redeemer!"

8 How was the Father's friendship restored?

God's work of restoring creation was a very gradual process. It was achieved through the Jewish people and was recorded in the writings of the Old Testament. The Exodus, in which the Jews escaped from the Egyptians through the Red Sea to be given the Ten Commandments by God on Mount Sinai, always remained the formative event in their lives and memories. Each year every Jewish family relived the event in the Passover meal.

"Sticks and stones may break my bones but words will never hurt me!" Not very many of us can say this of ourselves and really mean it. We know from experience that the spoken word is very powerful indeed.

Words can bring us happiness or extreme dejection. Try for a moment to recall just one occasion in your life when you perhaps overheard someone criticize you or were on the receiving end of a verbal lashing. The effect was probably devastating, and it is an experience we all dread. On the other hand, just one word of encouragement or praise is all most of us need to face and overcome any amount of hardship in our lives.

The Jews believed that a word was far more than just a sound emitted by the mouth. "The spoken word to the Hebrew," writes Professor John Paterson, "was fearfully alive. . . . It was a unit of energy charged with power." To the Jew a word was so alive that it actually did things. Now just think again about those critical words that were aimed in your direction and you will begin to understand the Jewish mind. Were they not like viruses which slowly wormed their way into you and really upset you?

When we remember this Jewish idea that words can actually do things, a new way of looking at the Bible opens up before us. We begin to see the Bible as a conversation between the Father and humankind. It is God who begins the conversation, and at his word creation springs into being. "God said, 'Let there be light,' and there was light. . . . God said, 'Let us make man in our own image, in the likeness of ourselves' . . . and so it was" (Genesis 1).

Perhaps we can see now what we mean when we say that God's word is *creative*. And every page of the Bible adds to the splendor of this teaching by reminding us that God is love. His words are the very opposite to those virus-type words which gradually destroy us. They are words of love in which he gives himself, shares his secrets, and reveals himself to those who listen.

As the Bible story unfolds, however, we see people turning a deaf ear to God's word. There is no reply of thanksgiving, no worship. But the Father keeps on talking, keeps on offering his love. It is his creative word which gradually forms the Jewish people into a worship community, a community fit to receive into its midst the One who alone can make an adequate reply to God's words of love: Jesus Christ, the Word made flesh, the true worshiper.

How, then, was creation restored? In the same way in which it came into being — by God's word. "At various times in the past and in various different ways, God spoke to our ancestors through the prophets; but in our own time, the last days, he has *spoken* to us through his Son" (Hebrews 1:1-3).

The various stages of Jewish history are reflected in the preaching of the prophets such as Isaiah, Jeremiah, Amos. Sometimes they condemn. Sometimes they coax. But always they speak in God's name, leading his people to love the one living and true God.

This love reaches its highest point in the Old Testament in the poetic literature, especially the Psalms. These hymns of worship reflected the Jewish longing for God and prepared them for the coming of Christ.

9 Is Jesus Christ the Son of God?

Jesus Christ fulfills the promise of the Old Testament. The history, the prophecies, and the worship of the Jewish people are explained in the life and teaching of Jesus Christ. "He cured all who were sick. This was to fulfill the prophecy of Isaiah: 'He took our sicknesses away and carried our diseases for us'" (Matthew 8:17).

The words and miracles of Jesus confirm that Jesus is truly the Son of God. The crowning sign was his exaltation when the Father lifted up Jesus to himself. Our friendship with God was restored. All people, when united with Christ, could now worship the Father perfectly.

At first in the Church the truth that Jesus was God was never denied. In the Arian heresy, however, many Christians — including bishops — maintained that Jesus was half human, half divine. The true teaching was expressed in the Council of Nicaea (A.D. 325): "I believe in one Lord Jesus Christ . . . of one being with the Father." The Arians failed largely through the efforts of Saint Athanasius.

"Truly this man was the Son of God." This confession of faith by the Roman centurion as he watched Jesus die was the last of several similar expressions repeated during the life of Jesus. It is certain that many people who met Jesus, including the centurion, recognized him as being very close to God. But it is equally certain that until Jesus had risen from the dead no one recognized him as God himself.

When we say that Jesus is the Son of God, we mean that Jesus *is* God. This is the central claim of Jesus' life and our belief. It is the truth which underlies every word written in this *Catechism*. Perhaps we may be drawn only rarely to confess: "Truly, Jesus is the Son of God." But the fact remains that in every single expression of our faith, that is *the* truth which, if not explicitly uttered, is nonetheless taken for granted.

And here, perhaps, we are faced with a problem — just as the Church was faced with a problem in her early days. When we begin to take something for granted there is a danger that we will eventually forget about it altogether. In Lesson 4 we saw how Jesus claimed to be the Son of God. Although Jesus' claim is really the subject of every question in this *Catechism,* we will briefly look now at how the Church came to the explicit understanding of this truth.

For it is undoubtedly true that the Church did begin to take the truth for granted — with disastrous consequences! For a time, the greater number of bishops in the Church "forgot" that Jesus was God. More, they denied it!

This was not, of course, while the apostles were still alive nor immediately after their death, when the full impact of Christ's words was still felt. The trouble came when the Christian faith began to make itself "respectable" and efforts were made to make it "reasonable."

The man immediately responsible for what was probably the most dangerous heresy in the Church's history was Arius (256-336), a priest of Alexandria. He taught that because the Godhead is unique it cannot be shared or communicated, so that the Son cannot be God. When Jesus was called God, in other words, he was being given only a courtesy title. So widespread did this heresy become that the Emperor Constantine's son, Constantius, confronted Pope Liberius with the question: "Who are you to stand up against the whole world?"

The "whole world" wrestled with the problem of the Blessed Trinity; and, not surprisingly, got it wrong! The truth was crucified as it had been 300 years earlier. And only very few lone figures in the Church came forward to uphold Catholic belief.

We recall that belief every Sunday in the Nicene Creed which was formulated to combat the Arian heresy. The Creed remains an explicit reminder that Jesus is the Son of God. That is the truth which we can never afford to take for granted or forget.

10 Is Jesus Christ truly man?

Jesus Christ, the Son of God, was "born of a woman" (Galatians 4:4). His mother was Mary, a "virgin betrothed to a man named Joseph" (Luke 1:27). Mary conceived by the power of the Holy Spirit to become "Mother of God." Jesus, in other words, "is equal to the Father according to his divinity, less than the Father according to his humanity" (*Credo of the People of God,* Paul VI).

Very quickly some began to deny that Jesus was truly man. The Docetists (from the Greek verb, "to seem") claimed that Jesus only "seemed" like a man and was in reality only a walking spirit, like a ghost, and that he did not really suffer in the same way as we suffer.

Read the following two statements carefully:

"I said that you are a liar, it is true, and I am sorry for it."

"I said that you are a liar. It is true. And I am sorry for it."

The first statement is an apology; the second is an accusation. They *mean* totally different things, yet the difference arises simply from the punctuation.

"What do you *mean*?" is a question we often ask. The same words can have quite different meanings. And this is why, over the centuries, the Church has tried to make the *meaning* of Christ's teaching as clear as possible. The process has always been (and continues to be) a difficult one; yet it has helped us to understand our faith more deeply.

In Lesson 9 we saw how some tried to change the meaning of the Church's belief that Jesus is God. "Jesus is only God in *name,*" the Arians claimed. "No," the Church replied, "Jesus is God in *nature.* . . . He is one *in substance* with the Father."

That great struggle for true doctrine was hardly over before others began to question the sense in which Jesus was truly man. This, in fact, was a question which began among the first generation of Christians (see *illustrations*), who maintained that human flesh was evil and so God could not have assumed a human nature. By the fifth century, however, the problem had taken on quite a different and more difficult character.

Under the Patriarch Nestorius (381-451), some Christians, while continuing to accept that "Jesus Christ is true God and true man," explained this by saying Jesus had a "dual" personality. The consequences of such a teaching are far-reaching. It meant that God and man were *not* actually united in Christ. The two natures were *close,* yes, but not *united* in one person.

The truth is totally different. Jesus did not simply bring God and people *close* together. He actually *united* them. As the priest says in every Mass: "By the mystery of this water and wine may we come to share in the divinity of Christ, who humbled himself to share in our humanity." Just as the water is united with the wine, so is the divine nature united with human nature in Jesus Christ.

How did the Church express this vital truth? Toward A.D. 100 Saint John told us: "The Word was made flesh." Toward A.D. 200 Saint Irenaeus told us: "In Jesus the blending and communion of God and man took place according to the good pleasure of the Father . . . in order that man, having embraced the Spirit of God, might pass into the glory of the Father."

In 431, however, the Church stated the truth in a new and startling way. She simply declared Mary to be "Mother of God." The union of divine and human natures in the person of Jesus. Christ was such that because Mary was "Mother of Jesus" she was "Mother of God." The Church's *meaning,* at last, was clear!

It was partly to combat such errors that Saint John wrote his Gospel toward the end of his life (about A.D. 95). "In the beginning was the Word," he wrote, "and the Word was made flesh." John accompanies this most sublime summary of our faith with its most important instruction: from the lips of Jesus' Mother at Cana, we are told, "Do whatever he tells you."

11 How does Jesus make us children of God?

Jesus is the Son of God. And he makes us children of God by uniting us to himself. He does this by offering us his Spirit who gave him his own power. Before Jesus began his work, Luke tells us: "Filled with the Holy Spirit, Jesus left the Jordan and was led by the Spirit through the wilderness" (Luke 4:1).

In the public ministry of Jesus we can only glimpse the Holy Spirit. The true power of the Spirit was fully revealed only when Jesus rose from the dead. Jesus' miracles — when, for example, he brought the dead Lazarus from the tomb — prepare us for the outpouring of the Holy Spirit on all humankind after the Resurrection.

Am I a "picture" person or a "drama" person? This is the question the American writer Raymond Nogar feels all of us should ask before we ever turn our attention to the doctrine of the Trinity.

He describes a "picture" person as someone who prefers to view the Gospel from a safe distance, as one would view Michelangelo's magnificent paintings on the ceiling of the Sistine Chapel in Rome. The "drama" person, on the other hand, is no mere spectator. He is caught up personally in the drama of Jesus' death and Resurrection just as a whole audience can become completely engrossed in a play or film.

True Christians are "drama" persons. They are not content to be mere spectators but desperately want to be caught up and involved in the life of God. So when Jesus tells us of a Father, Son, and Holy Spirit within the Godhead, we must be careful not to brush aside the implications of all this as mere abstract theology. If we believe in God and want to be involved with him, it is only natural that we should want to know everything we can about him. "Nothing," writes Frank Sheed, "could be less abstract than *the* reason for everything, nothing more relevant."

We have spent some time examining how Jesus gradually unveiled the mystery of God to his followers. Just what it meant to them when he spoke of a Father and Son within the Godhead, two Persons each knowing and loving himself for himself, we do not know. Probably they could not make head or tail of it. But in Matthew's account of this revelation (11:25-30) we are told how after it Jesus himself gave us some indication of just what involvement with God would mean for us. "Come to me, all you who labor and are overburdened, and I will give you rest."

Jesus repeatedly told his followers that he had come from the Father to bring the world to the Father. And here we have his invitation to become "drama" persons: to allow ourselves to be drawn into the love which he and the Father share.

When Christ began to speak of this love, his disciples were in for yet another surprise. He told them of a third Person in the Godhead whom he called the Spirit. This is the Holy Spirit whom the Church in her ordinary teaching, in her creeds, and in her solemn declarations — such as the First Council of Constantinople in 381 — describes as the Love which proceeds from the Father and the Son.

This love is a distinct Person who draws us into the very life of God. This is the Love who overshadowed Mary. And this is the Love who overshadows the Church, making us into "other Christs," children of the Father. "If anyone loves me," Jesus said, "my Father will love him and we shall come to him and make our home with him" (John 14:23). This is what it means to be children of God. This is why we are all able to shoulder the burden of Christ himself and find it easy and light.

It is through faith, the gift of the Holy Spirit, that we become the children of God. Jesus could only work where there was faith. To the woman who said to herself. "If I can touch even his clothes . . . I shall be well again," Jesus said that her faith had restored her to health (see Mark 5:25-34).

Faith is a gift of the Father. To the Jews, Jesus said: "No one can come to me unless he is drawn by the Father who sent me" (John 6:44). As a sign of this gift Jesus opened the eyes of the man born blind from birth: "Jesus spat on the ground, made a paste with the spittle and put this over the eyes of the blind man" (John 9:6).

Faith is one of those key words which so often creep into the everyday conversation of Catholics. Non-Christian bystanders, unaware that so humble a word seeks to describe the deepest of human experiences, are often surprised at the emotion it arouses.

The obvious dismay which greets the news that Tom has "lost" his faith is as much a puzzle to unbelievers as the spirited rejoicing over someone who has "found" faith. But, whatever else they may think, they are left in no doubt that this thing called faith is something highly valued by their Catholic friends. After all, only something one treasures can be lost in sadness and found in joy.

We certainly value our faith; and possibly that is why, for most of the time, we take it so much for granted. It is like an old coat that fits so snugly we hardly notice it. But, in much the same way as old coats tend to suddenly give way at the seams, life often takes us unawares. We find ourselves in new and changing situations which force us to ask such questions as, "Do I have faith?" and, not least, "What is faith?"

It was just such a changing situation which forced the first disciples of Jesus to question their attitude toward him. His torturous and degrading death on the Cross plunged them into despair. "Our own hope," the two disciples told the mysterious stranger on the road to Emmaus, "had been that he would be the one to set Israel free" (Luke 24:21). Their now fading hope echoed the intense devotion of Peter, who in happier days had defiantly asked, "Lord, who shall we go to? You have the message of eternal life" (John 6:68). But that life had been cruelly extinguished. Or had it?

The gift of faith unites us with Christ. Jesus then said to the blind man: "Go and wash in the Pool of Siloam." Through this washing the man received the sight to see Christ. He said: "'Lord, I believe,' and worshiped him" (John 9:38).

Somewhere on the road to Emmaus the stranger stopped and, in speaking to the two men, addressed himself to the whole world. "You foolish men! So slow to believe the full message of the prophets!" (Luke 24:25) Then he began to explain the Scriptures and, almost imperceptibly, they found welling up within them their former attitude of hope and confidence in Jesus. This attitude we call *faith*.

What, then, is faith? It is the stupendous divine gift which enables us to recognize the risen Lord in the face of the stranger of Emmaus. It is to recognize that nowhere in this wide world can we find more truth than in his words. In the attitude of faith our whole being — intellect and emotions — is impelled to join Peter in his confident assertion, "Lord, who shall we go to? You have the message of eternal life."

Our union with Christ enables us to profess the truth. We can profess our faith only when we have received God's Spirit. As Jesus tells us: "I shall ask the Father, and he will give you another Advocate to be with you for ever, the Spirit of truth" (John 14:16). And so when the man born blind recognized Jesus he professed his faith to the Pharisees: "If this man were not from God, he couldn't do a thing" (John 9:32).

Faith prompts us to follow Christ. Many recognize the wisdom of his words and perfection of his life. As Jesus began his public ministry the impression he made on men, such as Simon and Andrew, was so deep that they left their nets and "followed" him.

"Every person," writes Bishop Fulton Sheen, "carries with him a blueprint of the person he loves." And we know exactly what he means.

It is, perhaps, one of the more puzzling quirks of our human nature which leads us on occasion to take an instant like or dislike to someone on first meeting. "A tiny architect," muses Bishop Sheen, "works inside the human heart drawing sketches of the ideal love from the people it sees, from the books it reads, from its hopes and daydreams, in the fond hope that the eye may one day see the ideal and the hand touch it."

Perhaps we will never meet our ideal love. But that does not prevent us from recognizing these feelings within us and seeing in them a pale reflection of what the human heart most desires. In each of us there is a deep hunger and craving for the love of God.

Now such a statement may seem just a little too poetic and "up in the air" as we struggle out of bed in the morning to face another day of work and routine. But at some time, even on the bleakest of days, a little flicker of love is bound to stir in our hearts. Someone or something will remind us that we are a *thinking, feeling, loving*

being. And that is important. In a more reflective mood we will remember those moments and recognize that the ability to love and be loved has been planted in us by the supreme Architect, God himself. And only God himself can fully satisfy this love.

We really begin to understand just what this means only when it dawns on us just how important we are in God's sight. Saint Paul tried to drive this truth home to his Ephesian converts by telling them that, even before the world began, God chose us and determined that we should become his adopted children through Jesus Christ.

Saint Paul was not just making a general statement that doesn't concern *me*. He wanted me to understand that God really did choose *me* to be his child. This is the often unspoken desire planted by God in the heart of every man and woman. And until the hope is realized, no one can ever really understand what it is to be fully human.

How does God's gift of faith unite us with Christ? That is the question we have asked ourselves. Catholic teaching is quite clear in stating that so closely does the gift of faith unite us with Christ that he becomes our brother, and we children of the Father. But just how this union comes about will form the greater part of our continuing prayer and reflection in this *Catechism*.

But toward the end of his public ministry Jesus spoke of a deeper union for those who had "followed" him: "Make your home in me, as I make mine in you . . . I am the vine, you are the branches . . . If you remain in me and my words remain in you, you may ask what you will and you shall get it" (John 15:4-7).

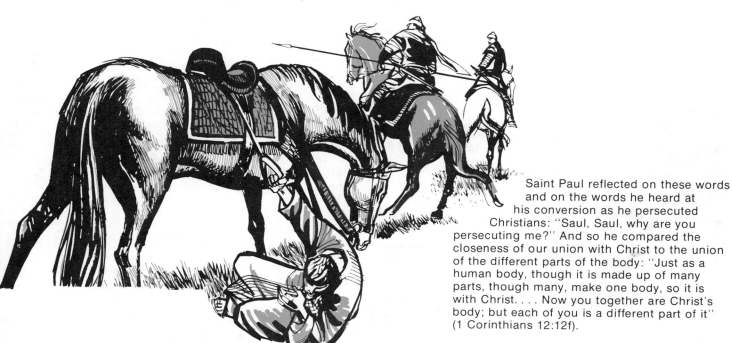

Saint Paul reflected on these words and on the words he heard at his conversion as he persecuted Christians: "Saul, Saul, why are you persecuting me?" And so he compared the closeness of our union with Christ to the union of the different parts of the body: "Just as a human body, though it is made up of many parts, though many, make one body, so it is with Christ. . . . Now you together are Christ's body; but each of you is a different part of it" (1 Corinthians 12:12f).

14 Where is Jesus Christ?

Jesus Christ is in glory with his Father in heaven. During his life Jesus gave us glimpses of this glory: "There are many rooms in my Father's house" (John 14:2). "Now, Father, it is time for you to glorify me with that glory I had with you before ever the world was" (John 17:5). "I shall send to you from the Father, the Spirit of truth who issues from the Father" (John 16:26).

Jesus Christ is in his Church on earth. As Jesus prepared to return to his Father he prayed: "I have given them the glory you gave to me, that they may be one as we are one" (John 17:22). The glory of the Church is the same as the glory of Christ.

Through God's gift of faith, Christians are united with Jesus Christ. And so they already enjoy God's heavenly glory, sharing in the life of Father, Son, and Holy Spirit. But this glory is not yet fully revealed. Reflecting on this great mystery, Saint John wrote: "We are already the children of God but what we are to be in the future has not yet been revealed; all we know is, that when it is revealed we shall be like him because we shall see him as he really is" (1 John 3:2).

"The greatest need of our time," said Thomas Merton, "is to clean out the enormous mass of mental and emotional rubbish that clutters our minds and makes of all political and social life a mass illness. Without this housecleaning we cannot begin to *see*. Unless we *see* we cannot think."

Time and time again we are faced with situations in life which test us with the challenge of finding some meaning in our existence. But so many and varied are the solutions offered that comparatively few people come to that moment when things finally fall into place. They live and die with no real solutions to the problems that so perplex them.

According to Catholic belief, however, there is one truth which can put meaning into life. It is the truth that Jesus Christ is still with us. Not that we are always blessed with a vivid sense of his presence. But, under the prompting of the Holy Spirit, there are moments when our overactive minds relax and we *see*. They are moments of faith which are to be treasured as precious gifts of God.

Such a moment of faith often comes to Catholics during Mass. The gift of faith enables us to see Jesus in all the ritual and the symbol. We *see* him offering himself and giving thanks to the Father. We *see* him in Communion sharing his life with us. And we know deep down that his life alone unites all people in their journey back to God.

The writer of the letter to the Hebrews reminds us very powerfully that "Jesus Christ is the same today as he was yesterday and as he will be for ever" (Hebrews 13:8). And it is at such moments as the Mass that we remember that Jesus Christ was no ordinary man. He is still alive. All people — those who have gone before us, those who are alive today, and those in heaven — are joined to each other and to God the Father through him.

Where is Jesus Christ? People can ask us and we find it almost impossible to put into words the real answer that we give to ourselves. Of course, we tell them we believe that Jesus Christ is glorified in heaven, that he is in the Church, and that he is in our brothers and sisters. But all these statements do not add up to the real, live person of Jesus whom we know has bound himself inextricably to our daily lives.

How, then, do we answer the question? In his book, *The Use of Praying,* J. Neville Ward reminds us that through the history of humanity "the offering of self, thankfulness, suffering, and sharing has always been connected with the ultimate glory and fulfillment of life." It is Catholic belief that only when we are close to Christ can we fully respond to these deep human needs.

Where, then, is Christ? He is with us in our daily self-offering, our thanking, our suffering, and our sharing. And because he is there all these moments of life give glory to God.

Jesus reveals his Father as the one who sends. "When the appointed time came, God sent his Son" (Galatians 4:4). This revelation reflects the truth that "the Person of the Father is not made by anyone, nor created, nor begotten" *(Athanasian Creed).* Traditionally, the work of creation is appropriated to the Father.

More than fifteen hundred years have passed since that famous occasion when, according to legend, Saint Patrick plucked a shamrock from the ground to explain its triple leaf and single stem, in some rough way, the great doctrine of the Blessed Trinity. The assembled chieftains were convinced, and they converted.

Many times in his life Patrick bravely faced a hostile and pagan people. Yet never was he more brave, we may think, than when he attempted a sermon on the Trinity!

There can be little doubt that many Christians dismiss the mystery of the Blessed Trinity as simply "a truth which is above reason, but revealed by God." Some people even regard Christ's revelation that he came to take us to the Father by giving us his Spirit as no more than "a little bit of extra knowledge about God" which, insofar as living the Christian life is concerned, we could manage equally well without.

Nothing could be further from the truth! Jesus did not reveal the life of God in order to confuse us. He revealed the life of God in order that he might share it with us. And this life of God is nothing less than the life of the three Persons of the Blessed Trinity.

Traditionally, the Church uses the word *grace* to describe this life of God offered to us. And of grace, one thing is certain: it cannot be received simply by applying the mind in the right direction. Our minds applied in the right direction can *recognize* God; they can help us to understand his revelation. But they cannot *reach* him.

Various analogies or comparisons have been attempted to describe the relationship between Father, Son, and Holy Spirit. St. Basil, for example, suggests that the Son proceeds from the Father as "our word proceeds from our mind." And the Holy Spirit is regarded as "the personal Love of both the Father and the Son." These analogies undoubtedly help our understanding. But we can never forget that we receive the life of God because *he has reached down to us.* Our relationship with him is deeply personal.

How, then, can we receive God if we cannot fully understand him? Jesus, the Son of God, shows us the way. The answer is strangely simple. We must experience sonship, as Jesus did. "Unless you change and become like little children, you will never enter the kingdom of heaven" (Matthew 18:3). It is as "simple" as that! We enter into the personal relationships of the Trinity by becoming "like little children."

We can now see why the Trinity is the fundamental truth of our faith. The Trinity is a life of relationships between the divine Persons. We enter their life by allowing God's Spirit to adopt the right relationship within us: the relationship of a child to our heavenly Father; of a brother or sister to his only-begotten Son. If we enjoy the right relationship with the divine Persons, their life is ours.

Jesus reveals himself as the Son who is sent: "I have come here from God . . . not that I came because I chose, no, I was sent, and by him" (John 8:42). This mission reflects the truth that "the Person of the Son is from the Father alone, not made, not created, but begotten" *(Athanasian Creed).* The Son alone became man.

Jesus reveals the Holy Spirit as one who proceeds from the Father and the Son: "When the Advocate comes, whom I shall send to you from the Father, the Spirit of truth who issues from the Father, he will be my witness" (John 15:26). This mission reflects the truth that "the Holy Spirit is the uncreated Person who proceeds from the Father and the Son as their eternal love" *(Credo of the People of God).* The Holy Spirit completes the work of creation and salvation: "God has sent the Spirit of his Son into our hearts: the Spirit that cries, 'Abba, Father'" (Galatians 4:6).

The three Persons of the Holy Trinity are one in substance, coeternal and coequal with one another. At critical moments of Jesus' life the unity of the three Persons is revealed. When Jesus was baptized "heaven opened and the Holy Spirit descended on him in bodily shape, like a dove. And a voice came from heaven, 'You are my Son, the Beloved'" (Luke 3:22).

The mystery of the Trinity is beyond our understanding. Over the centuries the Church has upheld true doctrine against errors which denied either that the three Persons are really distinct or exaggerated that distinction. In 1968, Pope Paul reaffirmed: "In the three divine Persons the life and beatitude of God is realized and fulfilled with overwhelming plenitude in the supreme excellence and glory which is proper to him who is the uncreated Being, in such wise that 'unity in the Trinity and Trinity in the unity must be humbly acknowledged'" (Credo of the People of God).

Many Christians never quite manage to get rid of the idea that God is "out there." We "look up" to heaven where, since our childhood, we have firmly placed him. We imagine the coming of Christ as a kind of "excursion" which God made to our world; and so, when we think of Jesus, we picture a shadowy figure with whom we try to get in touch, almost in the same way as a medium at a seance tries to contact some ghostly figure from the past. It requires a lot of effort on our part and no small amount of imagination!

This caricature may bear the marks of exaggeration. But many of us will surely recognize at least the bare outline of the problem. It is a problem founded on one totally false idea. We make the mistake of looking at God as *something*, rather than as *someone*.

With *something* it is impossible to form any relationship at all. It is an object outside us which we can admire or fear or find useful or be indifferent to. With *someone*, however, we are forced to form a relationship. And a relationship — whether of friendship, of marriage, or of blood — *changes* us. That someone becomes *part* of us. We become different persons.

God calls us to a personal relationship with him. He asks to become *part* of us. We are invited to enter into the life of Father, Son, and Holy Spirit — not as intruders standing awkwardly on the outside of an exclusive gathering, but as persons who have been adopted in the most intimate way into a gathering where we can truly belong.

Our union with God, then, is not the fruit of a vivid imagination by which we have successfully pictured him in a way that seems most suitable to us. Our union with God is the result of recognizing him for who he is and for how he has revealed himself: three Persons who together have worked to make us children of God. He becomes *Someone* who is part of us; we become different persons.

The Trinity is a revelation which we can never lose sight of without totally destroying our faith. We shall return to it constantly, as Jesus did in his teaching. His last prayer before his arrest and crucifixion was simply: "Father, may they be one in us, as you are in me and I am in you. . . . I have made your name known to them . . . so that the love with which you loved me may be in them, and so that I may be in them" (John 17:21,26).

So far in this *Catechism* we have seen how God calls us to enjoy his own life by faith in Jesus Christ. Now we can go on to consider more fully how that call is continued in the Body of Christ, the Church.

The Trinity is a community of Persons, eternally bound together in perfect understanding and love. As adopted children of the Father, coheirs with Christ, filled with the Spirit of the Son, Christians are caught up in the divine life of the Perfect Community.

We present, in summary form, the vision of God revealed to us which has been our concern up till now. It is a vision of love into which we are invited to enter. We must keep this in our minds and hearts throughout the *Catechism,* recognizing the truth outlined in the Introduction: that it is a vision reached only through prayer.

We all search into the meaning of life. We can never escape the questions: Where did I come from? What am I doing? Where am I going? (Lesson 1)

Jesus Christ claims to answer these questions. His Resurrection, if true, confirms that he is the Lord of life (Lesson 2).

The claims of Jesus are supported by history. The Old Testament history of the Jewish nation, the New Testament writings of those who witnessed his life, and the present-day experience of his followers point to the truth of Christ's Resurrection (Lesson 3).

Jesus reveals the life of God and offers us a share in this life. His teaching is summarized in three statements: that God was his Father; that he was the Son of God; that he could make us children of God (Lesson 4).

Jesus Christ reveals that the God of creation is his Father. We can prove the existence of God from created realities. Jesus reveals this God as his Father (Lesson 5).

We are the summit of the Father's creation. Everything created by God was good. We were created "in the image" of God (Lesson 6).

Our first parents were responsible for bringing evil into the Father's creation. "Original sin" destroyed the Father's ordered plan for our happiness. It separated us from God (Lesson 7).

The work of restoration began and is recorded in the history and writings of the Old Testament. The Old Testament prepares for the coming of Jesus (Lesson 8).

The life of Jesus confirms that he is truly God and truly man. Jesus therefore restores the break between us and God (Lessons 9 and 10).

Jesus offers every person a share in the life of God. This sharing is through the gift of the Holy Spirit who makes each of us a child of God, as Jesus is his Son (Lesson 11).

We receive Christ's gift of the Holy Spirit through faith. God's gift of the Holy Spirit identifies us with Jesus in the deepest way possible. Faith changes us so that we become part of Christ's Body (Lessons 12 and 13).

As members of Christ's Body, Christians already share his glory in heaven. This glory is not yet fully revealed. But all Christian actions are actions of Jesus Christ (Lesson 14).

Christians share in the relationships of the Persons of the Trinity. Through the Father's gift of the Spirit of Christ, Christians enter into the life of the Father, Son, and Holy Spirit: three Persons in one God (Lessons 15 and 16).

The traditional catechisms had a lot of advantages. They answered clearly and concisely the kind of questions asked by every Catholic and also by a good number of people who are not Catholic. "What is the Catholic Church?" was one question. The answer, simply, was: "The Catholic Church is the union of all the faithful under one Head."

Everyone, of course, recognized that, as an answer, such a simple statement had many limitations. But it was easily understood; it formed a valuable basis for further explanation by the teacher — especially when this explanation was surrounded by an atmosphere of faith. It was also "memorable." Memorizing the answers was often a painful process, but everyone brought up on the traditional catechism is grateful for the sound foundation in the faith that it provided. The hundreds of questions and answers formed a generation of Catholics. And, by and large, the catechism formed them well.

There is one question, however, which the traditional catechism didn't ask. This is the question: Why do you believe in God? It is the question which each person can answer only for himself or herself. It is the most difficult question of all. And it is also by far the most important. If we cannot answer this question, knowing the answers to all the others will serve no purpose whatever.

Why do you believe in God? The answer doesn't come easily. For it isn't an answer we can memorize from reading all the right books, least of all, a short catechism. We have to think it out for ourselves. More, we have to make it *part* of ourselves.

Other questions about God and the Church are concerned with dogmas and definitions and descriptions. This question — why do you believe in God? — is concerned with a deeply personal relationship.

Other questions deal with *problems.* A problem can be solved by research and logic. But this question — why do you believe in God? — takes us into the *mystery.* And a mystery is not something to be solved but to be entered into.

So far, this *Catechism* has attempted to present something of the *mystery* of God. We have shown how God has taken us *into* himself. In other words, this *Catechism* has tried to reflect the vision of God that God himself has revealed. In short, we have tried to help you answer the question: Why do you believe in God? That is the question, we believe, that a good catechism *should* help you to answer.

Now we present, in summary form, the vision of God revealed to us which has been our preoccupation so far. It is a vision which we will only fully realize on that day when we see God "face-to-face." But it is a vision which we must never lose sight of in our questionings in the faith.

18 What is the Church?

The Church is the continuing presence of Christ leading people to the vision of God. The Church shines forth as "a people made one with the unity of the Father, the Son, and the Holy Spirit" (*The Church,* #4).

The Church shines forth as a people, that is, she is a visible community with a structured ministry.

She is a people made one, that is, the Church has one "soul." This is the Holy Spirit given by Christ to make every Christian an adopted child of the Father. The inner life of the visible community is best expressed in her worship.

"And I love supremely, solely for the sake of him alone, Holy Church as his creation and her teachings as his own." (From a hymn by Cardinal Newman)

What do you think of when you hear the word *Church*? Is it the building down the road where you were baptized and confirmed? Where you went to Mass on Sunday? Or does it bring before your mind's eye Pope John Paul II and all the bishops, priests, and people scattered throughout the world?

The word *Church* has many different meanings. The few lines from Cardinal Newman's hymn, however, help focus our attention on what we want to consider here: that the Church is the visible presence of Christ in the world.

Recently, theologians have begun to describe the Church as the *Sacrament of Christ*. Now we learned as children what a sacrament is. It is a visible action that indicates and brings about an invisible effect. In the sacrament of Reconciliation, for example, the visible action of absolution brings about what it suggests, namely, the forgiveness of sins. But these words and actions have such a tremendous effect only because it is Christ who is acting in his Church.

But why call the Church the *Sacrament of Christ?* Well, it goes without saying that the sacraments are the high points of the Church's life. When we celebrate the sacraments, the Church is doing most clearly what she exists for: worshiping God and bringing Christ to people. But Jesus Christ *is* the life of the Church. Not only in the seven sacraments, but wherever she is, she worships God and brings grace to us, because Christ is in her.

The phrase *Sacrament of Christ,* then, helps to bring home very forcefully to us that the whole of the Church's life is to make Christ present in our midst. That is what the Church is, the visible presence of Christ. That is why she exists, that Christ may be heard and known and loved.

In the seven sacraments, Christ needs the voice of the minister of the sacrament. If Jesus Christ is to be heard clearly in our world, he needs a human voice. And so when we turn our attention later in this *Catechism* to the different functions in the Church — to the bishops, priests, married people, and so on — we should all the time see in our mind's eye Christ calling us to be his voice, to be his witnesses.

What, then, is the Church? The Church — called Mother by Catholics — is the presence of God in our world, the action of God saving us from sin, giving us his life. In this visible community we meet God, not because the Church is the biggest or best or anything else, but because God has given her life. In the Church we find Jesus our Lord. Without her teaching we would not know him. Without her sacraments we would not receive him. In the last analysis, we Catholics are not interested in learning *about* the Church: We want to learn to *be* the Church.

She is made one with the unity of the Father, the Son, and the Holy Spirit; that is, the Church is the community of all those who have been drawn into the life of God himself. The Church is the visible sign of God's presence in the world. The sign of the cross traced on the body reminds us of the life of the Trinity which is ours.

Jesus established his Church by bringing together a group of disciples, led by Peter, who witnessed his teaching and miracles. These words and actions of Christ were a sign (or sacrament) of God's presence in the world.

Jesus entrusted these visible signs of God's power to his disciples to be continued among his followers after his return to the Father. His bodily presence was removed, but his life remained. For, by the power of the Spirit who was given at Pentecost, these words and actions of the Church became infallible signs of God's continuing power in the world.

The Church is the Body of Christ whose words and actions are the same as the words and actions of Jesus. Christ's words are continued principally in the Gospels and in the tradition of the Church.

It is a commonplace of Catholic theology to state boldly that Jesus Christ is present in the Church. This teaching of the Church is contained, of course, in the documents of the Second Vatican Council. But in coming to grips with the question "How did Jesus establish his Church?" we will summarize three other important documents: one from the sessions of Vatican I and the other two from Leo XIII and Pius XII.

The Fathers of the Church and the medieval theologians never actually set out to write a treatise on the Church as a separate subject which could be treated in isolation from the saving work of Jesus Christ. For them the whole of Scripture spoke of Christ and his Church. They taught that the life of the Church is inseparable from the life of the Holy Spirit. Saint Irenaeus puts it rather beautifully: "Where the Church is, there is the Spirit of God, and where the Spirit of God is, there is the Church and all grace, and the Spirit is truth."

The Spirit comes to us, of course, only because Jesus Christ sends him to us. In one sense, then, we can answer the question "How did Jesus establish his Church?" by pointing to the moment of Pentecost when Jesus sent his Holy Spirit among us. It is the Holy Spirit, we are told, who "will lead you to the complete truth" (John 16:13) and "remind you of all that I have said to you"

(John 14:26). But we have here only the starting point of our journey into the mystery.

We know Jesus wanted a community to grow up because he gathered disciples around him of set purpose. He called them his "little flock" and spoke to them of his mysterious kingdom. He taught them the message they were to proclaim and appointed twelve of them as *apostles.* The word *apostle* means "he who is sent," and denotes someone who is sent not just as a messenger but as an envoy with full powers.

It was the Spirit who transformed this little group of apostles at Pentecost from being confused men into courageous witnesses who grasped the meaning of Jesus' teaching. They came to understand that they were much more than just an organized body. "I live now not with my own life," Saint Paul was to write, "but with the life of Christ who lives in me" (Galatians 2:20). They came to understand that "all of us, in union with Christ, form one body" (Romans 12:4).

To come to the Catholic faith is to recognize that Christ acts in his Church. His words and actions are really continued in the sacraments, the Gospels, and the tradition of the Church. "We must accustom ourselves," wrote Pope Pius XII, "to see Christ who lives in the Church, who teaches, governs, and sanctifies through her."

Christ's actions are continued principally in the sacraments of the Church.

20 What is a Gospel?

The written Gospels record the words of Jesus Christ. They faithfully hand on what Jesus, while living here on earth, really did for our eternal salvation. The Gospels were built up in three stages:

STAGE ONE: The public life and teaching of Jesus is witnessed by the apostles.

STAGE TWO: While the apostles lived, written records were not necessary. Through preaching and discussing among themselves they lived and proclaimed the Good News (or Gospel). In this way they built up a deeper understanding of the life of Christ.

STAGE THREE: Under the inspiration of the Holy Spirit the evangelists — Matthew, Mark, Luke, and John — expressed this faith of the Church in written form. All four written Gospels were completed by about A.D. 95.

Many people are disappointed that the Gospels do not tell us more about the life of Jesus. The 30 years up to the beginning of his public ministry are almost a complete blank. Details of his appearance and even an accurate timetable of his work are nonexistent.

The reason for this is simple. The Gospel writers did not attempt to write a biography of Christ. Nor did they set out to write a history book. What, then, was their intention when writing the Gospels?

Saint John gives the answer. Toward the end of his Gospel he tells us: "These [signs] are recorded so that you may believe that Jesus is the Christ, the Son of God, and that believing this you may have life through his name" (John 20:31). John wanted his life of Christ to be more than just a list of facts. He wanted it to lead people to *believe* in Jesus; he wanted his Gospel to give *life*.

The illustrations show us how the life-giving words of Jesus were built up into the Gospels. At first they were preached by the apostles, whose intimate knowledge of Jesus meant that they could give their hearers a vivid picture of his life and teaching. They could accurately describe his miracles and repeat his teaching.

But that was not enough. How could they best show that these words pointed to something deeper — that Jesus Christ was the Savior of the world?

It would be no use just telling random stories of his life and death. The apostles were teachers, and any teacher knows you cannot teach well in a disorderly way. And so, for maximum effect, the apostles put their belief in Jesus into an orderly system. In their preaching they grouped miracles together to show how everyone could share in this new life. They selected parables, miracles, and, above all, the Passion story, which urged their listeners to follow Christ.

So, we see emerging a most important fact about the Gospels. *Even before the first Gospel was written, the life and teaching of Jesus was being put into an accepted order.* And this was being done by the apostles and disciples, the men who really knew our Lord, the men he had chosen to be his chief witnesses.

The Gospels, then, by putting before us the preaching of the early Church about the public life, death, and exaltation of Jesus, give us a true witness and interpretation of Jesus' life. In short, they give us Jesus' life.

Just as the words of Jesus when they were first uttered attracted followers who formed the beginnings of his kingdom, in the same way those words as they have come down to us in the Gospels continue to draw people into his Church. Through the action of the Holy Spirit, the words of Jesus first uttered two thousand years ago and recorded by the Gospel writers are still effective today. They still give life.

21 What is tradition?

Tradition preserves the words of Jesus Christ as preached by the apostles. Tradition is built up in three stages. Stages one and two are similar to the first two stages of the formation of the Gospels (Lesson 20).

STAGE ONE: The public life and teaching of Jesus was witnessed by the apostles.

STAGE TWO: While the apostles lived, written records were not necessary. Through preaching and discussing among themselves they lived and proclaimed the Good News (or Gospel). In this way they built up a deeper understanding of the life of Christ.

The message of Jesus Christ is a message for all people in every age. During his life on earth, Jesus revealed his Father to the men and women of his time: he told them about God; he showed them what God is like. But what about us, the men and women of the 20th century? How are we to hear the true and authentic voice of Jesus?

In the preceding lessons we have examined closely the manner in which God gradually revealed himself to the world and found that he made his revelation in the setting of a community, the people of Israel. It is clear that the stories of the Exodus and other saving interventions of God on their behalf were preserved in the memory of the community long before they were committed to writing.

We refer to these stories, memories, and reflections of the community on God's gracious intervention in their daily life as *oral tradition.* They are obviously very important because they preceded the *written tradition* collected together into Sacred Scripture.

It was the same in the early Church. The early leaders of the Church, the apostles, were men who had listened to the teaching of Christ at firsthand, both before and after his Resurrection. It was these men who were the first to take up Christ's command to teach all nations. They did so eagerly, confident in the belief that the Holy Spirit — sent to them by Christ at Pentecost — would bring to their minds, and help them to understand, everything he had taught them. In the early Church, then, there was an *oral tradition* which preceded the *written tradition* of the New Testament.

In a real way we can say there was a gospel before the Gospels were written. "For by no others have we known the method of our salvation," wrote Saint Irenaeus about the year 180, "than those by whom the gospel came to us — which was both in the first place preached by them, and afterwards by the will of God handed down to us in the Scriptures, to be the ground and pillar of our faith." Irenaeus was convinced of the importance of the law of tradition and taught that even without the Bible we should still have in the present teaching of the Church the authentic teaching of Christ.

The theologians speak about three types of tradition, namely, *divine, apostolic, ecclesiastical.* We have already seen how Christ, God-made-man, initiated divine tradition by revealing God in a human way right at the heart of a community. In the next few lessons, we will see the importance of the apostolic tradition begun by the "Spirit-filled" apostles, and the ecclesiastical tradition which began in the Church after their death. But let us always remember that the Scriptures and tradition are not totally distinct. Each is part of the other. For both preserve the same Word of God.

STAGE THREE: Under the inspiration of the Holy Spirit the Church continues to grow, through preaching and discussion, in her understanding of the life and teaching of Jesus Christ as first preached by the apostles and handed down from age to age.

A sacrament is a saving act of Jesus Christ. In the celebration of every sacrament it is Jesus Christ who makes the first move in coming to lift up the person in need of salvation — just as he came to lift up his friend Lazarus in the village of Bethany.

It is an act celebrated in and through the Church which unites us with Christ's worship of his Father. In the celebration of every sacrament of the Church, Jesus Christ lifts up those who believe in order to unite them with the Father — just as he revealed the glory of God when he raised up Lazarus with the words, "Father, I thank you for hearing my prayer" (John 11:41).

It is an act by which we receive the Spirit of Christ and so are formed in his image — just as Lazarus was formed in the image of Christ when he emerged from the tomb with new life.

"Since the Lord is no longer visible among us," wrote Saint Leo the Great about the year 450, "everything of him that was visible has passed into the sacraments." When we think about it, that really is a startling claim! But startling or not, it is harder to find anywhere a clearer expression of just what the sacraments mean to Catholics.

Our life of faith, of course, revolves around the belief that Jesus Christ, who walked the dusty roads of Palestine all those years ago, is still with us. It is obvious that any faith which rests secure in the belief that Jesus — who died twisted in the agony of torture — is still alive must be a joyous and exuberant affair. But the joy seems to elude us so often; and if our minds turn at all to Christ in the apparent drabness and weariness of the daily round, it is often simply to give way to nostalgia: "Oh, it would be so much easier if I had actually seen Christ."

Saint John wrote of the Jesus he saw with his own eyes and touched with his own hands: "The Word was made flesh, he lived among us, and we saw his glory" (John 1:14). True, it is only natural to think it must have been so much easier for John. But it is much more to the point to try and discover in his writings the reason for his exuberant and joyful faith. And that can be summed up in one word: *love*. John saw the love of God revealed in Christ as a love which had no other object than to share its own delight. As Saint Athanasius put it, "Christ became man that man might become God." That belief was the mainspring of John's life.

Perhaps it seems obvious and rather silly to say that Jesus Christ was the first to live the Christian life. But it does bring home to us that it is meaningless to talk about a Christian life which is not an actual sharing and participation in Christ's life. That is where the sacraments come in. Christ is continually seeking to share his divine life with us, to be born again in each one of us.

And the place of our meeting is in the sacraments. As Saint Ambrose expressed it: "You have shown yourself to me, Christ, face-to-face. I meet you in your sacraments."

"A sacrament," writes Louis Evely, "is a gesture of Christ, a place where he begins to exist again and to act for all those who are gathered around him in faith." And the same writer brings home to us very forcefully that the sacraments are not just ceremonial commemorations of Christ's healing gestures but the way of abolishing time and making Christ alive today. "Do you wish," he asks, "to be present at Christ's birth, at the Passion, at his Resurrection? Go to a Baptism, attend a Mass, enter a confessional to tell your sins."

23 What is the visible effect of Christ's words and actions?

The words and actions of Jesus are expressed in the Gospels and tradition of the Church and in her sacraments (Lessons 19-22). These words and actions mold us into Christ's image.

This image is best expressed in communion (comm-union). Saint John, the disciple Jesus loved, tells us that before his Passion, Jesus prayed to his Father: "May they all be one. . . .may they be so completely one that the world will realize it was you who sent me" (John 17:21,23).

In the Church the communion or unity of Christians is achieved primarily in the Eucharist which, among the first Christians, led to communal ownership and collections organized for needy brethren.

Love for God and neighbor is the first and greatest commandment; for such love visibly expresses what God has done in us. The communion of God's love, which is the Church, is fractured by failure to love God through worship and failure to love neighbor through charity.

There is a story told of two French generals who were of equal age, equal rank, and equal years in military service. A dispute arose between them as to who should salute the other first. Eventually, the quarrel became so bitter that the matter had to be referred to the Marshal of France. His decision was immediate: "The one should salute first who is the most courteous."

The generals' preoccupation with how they could best express their rank blinded them to the most important truth of all. Their true status surpassed badges and ribbons; it even transcended their personal achievements. Their true greatness, rather, was founded on the qualities of human gracefulness and graciousness. Without such a foundation, we can say that their outward marks of rank were no more than signs of deceit.

In the last four lessons we have sketched the true nature of the Church by considering (at this stage, very briefly) the signs of the Church's greatness. Her tradition goes back to Christ so that her words and actions, contained in her Scriptures and her sacraments, are the words and actions of Christ himself. Every time the Scripture is read and every time a sacrament is celebrated it is Jesus who speaks and who acts. The Church is grace-full: she is "full of grace." Her life is the life of God himself. This is the foundation of the Church's true status.

And every action of every member of the Church at every moment must express her status. Every word must be a "graceful" word. Preoccupation with outward signs and external splendor will always lead us to forget this truth, so that our words and actions will be reduced not to signs of graciousness but to signs of deceit.

In short, in every conflict within the Church, or even between the Church and those outside her immediate fold, the more "graceful" is always the winner! For the true life of the Church is never better expressed than when her members allow the love of God within them to build a "communion of saints." This is why Saint Ignatius in the year A.D. 106 referred to the Church as "an assembly of love."

As we develop our understanding of the Church in this *Catechism* it is vital to keep this truth in the mind and heart. *The Christian's task is to make visible by word and action what is invisible – the love of God which is within.*

This does not mean that the truth is ever sacrificed. Often, as in the example of Saint Ignatius who was put to death at the teeth of lions, the truth will require the sacrifice of one's life. But, ultimately, there is no truth of dogma more important than the truth that Christ died to give life to *all* people. And so every word and action of the Christian must reflect the gracefulness — the courtesy — of Christ.

To enable all members of the Church to reach full communion with Christ, the Church has a variety of ministries — the episcopacy, the priesthood, and the diaconate.
Bishops — with the help of priests and deacons — preside as teachers of doctrine, priests of sacred worship, and officers of good order.

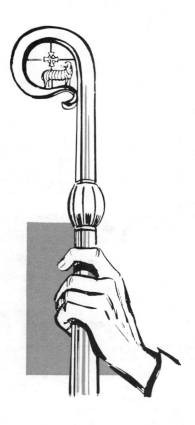

We have seen that the Church is a "communion of love." This is not a vague and hazy definition. It expresses the essential nature of the Church. Now we emphasize an equally important truth: *the Church is a communion governed by clergy who have a variety of ministries, each subject to the one above it.*

This structure is far more than a practical way of preventing chaos. It is of divine institution and is Christ's way of making the love of God (which would otherwise be hidden) visible to the world.

Many people today feel that they can do better without "organized" religion. They feel that they can approach God more effectively without the institutional Church. The truth, however, is that no person can ever approach God. It is God who does the approaching in his Son, Jesus Christ. He comes quietly to us today, as he did in Palestine, in human form. He comes in a way that we can *see* him — in his Church.

In short, we enter the invisible "communion of love" by entering into the visible "structured communion." The Church in her fullness is most surely found where there is a bishop in union with the Supreme Pontiff.

It should not really surprise us that Christ turns to people of flesh and blood to guide his Church. After all, he founded a visible Church so that down the centuries men and women could share in the joys of those who came into contact with the *Word made flesh.*

"A visible Church," writes J. P. Kenny, S.J.,"requires a visible head . . . a stand-in, a vicar . . . a doctrinal spokesman to gather together, represent, sanction and nourish the thinking of the Christian community." When the world turns to the successor of Peter, it can be sure of turning to the recognizable source of Christ's healing power.

For many people today, the Catholic Church stands or falls on the papacy. They point to the scandals of the past and suggest the Church is lacking today in constructive leadership. And here, of course, we are on serious ground. But it must be remembered that "by divine appointment" the Church is a Church of sinners and not saints.

The title "Vicar of Christ" means that the Pope is the spiritual father of all people. We believe, of course, that it is the Spirit and not the institution who is the Giver of life. But the frail figure of the Pope reminds us that Christ left the Spirit of Unity to a very weak Peter and even weaker apostles.

Jesus formed the apostles after the manner of a college or a fixed group. As he appointed Peter to be first among the apostles, so his successor (the Bishop of Rome) is first among the bishops. This apostolic body continues without a break in the order of bishops. The bishops assembled under one visible head, the Pope, express the unity of Christ's flock.

Those communities which have become "separated from full communion with the Catholic Church but whose members believe in Christ and have been properly baptized are brought into a certain, though imperfect, communion with the Catholic Church" (*Ecumenism,* #3).

The Church also recognizes that people can reach salvation "who through no fault of their own do not know the Gospel of Christ, yet sincerely seek God and, moved by grace, try by their actions to do his will as it is known to them through the dictates of conscience" (*The Church,* #16).
Such people are not visibly united with Christ's Church, but they enjoy in some degree the invisible life of the Church — the grace of the Holy Spirit.

The Church is an infallible sign of the presence of Christ, for the Church is given life by the same Holy Spirit who gave life to Jesus Christ. Jesus promised that the Father would send the Holy Spirit who "will teach you everything and remind you of all I have said to you" (John 14:26). The whole People of God cannot err in belief when from bishops to the last lay person they show universal agreement in matters of faith and morals.

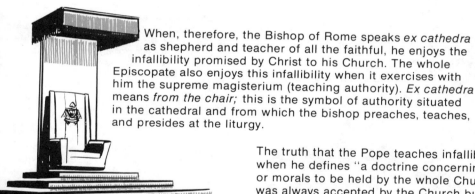

When, therefore, the Bishop of Rome speaks *ex cathedra* as shepherd and teacher of all the faithful, he enjoys the infallibility promised by Christ to his Church. The whole Episcopate also enjoys this infallibility when it exercises with him the supreme magisterium (teaching authority). *Ex cathedra* means *from the chair;* this is the symbol of authority situated in the cathedral and from which the bishop preaches, teaches, and presides at the liturgy.

The truth that the Pope teaches infallibly when he defines "a doctrine concerning faith or morals to be held by the whole Church" was always accepted by the Church but was explicitly defined by the First Vatican Council (1870).

In recent years there has been a growing awareness, both within the Church and society, of the importance of the "group." People seem to feel more than ever before the need to come together to share the interest and effort to further some political, spiritual, or cultural cause. Prayer groups, for example, can be found in many parishes throughout the world.

It isn't hard to find reasons why people feel so attracted to smaller groups. Perhaps one main reason is that in a large and impersonal society they help us to understand more easily both ourselves and our relationship to other people.

One way of looking at the Church is to view her as a large impersonal group in which it is impossible to know everyone. But this is not strictly true. In reality, the Catholic Church is made up of a whole series of smaller groups which we call "local churches" or dioceses. The Fathers of the Second Vatican Council put it this way: "In and from such individual churches there comes into being the one and only Catholic Church. For this reason each individual bishop represents his own church, but all of them joined together in union with the Pope represent the entire Church joined together in the bond of peace, love, and unity" (The Church, # 23).

But the bishop cannot undertake his task alone. And so he will normally establish smaller groupings of the faithful, which we call parishes, under the guidance of the priest who takes the place of the bishop. These small groups are very important. In a certain way they represent the visible Church as it is established throughout the world.

It is in the small, lively parish group that Catholics come to understand the meaning and mystery of the doctrine of infallibility. For it is here they share with their brothers and sisters in the Lord the same belief, hope, and love. God alone is completely infallible. But in the experience of true Christian living we come to understand that the body of the faithful as a whole, anointed as they are by the Holy Spirit (see 1 John 2:20), cannot err in matters of belief. And this is because God has given us in the Spirit a share in his own infallibility.

If we examine in any given parish the young married couples, the single, the old, it is not hard to imagine the Church as a band of pilgrims on their way through life under the leadership of Christ. Surely, then, there can be only one answer to the question: Can she err from the true path?

We have been promised that as long as we are sensitive to the Spirit within us our following of Christ will not fail, will be *infallible.* And the promise that we shall not lose the way includes the promise that our leaders, the Pope and the bishops, will not fail in leading us.

The Church is one. That is, she is made one with the unity of the Father, Son, and Holy Spirit (see Lesson 18).

The Church is holy. That is, her words and actions — Scripture, tradition, the sacraments — infallibly lead men and women to the Father (see Lessons 19-22).

The Church is catholic. That is, she leads all people in every age into the communion of the life of Father, Son, and Holy Spirit (see Lesson 23).

The Church is apostolic. That is, the life of the Church enjoys unbroken succession with the structured communion instituted by Christ and established by the apostles (see Lessons 24 and 25).

It is sometimes suggested that one can equally well worship in the privacy of one's home as in church — the implication being that attending Sunday Mass is unnecessary.

Illness or some other obstacle does, of course, prevent many from attending their church. Their prayer can certainly be as effective (sometimes more so) as the prayer of those who attend Sunday Mass. But the truth is that although one *can* worship God effectively in one's own home, very few people actually *do.* In other words, there *are* people who worship God without sharing visibly in the life of the Church; but they are very few.

The life of the Christian must be seen to be believed. And this is equally true of the Church as a whole. Where the life of the Church cannot be seen there is nothing to excite belief. This is the importance of the visible marks of the Church outlined in the illustrations which summarize our *Catechism* in the past eight lessons. They are the marks that can be *seen* as signs of the Church's life.

Our proud profession of belief every Sunday in the Creed in "one, holy, catholic, and apostolic Church" brings home to us her essential nature. She is not always larger than other religious communities; her ceremonial is not always more magnificent; she is not always the most politically astute among Churches. But such visible signs of power are unimportant. The Church's visible power is displayed by these four characteristic marks.

We have been emphasizing in this *Catechism* that the Church, which is the Body of Christ, infallibly leads us to the intimate friendship of the Father. However, it is also important to remember that the Church does fail. And she fails insofar as her members conceal her marks from the sight of other people.

The unity of the Church has been fractured by division between large communities. Her holiness has been spoiled by the sin of individuals. Her catholicity (or universality) has been hindered by failure to spread God's Word beyond a world of selfishness. Her apostolicity has been hindered by a concern, sometimes amounting to an obsession, with what is basically trivial and has little to do with the tradition of the apostolic Church.

As Christians, then, there can be no doubt where our priorities lie. We are to work for the unity of all Christians; we are to take God's Word to all people and every nation, beginning in our own homes. As Louis Evely reminds us: "The Church is 'a light for revelation to the Gentiles,' not a bedside lamp for Christians." Smug self-satisfaction in one's possession of the true Church is the greatest possible betrayal of the truth. For it prevents the one, holy, catholic, and apostolic Church from revealing herself in her true character.

27 How do we enter into the communion of the Church?

We enter into the communion of the Church by Baptism. In the adult this requires repentance. As he began to preach, Jesus taught: "Repent, for the kingdom of heaven is close at hand" (Matthew 4:17). *Repentance* means "change of heart." This change of heart is perhaps best explained in Jesus' words: "I tell you solemnly, unless you change and become like little children you will never enter the kingdom of heaven" (Matthew 18:3).

The sign of this repentance is Baptism. Peter began his first sermon with the words: "You must repent . . . and every one of you must be baptized in the name of Jesus Christ for the forgiveness of your sins, and you will receive the gift of the Holy Spirit" (Acts 2:38).

The usual sign of repentance is "Baptism of water." The early Church quickly recognized, however, "Baptism of blood." This martyrdom for their faith was a sign which many catechumens, preparing for Baptism, were called upon to make in the fierce persecution against the Church.

The dramatic conversion of Saint Paul (see Acts 9) to the Christian faith was without question one of the great turning points of history. The "light from heaven," the "voice speaking in Hebrew," Paul's blindness which lasted three days were the signs which accompanied the event; and the world has not been the same since.

Many of us wish that our own conversion had reflected something of that drama. Like Paul, we didn't know what was happening to us. But that was because we were only babes in arms at the time the Church welcomed us into her fold. Most of us were baptized as infants, when we were still incapable of giving ourselves either to God or to our fellow human beings.

Saint Paul well expresses our frustration. He quotes "words of the Lord" which were not recorded in the written Gospels and were evidently passed down by word of mouth. He recalls the words of the Lord Jesus who said, "There is more happiness in giving than in receiving" (Acts 20:35). The trouble is that at the time of our entry into the Church we were incapable of *giving* anything. The priest and our parents and godparents, who represented the whole society of saints and believers, gave their assent on our behalf. *Giving* was the Church's role. Our part in the ceremony was to *receive*.

The fact is that although it may be more blessed to give than to receive, it is equally true that it is often a lot easier! Those who have spent weeks in a sickbed receiving care and attention from those around them, incapable of giving anything in return, will recognize this truth.

Our entry into the communion of the Church begins, then, at the moment of recognition that we need God. That is the moment when we realize that we cannot give God anything but, rather, that God has given himself to us. Our role is to *receive* him.

In the eyes of others, that moment is rarely world-shattering. But for the person the change is dramatic, for it means a complete change of heart. For some, as for Saint Paul, the change comes suddenly. But for others, such as Saint Augustine, it is a more gradual and painful process, typified in his youthful prayer: "Lord, give me chastity, but not yet."

One of the greatest "converts" of recent years, Monsignor Ronald Knox, whose name was given to his translation of the Bible, illustrated the "change of heart" required by the Lord. When asked if the Church of Rome came up to his expectations he admitted that she did not. "But," he went on, "thank God she didn't. Because I was expecting the wrong things. The Church is better than my expectations, because she put my ideas right about what I ought to expect."

"Unless you change and become like little children you will never enter the kingdom of heaven."

28 What is Baptism and what are its effects?

Baptism means "plunging." Jesus was baptized in the Jordan by John. The sign of the Spirit was seen. And the Father's voice was heard: "This is my Son, the Beloved; my favor rests on him" (Matthew 3:17). Jesus called his death and Resurrection a "baptism." In his baptism, he was "plunged" into death, but the Father raised him up by giving him the Holy Spirit.

Baptism is the sign instituted by Christ to unite us with his own baptism. What happened at Christ's baptism (of death and Resurrection) is what happens at ours. Our Baptism confers the character of Christ; it is permanent and irrevocable. When the sacrament is celebrated validly, the baptismal character is always conferred. Therefore, the sacrament can never be repeated.

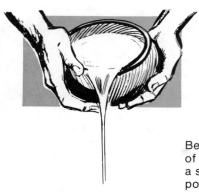

Because Baptism confers the character of Christ, it gives the baptized person a share in Christ's priesthood and the power, therefore, to worship. We must, therefore, be baptized before we can celebrate any other sacraments.

If Baptism is received with proper dispositions, the sacrament confers sanctifying grace (see Lesson 29). For an adult, the effect of the sacrament depends on the strength of the intention, the contrition, and the faith of the person receiving it.

John the Baptizer administered a "baptism of repentance" that demanded a moral reform and introduced its recipients into a new community that looked forward to the coming of God's kingdom. Unfortunately, even two thousand years later, many look upon their Christian Baptism as little more than a ritual initiation into a community or society, which we call the Catholic Church, whose members, as in every society, must keep the rules.

The fact is, however, that such a Baptism would be completely useless in its power to save, for it suggests that the waters simply wash over us to leave us as we were before: poor creatures knowing God but powerless to do what he requires. The person who is plunged into the baptismal font emerges from the waters a new creature with a new life. This new life is the Holy Spirit, who makes his home in us and gives us the power not only to know God but to do all that he requires. The baptized Christian shares in the nature of God and thus shares in the power of God.

Our difficulty in fully understanding what happens at Baptism is that the full Light can only dawn on us gradually. When we suddenly emerge from darkness into the light we instinctively shield our eyes, so great is the impact. Yet the difference between the baptized and the unbaptized is precisely the difference between darkness and light.

Many people still tend to regard Baptism as a private family affair. But such an attitude is so very misleading that it can badly warp our whole approach to the faith. That Baptism is a celebration for the whole parish, and not just the family or individual concerned, is clearly indicated in the revised rite for the sacrament. Even as far back as the year 1439, the Council of Florence described its effects in this way: "By it we are made members of Christ and of his Body, the Church."

So, if Baptism really does make us members of Christ, then it is our belief that the baptized are much more closely linked to each other than if we had been born into the same family. Surely, then, any Baptism and anyone baptized in our parish is very definitely our concern.

Catholics might well ask themselves how they welcome the newly baptized into their community. Is theirs a community which looks beyond its own salvation to the salvation of the whole world? A community of prayer and worship? Because of our Baptism such a community is a real possibility in our world. Jesus Christ unites us so closely with himself that we are able to repeat in our lives the great events of his life, particularly his dying to self and his Resurrection.

29 Is one obliged to seek Baptism in order to be saved?

Baptism is a sign of salvation, for it is the sacrament instituted by Christ to incorporate us into his Body, the Church. "I tell you most solemnly, unless a man is born through water and the Spirit, he cannot enter the kingdom of God" (John 3:5).

Water is a sign of cleansing. The baptismal water, accompanied by the invocation of Father, Son, and Holy Spirit, cleanses the person of original sin and of all actual sin committed prior to Baptism. Water is also a sign of new life. Those baptized receive the new life of the Holy Spirit, which we call "sanctifying grace."

The adult is obliged to seek Baptism in order to be saved, for Baptism alone is the sign which infallibly unites us with Jesus Christ. In the Baptism of infants the faith and desire of the Church is sufficient. This desire is expressed by the parents, assisted by the godparents. The Church recognizes adult "Baptism of desire." This desire may be explicit or simply implicit.

The physical appearance of Christ is no longer with us, but his words and gestures remain. And, because they are the words and gestures of the Spirit-filled Body of Christ — the Church — they retain the power of Christ. They continue to reveal his glory. What they signify infallibly comes to be. Or, in terms which theologians have come to use, sacraments "effect what they signify."

The sacraments, then, do not just tell us *about* something. In the very telling they make the event happen. They are signs which *work*. The sign tells us precisely what is happening.

If we want to know *what* is happening, we must therefore look at the sign. In Baptism the sign is the pouring of water accompanied by the words: I baptize you in the name of the Father, and of the Son, and of the Holy Spirit.

Having sought Baptism for themselves in order to be saved, Christians may well wonder about "Baptism of desire." Does it really matter whether or not they try to win converts? If following conscience is all that is required to be saved, wouldn't it be so much easier to leave others well alone in their comfort?

To answer these questions, it is well to remember that one word of God was sufficient to redeem the world. And here we approach the great mystery of faith. For the word of God that we needed for our redemption couldn't be "bottled up" in the secrecy of the Godhead. Such an unspoken word is worthless. The truth is that *the uttering of a true word means nothing less than the giving of oneself.* "And the Word was made flesh." Jesus Christ, the Word of God, was born.

Now, as followers of Christ we have received the Word of God into our own hearts. And we can do no less than God himself. We can only give that Word to others. This means nothing less than the giving of ourselves.

At first glance all this may seem very unfair. Life for the Christian seems more painful than for others who, not having received the Word of God, nonetheless win the same salvation provided only that they follow their conscience. The truth is, of course, that at no time did Jesus claim that his followers would enjoy an easier life. Quite the reverse! But in so giving ourselves we follow God; and all humanity becomes more like God.

What happens to unbaptized infants? Limbo, a state where they enjoy a purely "natural" happiness, was accepted in the Church in the past as a solution to this question, but never held universally. Such children are entrusted to the mysterious but infinitely kind and powerful love of God.

30 How is Baptism celebrated?

Baptism is celebrated by pouring water on the head of the person, saying at the time these words: **"I baptize you in the name of the Father, and of the Son, and of the Holy Spirit."** The ordinary minister of Baptism is a priest; but anyone may baptize in case of necessity, when a priest cannot be had.

In solemn Baptism the priest anoints the newly baptized with the oil of chrism. This anointing is a sign that God himself is "marking us with his seal and giving us the pledge, the Spirit that we carry in our hearts" (2 Corinthians 1:22). It is a sign that the baptized person shares in the kingly and priestly power of Christ.

The proper time for the celebration of Baptism is Easter when the Church commemorates the Lord's Resurrection. (Lent is traditionally and primarily the time of preparation for Baptism.) For this reason the paschal candle is placed in the baptistry so that in Baptisms throughout the year the candles for the baptized may be lit from it. The candle is a symbol of the light of Christ which is to be kept burning brightly.

A priest, writing a few years ago in a Catholic periodical, pointed out how Baptism can sometimes be downgraded by the way we approach the actual ceremony: Dad watching a sports program on TV; Mom cooking the dinner; baby handed over to a teenage daughter with instructions to take him or her to church at 2:30 p.m. to be "done."

He was obviously describing an extreme case of carelessness. The Church, however, still feels the need to issue constant reminders about the need to prepare well, both on an individual and parish level, for the celebration of the sacrament. And so it is useful to follow step-by-step the ceremony in which children become members of the Church, are united to Christ, and freed from all sin.

The celebrant first greets those present. The greeting is an informal one; it helps to put everyone at ease and allows the priest to express in his own way the spiritual welcome the Church is offering through his ministry. Usually, he will remind the parents that their child is a wonderful gift from God and that their happiness and joy will come from doing God's will for the child.

Then it is the turn of the parents and godparents to speak. They must answer some very direct questions. What do they seek from the Church? Are they aware of the obligations they are undertaking? Will the godparents be prepared to assist the parents?

The priest now invites everyone to join in the liturgy of God's Word. The reading and the preaching of this Word (see Hebrews 4:12) is "something alive and active," is meant to stimulate the faith of everyone present. This is the living faith of the Church from which the child will in due course draw his or her own faith.

The prayer of exorcism and the anointing with the oil of catechumens which follow represent the withdrawal of the child from the forces of evil. Tradition compares the anointing with oil to the custom of anointing athletes. The child is prepared by this anointing for the combat of the Christian life.

When parents bring their child for Baptism, they undertake to pass on to the child their own Christian outlook. Before the central moment of Baptism, then, they give expression to their own attitude to life by renouncing Satan and professing anew their faith. This renunciation of Satan is followed by the climax of the celebration, the Baptism itself, which binds the Christian to Christ.

After the Baptism, three traditional ceremonies take place: the anointing with chrism, the clothing with the white garment, and the giving of the baptismal candle. They underline our belief that our Lord has freed us from sin, given us a new birth by water and the Holy Spirit, and welcomed us into the People of God.

31 What is the sacrament of Confirmation?

Confirmation is the fulfillment of Christ's promise to send the Holy Spirit on all his followers to enable them to be his witnesses "to the ends of the earth" (Acts 1:8). In the synagogue, as he began his own public ministry, Jesus unrolled the scroll of the prophet Isaiah and told the crowds: "The spirit of the Lord has been given to me, for he has anointed me . . . ." (Luke 4:18).

The word "witness" means one who testifies to the truth at the expense of his or her life. In Confirmation Christians are "anointed" with the power of the Holy Spirit to profess their faith within the Church and to testify to the truth to those outside it.

Because of the close connection between Baptism and Confirmation the early Christians normally conferred them together in one rite. In the New Testament, nonetheless, the foundation for the clear distinction between them is evident. For example, Philip the Deacon sent for the apostles Peter and John to "come and lay hands" on some men and women whom he had baptized (Acts 8:14-17).

Confirmation, surely, is the sacrament which is least understood by Catholics. The reason partly lies in the fact that Confirmation has always been so closely linked with Baptism. Indeed, in periods of the Church's history they have often been conferred together. Why, then, *two* sacraments? What is given in Confirmation that has not already been given in Baptism?

The truth, of course, is that the Holy Spirit is given in both sacraments. But the function of the Holy Spirit in each is different. The kind of difference is hinted at by Saint Augustine when he explains that in Baptism we are mixed with water so that we might take on the form of bread, the body of Christ. But bread, he points out, then needs to be baked in the fire; and this fire is supplied by the chrism which is "the sacrament of the Holy Spirit" who showed himself in tongues of fire.

At Baptism, in other words, we are made members of Christ's Body. But at Confirmation we are given the power of God to bear fruit in our Christian life and to speak before the world boldly, and so draw others into the Church. It draws us deeper into the life of the Church, the Love of God, which is the Holy Spirit.

Our entry into the Christian life, then, is no sudden "overnight" experience. It is a process of gradual maturing until we meet Christ face-to-face in death. The sacraments of Baptism and Confirmation, together with our frequent celebration of the Eucharist, are the crucial moments of our birth and growth. As a theologian of the 14th century explained: "Baptism is birth; Confirmation means for us operation and movement; the bread of life and the cup of blessing are true food and drink."

The difference between Baptism and Confirmation is reflected in the age at which, traditionally, they have been conferred. The Baptism of infants has been an accepted practice in the Church from the earliest times. But not so with Confirmation. This sacrament gives the strength to publicly confess the name of Jesus. In normal circumstances its conferring on infants would seem inappropriate.

The ideal time, then, for the conferring of Confirmation is when the person is most ready to receive the Holy Spirit. This does not mean that the sacrament has no effect if the person is not receptive; but it does mean that the full effect can only be experienced when the person is consciously disposed to receive the Holy Spirit.

The revised Rite of Confirmation says episcopal conferences may designate the appropriate age for Confirmation. In the United States, practice in this matter varies. Formerly, young people were confirmed around the age of 10 or 12. More recently, emphasis on Confirmation as the sacrament of Christian commitment has led to postponement until the age of 12, 14, or even 17 years.

(For further information, see Supplement page S10.)

32 How is Confirmation celebrated?

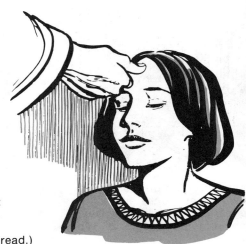

The sacrament of Confirmation is conferred by the imposition of hands followed by the anointing in the form of a cross with chrism on the forehead. The chrism must have been consecrated by the bishop. (Chrism is olive oil mixed with balsam: the oil is a symbol of strength; the perfume is a symbol of the "fragrance of Christ" which the Christian must spread.)

As he anoints, the minister of the sacrament says these words: ***"Name, be sealed with the gift of the Holy Spirit."*** It is normally the bishop, the leader of the community, who administers the sacrament (although a priest may do so under certain circumstances), symbolizing that Confirmation is a "confirming" of the Christian's initiation into the community.

In Confirmation the sponsor places his or her hand on the candidate's shoulder as a sign that he or she is presenting the candidate for Confirmation on behalf of the whole Christian community. Each sponsor undertakes to encourage the confirmed Christian to fulfill his or her promise to be Christ's witness.

The "slap on the cheek" is probably the part of the Rite of Confirmation which older confirmed Catholics remember best. However, like many other little ceremonies in the Church's liturgy, this disappeared in 1971 when the new Rite of Confirmation was promulgated. Today, the bishop says simply, "Peace be with you"; and the newly confirmed replies, "And also with you."

The gentle blow on our cheek given us by the bishop reminded us, we were taught, that in Confirmation we receive the strength to fight as soldiers of Jesus Christ. This strength we undoubtedly did receive. But such was not the original meaning of the blow. It is far more likely that it derived from the bishop's kiss of peace. When in the early Middle Ages, however, infants came to be confirmed, such a kiss was impossible, and so it developed into a caress or a gentle pat.

Such developments in rites are a common feature in the Church's liturgy. And it is such *changeable* elements in the celebration of the sacraments that has led the Church to try to establish the *unchangeable* elements.

When, for example, Jesus instituted the sacrament of Confirmation by his promise of the Holy Spirit, he did not lay down explicit instructions on how the gift of the Spirit was to be conferred. That was left for the Church to work out. What, then, is *unchangeable* in the sacrament of Confirmation? What is *essential* for its celebration?

A sacrament is an action of Christ. It is a work of God made visible to human eyes. And so it is not surprising that early in her history the Church began to speak of a sacrament as "the bringing together of an earthly and a heavenly element." The earthly element is what can be seen; the heavenly element is God's all-powerful word.

Every sacrament is composed of these two essential elements — an outward sign which by the power of God's word confers God's grace on the receiver. In some sacraments the elements of the sign were laid down by Jesus himself during his earthly life. In the Eucharist, for example, bread and wine with the words of consecration were exactly specified. But in Confirmation the elements were not so clearly defined.

Nor is it easy to trace the development of these elements in the sacrament of Confirmation. At first, there were, clearly, many variations from region to region. But two facts are clear. Confirmation was generally conferred with Baptism in one continuous rite. And there was always some form of anointing with oil.

And always, of course, there was the accompanying words — the heavenly element — with the minister speaking in the name of Christ. One of the earliest texts goes back to A.D. 213: "I anoint you with holy oil in God the Father almighty and Jesus Christ and the Holy Spirit."

33 How is the Eucharist a form of worship?

Through Baptism and Confirmation, the faithful are authorized to share in Christ's worship of his Father. This worship is celebrated in the Eucharist, where Jesus Christ in his supreme act of worship is substantially made present. The two essential elements in Christ's worship are sacrifice and Communion.

In his sacrifice on Calvary Christ offered himself to the Father. We share in Christ's offering of himself by assisting the priest in the offering of the divine Victim, to which we join the offering of our own lives.

The Father signified his acceptance of Jesus' offering by raising him from the dead through the power of the Spirit, so that Father, Son, and Holy Spirit live in perfect communion. By our Communion at Mass God's acceptance of our offering is signified and we enjoy a share in the life of God.

Worship is creation's reply to God's creative word. In the beginning, God's creation reflected his word perfectly. But original sin destroyed the harmony between God's word and God's creation. The Old Testament records many attempts to find an adequate reply to God's creative word. But creature sacrifices for sin were totally inadequate worship.

Jesus is the Word made flesh. He is the true worshiper of the Father. His life fulfilled all that was aimed at in Old Testament worship. As the representative of all people, his prayer is the perfect reply to the Father. And in the Liturgy of the Eucharist, we join ourselves to Jesus who continually gives thanks and praise to the Father.

Anyone who reads the Scriptures regularly soon becomes familiar with the vivid word-pictures employed to describe God's action in our world.

Striving to describe the unfathomable mystery of God in mere human words, the sacred authors turn to the Father's creation. They speak of God as the *water* which gives life and the *light* that shines for all people. He is the *food* that nourishes us, and under the *shade* of his hand we are kept safe.

Sometimes they speak of God as the *Word.* Perhaps that strikes us as being a little unusual, and in a way it is. But here in this image of God as someone who frequently engages in long conversations with his creatures we find the key to the meaning and mystery of worship.

Has it ever struck you that human words can and do transform us? A word of praise, for example, can turn even the most nervous of us into a confident, outgoing person. The critical remark, on the other hand, can worm its way into us and utterly destroy our equilibrium.

Our words are so often misleading and destructive. But God's word is never deceptive. It always performs his will infallibly. And his will is simply that we should be filled with his love — that we should become like Jesus Christ, God-made-man.

Almost every page of the Bible is a record of God's "speakings" to his people. And when God speaks, things start to happen! At his word the whole creation springs into being. Victories and defeats, plagues and famines are seen by the sacred writers as "God's word to men." In fact, as the drama unfolds we notice that God's words come to be regarded in a very personal way (see Isaiah 55:10). God's word is looked upon as a personal messenger of God himself.

All this, of course, was a preparation for the coming of Jesus Christ, the *Word made flesh.* "In these last days, he has spoken to us through his Son" (Hebrews 1:1). This is our Catholic belief. The Father is constantly speaking to us, through his Son, in the Church, the sacraments, and the liturgy. The question is: How can we reply?

The Christian response to this question is *through Christ our Lord.* Just as the Father speaks to us through his Son in the liturgy, we dare to speak back to the Father through that same Son.

This is what worship is all about: being so closely united to Jesus in every area of our lives that we are able "through him, with him, in him" to speak to the Father. And because Jesus, God-made-man, is head of the human race it is now possible for us to give adequate thanks and praise to the Father, especially in the Eucharist.

34 Is the Eucharist the perfect worship of the Father?

In the Eucharist Jesus Christ is truly present "whole and entire, God and man, substantially and permanently."
And in the Eucharist we are united with Christ through the power of the Spirit and so united with the risen Christ's worship of his Father.

The Eucharist gives perfect honor and glory to the Father, for it is the presence of Christ in his act of offering himself to his Father. That is, it makes present in a sacramental way Christ's sacrifice on Calvary.

All, ministers and faithful, who are anointed by the Holy Spirit in the sacraments of Baptism and Confirmation and who take part in the Eucharistic sacrifice offer the divine Victim to God, and offer themselves along with it.

At the Last Supper with his closest disciples, Jesus took bread and wine saying, "This is my body . . . this is my blood poured out for you."

To the ancient world the Eucharist seemed "intolerable language" (John 6:60). It appears no more reasonable to the modern world. Jesus' claim seems to defy reason: "How can this man give us his flesh to eat?" (John 6:52)

Here we must be clear about two things. First, in the Eucharist we are going beyond *appearances*. In the Eucharist Christ is as truly present as he was in Palestine nearly two thousand years ago. Second, Christ's presence among us was not, in itself, sufficient to save those who met him. To be saved, they had to approach him in faith. We have to *communicate* with him. He is present as our food, the eating of which gives us a share in his saving sacrifice and Resurrection.

How does the Church describe the vital change which takes place in the bread and wine at the words of consecration at Mass? Since the 12th century the Church has used the word *transubstantiation* to describe this

change. The *substance* of the bread changes; but the *accidents* do not.

Accidents are those qualities which are perceived by the senses — taste, touch, sight, etc. The *substance* is what is grasped by the mind. Only an intelligent person can say "what" a thing is.

Usually, when the senses perceive the qualities of whiteness, softness, etc. the mind, left to itself, says, "that is bread." But Jesus Christ has not left the mind to itself. He tells us that by the power of his word the bread and wine are changed into his body and blood.

The Mass perpetuates Christ's sacrifice on the Cross; it is the same sacrifice as that of Calvary. How do we explain this statement?

On the Cross Jesus chose to offer himself to the Father, in the supreme sacrifice of the giving of his blood. But then, into Jesus' lifeless body the Father poured his life-giving Spirit. The Son now sits at the right hand of his Father, raised up as Lord.

On the night before he died Jesus had instituted the Eucharist to be a sign of his true and continuing presence. To under-

stand the full significance of his presence, then, we look at the full meaning of the sign. We see the sign of Christ's body and blood on our altar offered to the Father by the priest. In the name of Christ he consecrates the bread and wine, changing them into Christ's body and blood.

On our altar at Mass, then, Christ is present in the moment of offering himself to his Father. Jesus Christ is given for us. What happened in a bloody manner on Calvary takes place in a sign, but just as truly, at Mass.

What is the difference between the two offerings? On Calvary Jesus was offering directly in his own Person. But at Mass Jesus offers through the person of his priest and also in union with his followers, his Church. On Calvary, Jesus was alone, isolated from the people who had rejected him. But, at Mass, we are united with Christ's offering. We are part of his Body, the Church.

At Mass, in other words, Christ's offering becomes *our* offering. We are not spectators at the sacrifice of Mass. As members of Christ's Body, we offer the sacrifice through him, with him, and in him.

35 How does the Eucharist unite us with Christ and with others?

The consuming of the bread and wine, which are changed into the body and blood of Jesus Christ to be the food of eternal life, is the sign of our union with Christ (see John 6:54).

Jesus instituted the Eucharist on the night before he died. "Then Jesus took some bread, and when he had given thanks, broke it and gave it to them, saying, **'This is my body which shall be given for you; do this as a memorial of me.'** He did the same with the cup after supper, and said, **'This cup is the new covenant in my blood which will be poured out for you'**" (Luke 22:19-20).

The Eucharist is not a purely private action. Rather, it is the celebration of the whole Church as a society composed of different orders and ministries in which each member acts according to his or her own order and role. Thus through the Eucharist the Church constantly lives and grows.

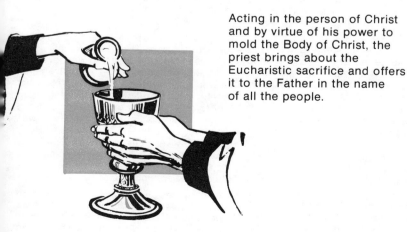

Acting in the person of Christ and by virtue of his power to mold the Body of Christ, the priest brings about the Eucharistic sacrifice and offers it to the Father in the name of all the people.

"The faithful join in the offering of the Eucharist by virtue of their royal priesthood. They likewise exercise that priesthood by receiving the sacraments, by prayer and thanksgiving, by the witness of a holy life, and by self-denial and active charity" (The Church, #110).

In the Eucharist, Christ has identified himself with us. The trouble is that we are reluctant to identify ourselves with him! This is why the change which takes place in us as the result of our Baptism is so often painstakingly slow. And it is also why our reception of the Lord in Communion is important. We should not attend Mass as onlookers at some social spectacle but as sharers in the Son's salvation. As Saint Augustine told us: "You have received that which you are; become that which you have received." Our Communion helps to seal our identification with the Body of the Lord.

When Jesus instituted the Mass at the Last Supper, he told us to repeat that meal: "Do this in memory of me." To the casual observer the Mass is nothing more than a ceremonial recalling of an event long past. But to those who have been given the gift of faith, it is much more. It is a meal which actually brings those who eat it into full contact with the saving power of God.

This is the full force of the phrase we find in each of the Eucharistic Prayers: "Father, we celebrate the *memory* of Christ, your Son. . . ." When Christ used the word *memory* he used it to signify the actual making present of a past event. In the Memorial Prayer, then, we are not simply recalling in a mental fashion the events of Christ's death and Resurrection: "Until the Lord comes, therefore every time you eat this bread and drink this cup, you are proclaiming his death" (1 Corinthians 11:26).

Christians are people who believe that Jesus is the Lord of the universe who alone can satisfy our craving for greatness. And nowhere are they more aware of his power to do this than when they are gathered around the altar in the Eucharist.

The Eucharistic Prayers encourage us to think bigger; we pray for the pope, bishops, priests, and all the People of God.

Jesus Christ died for *all* people. In the Eucharist, the Servant Christ teaches us that the way to true greatness is to be found in the unselfish love of others.

This is indeed a great mystery and paradox. But it is a fact that once we take just one step forward to help our neighbor we begin a journey which never ends. We have begun to imitate the Lord who loved all people, and we will slowly be drawn by the Lord into the unplumbable depths of the Trinity.

Whenever we bring to the altar our acts of selfless love, we join ourselves to Christ and break through the barriers of space and time. Christ is the *link* who unites past, present, and future. Around the altar we are brought into the life of the Trinity, united to all those who have died and to all the living. We begin to see the true goal of this drive toward greatness within us. In the Eucharist Christ gives us a foretaste of the love of heaven, and this is the only love that will ever satisfy the longings of our hearts.

36 What effect does the Eucharistic presence have on us?

All people are called to union with Christ, and in the sacrament of the Eucharistic bread the unity of all believers is both expressed and brought about.

In the Eucharist we are most closely united to the worshiping Church in heaven, as we join with and venerate the memory of Mary and Joseph, the apostles, martyrs, and all the saints. This is our promise of future glory. By way of foretaste we share in that heavenly liturgy in which Christ is sitting at the right hand of God.

These effects derive from the Lord's fourfold presence in the celebration of the Eucharist. He is present *in the body of the faithful* gathered in his name: "Where two or three meet in my name I shall be there with them" (Matthew 18:20). He is present, too, *in his Word,* for it is the Lord who speaks when the Scriptures are read in the Church. He is present *in the minister.* Acting in the person of Christ, the priest joins the offering of the faithful to the sacrifice of their Head.

He is present above all *under the species of the Eucharist.* This presence of Christ under the species is called "real" not in an exclusive sense, as if the other kinds of presence were not real, but *par excellence.* It is the presence which "is the most personal."

The Mass is the center of Catholic life. And what is meant by that? The meaning of the Greek word *Eucharist* can provide us with an answer. It means *thanksgiving.* Thanksgiving and gratitude, then, should be the hallmarks of our daily living.

"Christians are people who find ninety-nine reasons to say thank you before they find one to complain." That old saying is an excellent description of those who live the Mass.

As small children we became familiar with the phrase "to be in a state of grace." It is helpful to notice that *grace* and *gratitude* are two very closely connected words. To be in a state of grace is, in fact, to be a person of gratitude — one who, imitating the action of Christ in the Mass, sees everyone and everything as gifts from the Father.

In a world divided by selfishness, the Eucharist is the one sure sign of hope. Joined to Christ we can become unselfish and loving. We do well to recall that the sacrificial meal we have shared remains the one sure sign that peace in the family, peace in the community, peace in the world will surely come.

As far as one can gather from the Acts of the Apostles, those who had accepted Jesus as Lord tended to come together a great deal. But why? And what was it that led them to share everything in common?

An informal chat with these early followers of Christ would quickly reveal the basis of this communion of mind and heart. It would, in fact, be very hard to miss the constant references to the presence of Jesus Christ among them. He was their sole reason for coming together. They were of one mind and heart because right at the center of their community was the mind and heart and life of Jesus whom they believed to have risen from the dead.

Those early Christians believed, as do we, that Jesus continued to speak to them when the Scriptures were read. They recalled that he himself had told them that whenever two or three of them met together in his name, he would be there too. That is why to meet together for the reading of the living Word and for the breaking of bread became the center of the community's life. For it was then that the Father was glorified, the Body of the Lord was built up, and the Spirit was poured into their hearts. Here they received the strength to withstand the persecutions of those early centuries of Christianity.

Nothing has changed. Saint Paul warned the Corinthians that the world would think them mad to hold such beliefs, and he was right. But he also told them that they would find Christ to be the "power and wisdom of God." Once again he was right. That is why we share with those early Christians the belief that Jesus is still Lord of our community. His Word is still spoken, his sacrifice is still celebrated, and we have all shared in his communion of peace and joy.

37 How and when is the Eucharist celebrated?

In the early Church the Eucharist reflected the form of the Jewish synagogue service (which consisted of the offering of prayers, the reading of Scripture, and teaching); this was followed by the "breaking of bread" in the form of a meal (see Acts 20:7-12).

The form of celebration of the Eucharist has remained unchanged; it is divided into two principal stages.

The infant Church celebrated the Eucharist informally in the home of one of the Christian community. Nonetheless, a clearly defined form was already emerging.

The Gospel was preached and this preaching reached its climax in the "breaking of bread." In other words, the Christian community shared the Word of Jesus in the relating of the Gospel before proceeding to share his flesh and blood in the breaking of bread.

In those very early days, of course, there was no need for the Gospel to be written down. Many disciples had witnessed the life of Christ; others had heard it by word of mouth. The first Christians deepened their faith by talking and reminiscing about the Good News among themselves.

Similarly, in those very early days, the words of what we now call the "Eucharistic Prayer" would have varied from celebration to celebration and from place to place. It was not until the third century that the Church adopted a set form or "canon" in her celebration — although, naturally, the precise words of consecration remained virtually unchanged.

This is the form of the Eucharist — the preaching of the Gospel followed by the breaking of bread — which has been passed down to us. Today, this form is reflected in the two principal stages of the celebration — the Liturgy of the Word and the Liturgy of the Eucharist — which "are so closely connected as to form one act of worship" (*Introduction to Roman Missal*).

Christ's Resurrection is embedded in the memory of the Church. Yet it remains far more than a memory. It was a historical occurrence. But it is also a present event. Jesus is risen! And every moment of life is a celebration of Easter when Jesus rose from the dead.

This is why on the first day of the week we gather — as Christians have always done — to give thanks to God and to celebrate the first Easter. We recall, in a special way, the new creation of all things in Christ.

It is quite impossible today for the Church to lay down precise rules for the proper observance of Sunday, other than to state Christ's faithful "are bound to come together into one place to listen to the Word of God and to take part in the Eucharist." In recent years the Church in some regions (the United States, for example) has allowed the concession of fulfilling the Sunday obligation by attendance at Mass on Saturday evening. This is to enable the Christians of today to celebrate more easily the day of the Resurrection of the Lord.

Our attitude to Sunday invariably reflects our appreciation of Christ's Resurrection. Often, of course, it is necessary to work on Sundays; but for many it provides nothing more than an opportunity for double pay. Others enter the Sabbath Day as they would enter a tomb; for them it is solemn and somber. Both extremes equally lead us to forget that it is the Lord's Day — that Christ is risen.

Sunday is the day when we reflect upon the direction of our lives. We ask ourselves whether we are simply rushing through life without purpose or whether our lives proclaim the truth of the Lord's Resurrection.

In the *Liturgy of the Word,* the same Word who brought the world into existence and who saved us continues to mold us into the Body of Christ — so that Christ becomes truly present in each of us. In the *Liturgy of the Eucharist* the same all-powerful Word changes the bread and wine into the body and blood of Jesus Christ. Christ becomes truly present on the altar.

Whenever the Christian community gathers to celebrate the Eucharist it announces the death and Resurrection of the Lord, and looks forward to his return in glory. For the Jews the Sabbath was primarily the day given over to the Lord. Observed on the last day of the week (Saturday), it was a memorial of creation and a sign of God's promises. Christians, however, celebrate our Lord's Resurrection and his principal appearances to the apostles before his Ascension which took place on the first day of the week (Sunday). And so this day became a special day of "meeting the risen Lord"; a day of re-creation; a day of joy and rest from work.

38 Is our union with Christ truly completed in the Eucharist?

Plato, the famous Greek philosopher, liked things to be neat and tidy. And his ideas on tidiness and order applied as much to people as to things!

He makes this quite clear in his book *The Republic* where he sets down his idea of the perfect State. His plan was to divide the citizens of this dreamworld into three classes: the common people, the soldiers, and the rulers. He speaks of the rulers as being made of gold, the soldiers of silver, and the work people of brass and iron. His is a world which is permanently divided into those who have many privileges and those who have none at all.

Everything we have said up to this point about Baptism, Confirmation, and the Eucharist strikes at the very foundations of Plato's brave new world and any other brave new world which divides people into gold, silver, brass, and iron. Membership in the kingdom of God has nothing to do with being male or female, rich or poor. But it has *everything* to do with a special relationship with Christ.

Our union with Christ is truly completed in the Eucharist. For we are nourished with the Victim of the sacrifice of the Cross; we are led to unite ourselves with God each day in prayer; and thus we acknowledge and love others as brothers and sisters of Christ and children of God the Father. By such growth in prayer and charity the Body of Christ is built up.

On certain members a sacred power is conferred in the sacrament of Holy Orders so that the Body of Christ may be shepherded, nourished with the Word of God and, in the sacrifice of the Mass, offered to the Father. In this way, the priest cares for and strengthens the Church.

There can be hardly anything more foreign to the spirit of the Gospel than to judge by externals. Jesus himself knew exactly what it was like to be treated as a man of brass and iron. He was laughed at because of his rough Galilean accent and taunted with being a "carpenter's son." It is certainly a sobering thought to recall that when God came among us we labeled him a criminal. We constantly fall into the trap of judging by externals; but God never does. Jesus chose a simple fisherman to be his Vicar and a tentmaker to be one of his leading preachers.

The greatest consolation we have in life is that the story of men like Peter and Paul can be our story too. Their friendship with Jesus grew gradually deeper and deeper, so that in the end Paul could only describe the experience by saying, "I live now not with my own life but with the life of Christ who lives in me" (Galatians 2:19).

This gradual "growing into Christ" began with our Baptism and gradually deepens in our grace-giving contact with Jesus in the sacraments and our everyday life. The Fathers of the Church used to describe this growth as a daily invitation from Jesus to sit at one of his three tables: the table of life, the table of the Lord's Supper, and the final table in the kingdom of God.

It is the task of other members to increase and strengthen the Body of Christ by working in the world. By living in the ordinary circumstances of family and social life they order the world according to the plan of God. The power to build up a Christian society through family life is given especially in the sacrament of Matrimony.

Like Peter and Paul we can share the table of life with Christ. We can deepen this daily friendship in the table of the Eucharist by sharing the food which, as Father Durwell remarks, "puts the man of this world to death and resurrects him into the life of God." And when it comes to a place at that final table our accent or education will not matter. There are no reserved places for people of gold, silver, or brass. For Christ is the Alpha and Omega, the beginning and the end of all things.

39 What is a priest?

A priest is ordained to act in the person of Christ. The fullness of the ministerial priesthood belongs to the bishop, who is assisted by priests and deacons. The ring worn by the bishop is a symbol of the fact that he is wedded to his diocese.

A sleepy little girl, a rather battered teddy bear, and a very busy mother. Hardly, one might think, the best starting point for an investigation into the Church's understanding of the priesthood. Or is it?

The little girl, who was being put to bed, simply didn't want her mother to leave her alone. "When I'm gone," her mother whispered, "just cuddle your teddy bear and you won't feel lonely." To which came the immediate rejoinder, "When I'm lonely a teddy bear's no good to me. I need someone with skin on his face!"

When we think about it, this sleepy little girl was throwing more than just her teddy bear out of the window. She obviously would not give the time of day to the idols of gold and silver, the pyramids, and all the mumbo jumbo which litters the long road taken by people in their search for God. "I need someone with skin on his face!" This is what people have constantly sought, and this is what the Father gave us in Jesus, God-made-flesh.

That all happened, of course, nearly two thousand years ago. But a living faith leads us to understand that Jesus is not just a historical memory. His presence, if mysterious, is nonetheless very real and in some way part of our own inner life. In fact, the belief that we are all in some way united *internally* to the risen Lord is an essential part of our belief.

The earliest Christians were, perhaps, a little more conscious of this truth than we are. So in the Letter to the Hebrews (5:1-10) where the writer is at pains to show that Jesus is the one true priest forever, he is also careful to remind us that since we all share in Jesus' risen life we also share in his priesthood. But what exactly does this mean?

Saint Peter takes up the point in his first letter. He tells us that by offering his own life and death to the Father, Jesus reconciled everyone to God. Reconciliation is what priesthood is all about. So we who share in his life must also share in the task of mediation and reconciliation which led Christ to offer his life for others. We make his life and death our own. We shoulder with him the crushing burden of the world's sinfulness until, as Monika Hellwig writes, "our life is crushed out of us for others, as wine from the grapes."

The Body of Christ, of course, is made up of many different parts. Bishops, priests, and lay people all share in Christ's priesthood in their own special way. "I need someone with skin on his face!" said the little girl. What the world needs is a Christian community who can make their own the Redeemer's words, "This is my body and my blood."

The sacrament of Holy Orders confers the character of Christ in a special way. The ministerial priesthood differs essentially from the priesthood enjoyed by all the baptized; for the priest is empowered to "consecrate, offer, and administer the body of Christ" for the good of the Church and of the world. The office of the priesthood is a sacrament; for, irrespective of human failing, Christ is made present through the priest's actions. The stole of the priest is a distinctive symbol of his sharing in Christ's priesthood.

The priesthood is for the service of the Church. The priest is to gather and mold the whole family of his flock so that everyone may live and work in the communion of love which is the Church. In this the priest follows Christ who "came among us as one who serves." The celibacy of priests is a sign which enables them to more freely devote themselves to the service of God and people.

40 How does the priest act in the person of Christ?

The priest acts in the person of Christ in three principal ways:

He teaches: The priest's primary duty is the proclamation of the Gospel of God to all. In this way he fulfills the Lord's command: "Go out to the whole world; proclaim the Good News to all creation" (Mark 16:15). Thus he establishes and builds up the People of God.

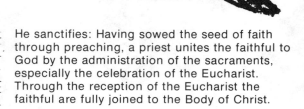

He sanctifies: Having sowed the seed of faith through preaching, a priest unites the faithful to God by the administration of the sacraments, especially the celebration of the Eucharist. Through the reception of the Eucharist the faithful are fully joined to the Body of Christ.

He governs: Having gathered together God's family into the one Body of Christ through the celebration of the sacraments, a priest shares in the office of Christ the Head and the Shepherd. Imitating him, he leads individuals under his care to a deeper understanding of their own vocations and so builds up a genuine Christian community.

"The Catholic Church," remarked Monsignor Ronald Knox, "manages to carry on by hook or by crook." He was referring, of course, to the hook of the fisherman — the pope — and the crook of the shepherds — the bishops. And it is true. The Church always looks first to the successor of Peter and his fellow bishops for guidance and inspiration.

Nonetheless, very few Catholics enjoy direct contact with the Bishop of Rome; it belongs to the privileged few even to be received into private audience by the pope. And it remains true, also, that Catholics not only rarely *see* their bishop but even more rarely *speak* to him. Most bishops today attempt more contact with their diocese, but the task of getting to know even a portion of those under their care is an almost impossible one.

The fact is that, on the personal level, it is to the *priest* that most Catholics look for guidance and inspiration.

The priest's principal duties are outlined in the illustrations. In these he assists the bishop, for which purpose he was ordained. For although we may not see him very often, it is the *bishop* who is the one appointed to shepherd and serve the diocese — the territory under his leadership and given into his care. Yet, the success or failure of the Church in any area depends so much on the relationship between priest and people.

This is a relationship founded on a very remarkable truth, instinctively recognized by every Catholic: the truth, quite simply, that the priest is the Church. We might not always state the truth in such a grand manner; the truth may often be concealed beneath a harsh exterior and an abundance of human failings. But the truth remains: the priest is the Church.

At no time is this more apparent, perhaps, than when the priest enters the home of one of his parishioners who is dying. All human comfort has disappeared. The harsh reality of the passing world has been recognized. The person is alone — surrounded only by four walls soon to enclose him and a few "get well" cards. Into the tomb which is the sickroom enters the priest.

In that instant the room is filled with a new life. It is not the personality of the priest, who may himself only be capable of muttering a few irrelevant pleasantries. It is the personality of Christ. The dying person has been visited by the Church. And, in a sacrament instituted for strengthening the sick, the priest touches the brow and the hands of the dying Christian and feeds him or her with the flesh and blood of Christ. From the tomb to a life of resurrection!

The priest has turned a lonely room, which was a kind of "limbo" between heaven and earth, into a place where the Church in heaven and the Church on earth meet.

(For further information, see Supplement page S11.)

41 How did Jesus Christ institute the sacrament of Orders?

Jesus Christ instituted the sacrament of Orders when he gave his apostles the authority to teach, to administer his sacraments, and to govern in his name. The College of Bishops, in union with the Bishop of Rome, are the direct successors of the apostles who were appointed by Christ and enriched with a special outpouring of the Holy Spirit. This gift has been passed down from the apostles by the imposition of hands in the sacrament of Holy Orders.

Soon after the Lord's Ascension a gradation of orders began to develop. Acts, chapter 6, tells us how "seven men of good reputation" were elected for the daily distribution of alms in order that the apostles could be freed for "prayer and the service of the word." Their number included Stephen, the first Christian martyr — stoned to death. The services performed by these men grew into the duties of the deacon.

Immediately after the death of the apostles, the distinction between bishops, priests, and deacons was becoming clearer. About A.D. 100 Saint Ignatius of Antioch wrote: "Be obedient to the bishop, as Jesus Christ was to the Father, and to the presbyterate (priests), as to the apostles. Have reverence for the deacons, as charged by God."

Our Lord had the nicest way of putting things. While preparing his first followers for his departure from this world, he told them: "I will not leave you orphans." These words of our Lord are particularly well chosen, because when we think of orphans we see in our mind's eye forlorn and faltering little children.

And when we think of the apostles we see that, at times, they behaved not like little children but like big children! They argued among themselves as to who was the greatest — as to who was the "king of the castle"! They made rash promises they couldn't keep. They got frightened and ran away. Toward the end of his public life they caused an exasperated Jesus to exclaim: "Have I been with you all this time and you still don't understand?"

Of course, while he was with them, the apostles *didn't* understand. Indeed, they *couldn't* understand. For while Jesus was with them they could only remain helpless onlookers. Only when Jesus was gone could they begin, literally, to take his place.

Christ had not only the nicest way of putting things but also the nicest way of doing them. He promised that through his Spirit he would remain with the apostles and with us. But he would remain in a way that we could easily understand. He would remain through signs or sacraments.

Christ remains with us through the sign of what came to be known as the "laying on of hands." To the present day bishops, priests, and deacons, in their differing degrees, are ordained, or impressed with the priestly character of Christ, by the imposition of hands.

Many people may be surprised to see *deacons* listed with bishops and priests. The fact is, of course, that in the early Church deacons quickly became important, as assistants to the bishops. But over the centuries their tasks were divided up and given to others. Today, their early caring role for the poor and the care of the finances are usually delegated to lay people like the St. Vincent de Paul Society, the Legion of Mary, and certified accountants.

Yet, the office of deacon didn't die out altogether. It was always a step — the last — before the priesthood; and Saint Francis of Assisi, for example, remained a deacon all his life. Today, with the reintroduction of the permanent diaconate, they are again becoming important in the life of the Church.

Deacons are chosen from a parish for work with the local priests or bishops. Most countries now have permanent deacons; some of these have other secular jobs, while others make it a full-time vocation. The deacon can baptize solemnly, visit the people, witness marriages, bring Communion to the sick, instruct the people, lead them in prayer, and generally be the leader of the area where he lives.

42 How is marriage a sacrament?

Marriage between baptized people is a sacrament, for married love is a sign of Christ's love. The mutual promises of the baptized man and woman and their life in accordance with those promises bring God's grace to one another. In the marriage ceremony, then, the man and woman administer the sacrament to one another. The priest, representing the Church, acts as a witness only.

Saint Paul identified the union between husband and wife with the union between Christ and his Church: "Husbands should love their wives just as Christ loved the Church and sacrificed himself for her to make her holy. . . . In the same way, husbands must love their wives as they love their own bodies; for a man to love his wife is for him to love himself. A man never hates his own body, but he feeds it and looks after it; and that is the way Christ treats his Church, because it is his body — and we are its living parts" (Ephesians 5:25-30).

In the Encyclical, *On the Regulation of Birth* (1968), Pope Paul VI indicated four characteristic features of married love: such love is fully human; it is total; it is faithful; and it is creative of life, or fruitful.

Baptisms, weddings, and funerals are the three occasions when, traditionally, everyone goes to church. And most people have little doubt which event they prefer. Baptisms generally focus on an infant — on a tiny baby only just alive and, literally, kicking! At a funeral we come together to pray for someone who has just died. But most weddings center on two people who enjoy the full vigor of youth. For the couple, the wedding ceremony is the beginning of a new life; and for those who witness their love it is a poignant moment fulfilling years of expectation and hope.

On their wedding day the man and woman are fully *alive*. For both, it is probably the most important decision they make in life. In the ceremony itself a mixture of shyness and nerves probably prevents the bride and groom from knowing what's happening to them! But they recognize the simple actions of the ceremony, rehearsed a hundred times in their minds, as expressing all that they are — and have — as man and woman.

As they are drawn together in marriage both the man and woman naturally come to ask themselves two basic questions: What have I to offer my partner? What has my partner to offer me? These are not the kinds of questions which we ask ourselves over the breakfast table or while we are enjoying ourselves at the local disco! Nor are they the kinds of questions which we ask ourselves when our marriage has already become lifeless, with the heart gone out of it. Yet they are questions which everyone — Christians and non-Christians alike — ask themselves in their quieter moments. For we recognize life in ourselves and in our partners. But what, we wonder, is the source of that life? Is it really worth exchanging with another?

These same questions are reflected in the documents of Vatican II. Believers and nonbelievers are agreed that we humans are the center on which all things on earth focus — the apex of nature — but who and what are we?

The Christian answer is clear. Created in the image of God, we are "appointed by him as master of all earthly creatures that we might subdue them and use them to God's glory" (*The Church Today*, #12). We need to recognize this answer before we can understand Christian marriage. For it is our dignity as human beings, created in the image of God, that makes the life we give and receive in marriage a worthwhile exchange.

When we were baptized in the name of the Father, Son, and Spirit we were lifted up into the life of the Trinity. That is the dignity of the Christian. And when two Christians come together in marriage they exchange not only their own life but the life, too, of the Trinity which they share.

On their wedding day, in other words, the man and woman who are baptized as Christians are *alive*, not with their own life but with the life of Christ. It is a happy occasion!

43 What do we mean when we say that married love is fully human?

Every human society recognizes married love as the usual means by which men and women reach their human fulfillment. And so every marriage is a public act, approved and witnessed by the society in which it takes place. In most countries this takes the form of the marriage being registered by the State.

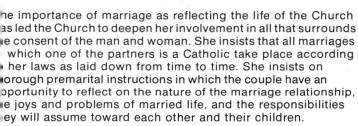

he importance of marriage as reflecting the life of the Church as led the Church to deepen her involvement in all that surrounds e consent of the man and woman. She insists that all marriages which one of the partners is a Catholic take place according her laws as laid down from time to time. She insists on orough premarital instructions in which the couple have an pportunity to reflect on the nature of the marriage relationship, e joys and problems of married life, and the responsibilities ey will assume toward each other and their children.

The purpose of such involvement is to help the couple to make a free, fully human consent, so that the giving of themselves to one another may truly reflect Christ's giving of himself to his Church. In the wedding ceremony the giving of the ring, as a sign of love and fidelity, seals the consent between husband and wife.

Carved on many a school desk for the benefit of future generations can be seen the simple outline of a heart through which runs the Christian names of two young lovers. Usually the carving is richly inlaid with blue ink! Thus are two names locked together in the first stirring of romantic love.

The roughhewn carving is symbolic of adolescent love — drawn with passion, yet awkward. It takes time for the sharp scratches to blend into the wood; only over the years are the rough cuts made smooth. And so it is with love. With the passing of the years it grows deeper but less obtrusive.

It is a very rare marriage indeed in which the maturing of love has not been won after much struggle and pain. It is as though the union of husband and wife can only be achieved after the friction of constant running together in daily life has smoothed out the more abrasive differences of character and outlook. And, to a great extent, that is what must happen in mar-

riage. The locking together in love, carved so naïvely in wood and achieved so painstakingly in reality, is the fruit of a lifetime of self-sacrifice.

The great majority of people discover this hardship in marriage. We draw on the love of our partner when we need someone to "lean on." And, at other times, when we have to make up for our partner's weakness by showing the strength of two people, we are forced to search for the hidden reserves of love. This is hard, yes; but isn't this how we become more fully human — by learning to depend on others and by being dependable? We are formed by our relationships with others. The depths of our being are formed by our most intimate relationship — our marriage.

Husband and wife, wedded in Christ, become more perfect by discovering the love of their partner and by revealing that love within themselves. And that love is God's love. Married people discover and

reveal God's love, in other words, in their everyday relationship with one another. By word and deed husband and wife encourage, build up, and perfect one another in the life of Christ.

The words of a partner in marriage can also cut deeply. Only people who know each other well know exactly where to put the knife to hurt most! This can be destructive. But it doesn't need to be if only we remain willing to learn — willing to learn about ourselves and our own failings; willing to learn about and to accept the partner's shortcomings; willing, in a word, to learn about love.

We are formed by God's Word, both when it comes to us in the Scriptures or through the partner in marriage. It is his Word, indeed, which carves out our hearts — a roughhewn image on our wedding day but which from day to day, year to year, cuts deeper into our being, growing more and more like the heart of Christ.

44 What do we mean when we say that married love is total?

Married love is total in that husband and wife generously share everything, allowing no unreasonable exceptions or thinking just of one's own interests. The capacity to give oneself in such a way — to love a person for his or her own sake rather than one's own — demands a certain maturity. This maturity can only be developed within a stable Christian family and community life.

"This love is uniquely expressed and perfected through the marital act. The actions within marriage by which the couple are united intimately and chastely are noble and worthy ones. Expressed in a manner which is truly human, these actions signify and promote that mutual self-giving by which spouses enrich each other with a joyful and thankful will" (*The Church Today*, # 49).

In controversy against the Pharisees Jesus emphasized the totality of married love. After reminding them that the Creator from the beginning had made them male and female, he said: "This is why a man must leave father and mother, and the two become one body. They are no longer two, therefore, but one body. So, then, what God has united, man must not divide" (Matthew 19:5-6).

Can the man and woman on their wedding day really understand what they are doing? In one sense, of course, they can't. They can't foresee the ups and downs of life. They can't be sure what burdens each will place on the other. They can't know when sickness, physical or mental, will test their union to the limit.

But even though they don't know the details of what lies ahead, they *can* understand what they are doing to the extent that they have already learned to love. They still have a lot to learn, of course! But, founded on God's giving of himself, the couple have learned already that loving is based on giving. Total loving means total *giving*.

As small children, we begin to love others because we are constantly *receiving* love from those around us. But as we grow up it gradually begins to dawn on us that love is not just a matter of receiving. Love means giving as well as receiving. It is a two-way thing. "In adult life," writes Father O'Neill in his book *About Loving*, "we must take a further step in love and discover that, when two mature persons love one another, they begin to reach out in generosity beyond themselves. Mature love must overflow to others."

Giving, then, is as much a part of love as receiving; and we have to be perfectly sure just what this rather unique form of giving entails. It is not just a question, as many of us might think, of "giving up" something. If we see love simply in terms of sacrifice, it can often mean that we have not progressed beyond seeing love as a child sees it. Our attitude is: "I have received lots of things. They are *mine*, but I will give something up for you."

What, then, do we mean when we say that in marriage one person gives himself or herself totally to the other?

Erich Fromm sums up the attitude of the Church beautifully in his book *The Art of Loving:* "He gives of himself, of the most precious he has, he gives of his life. This does not necessarily mean that he sacrifices his life for the other — but that he gives of his joy, of his interest, of his understanding, of his knowledge, of his humor, of his sadness — of all expressions and manifestations of that which is alive in him."

This may all sound a bit theoretical. A young wife, however, writing recently of her own marriage puts it all in more everyday terms. "You could say I am now a very different person to what I was two years ago. I think I can truthfully say I now share in Jim's capacity to feel for others and his sense of fun. Not that he hasn't changed. People also assure me that he has taken on some of my qualities — fortunately, my better ones!"

This is exactly what the Church prays will happen when a couple give themselves "freely and without reservation" in marriage. We pray that they will enrich each other with their own unique gifts. We pray, in other words, that love will produce love.

45 What do we mean when we say that married love is faithful?

Married love is faithful and exclusive of all other until death. Although such fidelity is often difficult, it is possible through the grace of him who "loved us first" (1 John 4:19). The appearance of Jesus at the marriage feast of Cana, where he performed his first miracle, was the fulfillment of the Father's desire to "betroth Israel to himself forever" (Hosea 2:21).

In the Sermon on the Mount Jesus laid down his New Law, emphasizing the importance of its inner spirit over mere external observance: "You have learnt how it was said: You must not commit adultery. But I say this to you: If a man looks at a woman lustfully, he has already committed adultery with her in his heart" (Matthew 5:27-28).

Jesus intended that faithfulness in marriage would be a sign of his own faithfulness. And so divorce in marriage was impossible: "The man who divorces his wife and marries another is guilty of adultery against her" (Mark 10:11). But Jesus also intended his own mercy to the sinner to be a sign of the mercy to be shown by his disciples. To those who wished to stone the woman caught in adultery he said: "If there is one of you who has not sinned, let him be the first to throw a stone at her" (John 8:7).

"Will you love and honor each other as man and wife for the rest of your lives?"

This is one of the questions that the minister asks the bride and bridegroom on their wedding day. What answer can they make? Wouldn't it be reasonable if they replied: "Yes, provided everything goes according to plan . . . Yes, if at all possible"? But that is not the answer the Church demands! She expects the reply: "I will . . . I will."

Should one of the partners — in pronouncing his or her vows — explicitly exclude lifelong faithfulness there would, of course, be no marriage. Regardless of how common divorce and remarriage have become, Christian married couples pledge themselves to imitate, and in a way represent, Christ's faithful love for his bride, the Church. The binding nature of this loving covenant is indicated in the words of consent given by each partner in the marriage ceremony: "I will love you and honor you all the days of my life."

Is faithful love truly possible? As the bride and bridegroom emerge from the church, in some places, confetti is scattered, a less expensive form of the sweets which were originally thrown. These sugared almonds, a mixture of sweetness and bitterness which today takes the form of the almond paste on top of the wedding cake, are a reminder of the nature of the life which follows. And for many couples who put so much preparation into the wedding day, the "bitterness" — the anticlimax — follows very quickly. Waking up, they realize that they are the same people.

The Christian husband and wife, however, realize that now they are *not* the same persons! Their love makes them not two persons but one body. They can now "honor" one another. Or, as the old English rite expressed it: "With my body I thee worship."

This is not idolatry, the worshiping of a "false God." It is the worship of the "true God" whose life beats in the hearts of the married couple who are bound in faithful love. The love two people have for one another in marriage is like the love God has for us. It *is* the love God has for us. It is the same love. And that love is faithful.

As Ronald Knox tells us: "Like swimmers carried away by a silent undertow that is too strong for them, a married couple are swept into the current of the divine love which reaches beyond time and sense; they are united, beyond their knowing, with that divine will which made them for one another." In faithfully loving one another, in putting their faith in one another, a married couple are drawn deeper into the love of God and reveal that love to the world.

This is what we mean when we say that marriage is a "sacrament." It is a "sign" of God's love, bringing about a new presence of Christ in the world. Faithful love *is* possible, for Christ has shown such love for his Church. And now, in the union of marriage, two people united in one flesh share and show his same love.

46 How is married love fruitful?

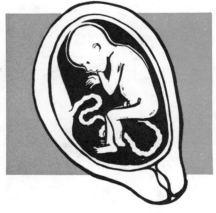

Married love bears fruit, through a deepening of love between husband and wife, to bring new life into being. "Marriage and married love are by their nature ordained to the begetting and educating of children" (*The Church Today*, #50). But marriage is not instituted solely for procreation. Another purpose of marriage is mutual support and growth of love between husband and wife. Therefore, marriage maintains its value and permanence even when offspring are lacking.

True married love is fruitful. We describe the act of sexual intercourse as "making love." And this is a good description to use. For intercourse is not only the physical expression of the total giving of husband and wife to one another, but it actually makes their love for each other grow.

The first fruit of married love, in other words, is a deepening of love. It brings the couple closer to one another as they are drawn to share one another's burdens; and it binds them closer to God, who is love and whose love they are called to share.

"Making love" is a couple's greatest activity. This activity is not limited, of course, to sexual intercourse but to all the experiences that a couple share. Besides these tender, affectionate experiences, it also refers to the sacrifices they make, as well as the mistakes, misunderstandings, and quarrels they have with one another. It remains true, nonetheless, that sexual intercourse is the climax of lovemaking. It is the moment when a new person can be conceived.

It is the moment, too, when man and woman share most intimately in God's lovemaking. The child of their love is the fruit of a unique partnership between God and them. Because they share in God's creative love, husband and wife are privileged to share in the most exalted part of God's creative love — the creation of a human being. Their generosity and love are surely a brilliant reflection of the Creator's love when he first brought the world into being.

This is a great privilege. But it is also a great responsibility! The Church reminds parents that they are "cooperators with the love of God the Creator, and are, so to speak, the interpreters of that love" (*The Church Today*, #50). Parents "interpret" the love of God to one another and to their children! Any act — such as artificial birth control, sterilization for that purpose, or abortion — which does not interpret his love is a lie.

Born of God's love, the children are to grow in God's love. As Father Gerald Vann, O.P., reminds us in his book, *The Heart of Man:* "The child's power of vision must be cherished, enlarged, deepened; to destroy it is a sort of murder." These words may strike us as harsh. But they are also true! The parents' responsibility to bring a child into the world does not cease with birth. It is wrong to destroy that life before birth. It is equally wrong to stunt the growth and development of a child after he or she is born.

"The child is the parents' love made flesh; and at the same time in the making of the child they make their own oneness." In these words Father Vann sums up for us the unique relationship between parents and children. "Making love" is creative. It creates a new man and woman, making them "one flesh." It creates a child. It creates a family. It creates the love of God in the world.

When there is a question of harmonizing married love with the responsible transmission of life, the moral aspect of any procedure must be determined by objective standards. Catholics may not, then, undertake methods of regulating procreation which are found blameworthy by the teaching authority of the Church (see *The Church Today*, #51).

In bringing children to birth and in educating them, parents are cooperators with the love of God the Creator. Responsible parenthood requires, then, that husband and wife — keeping a right order of priorities — recognize their own duties toward God, themselves, their families, and human society. In fulfilling these duties, parents are called to "interpret" the love of God.

47 Is the family the foundation of society?

The Church teaches that the family is the foundation of society: it is the "first and vital cell of society" (*Apostolate of the Laity,* #11). Married couples are to educate their children in a Christian manner and defend the dignity and lawful independence of the family. Parents are the first to communicate the faith to their children; they help them in the choice of their vocation and carefully promote any religious vocation which may be discerned in them.

Through the mutual love of the members of the family and the common prayer they offer to God, the family reflects the life of the whole Church. The activities of the family apostolate include the adoption of infants, hospitality to strangers, assistance in the operation of schools, help for the aged.

In this way, parents and children mutually support and educate each other for the strengthening of society as a whole; for it is in teaching their children that parents are themselves educated. The mutual support of parent and child is often particularly strong where there is only one parent.

Each morning he dons a sandwich board and sets out from his cramped basement flat to plod wearily around the streets of the city. "The end is nigh! . . . Repent of your sins! . . ."

The message is not a particularly consoling one. But Johnny Walking Gospel, as the song calls him, never stops to explain. This lonely old man with the crumpled coat and the leaking shoes just keeps on walking.

It is easy to write off Johnny Walking Gospel as an eccentric nonentity. But folk songs contain a great deal of human wisdom, and we would be extremely foolish not to recognize that his relentless circling of the city bears within it the kernel of a truth that no Catholic can ignore. We must all be "Walking Gospels."

This is a message we often hear from the pulpit. Perhaps this is because the preacher is more conscious than most that actions speak louder than words. He doesn't need to be told that no matter how carefully he prepares his Sunday homily it will be relatively ineffectual compared with the living love of a married couple in his parish.

This is not just pious talk. It is both faith and fact. When the Catholic Church was undergoing persecution in England, the hunted priests were the great sign of Christ's presence among his people. But this is not quite the case today. Ours is a world where people feel alienated and manipulated. In other words, they are hopelessly lonely. "For them," as Father C. Gallagher, S.J., writes, "the one sacrament today that has the greatest power to change the lonely crowd of society into a community of people who belong and who care is the married couple — people really living the sacrament of Matrimony."

It is a maxim in theology that a sacrament is never just for the sake of the one who receives it; it is always in the Church, of the Church, and for the Church. Once we set the sacrament of Matrimony in this context, it is not difficult to see why sacramental marriage is of its very nature a way of life.

The world is crying out for love. We all need to know that we are loved and wanted. We need to know most of all that there is Someone, a loving Father, who loves and accepts us totally. It was because God our Father wanted us to know just this that he sent his Son into the world as a man we could touch, feel, and acknowledge. The Incarnation was God's way of speaking our language. And so is the sacrament of Matrimony.

The married couple speak to the world. In their love for each other and their children they are saying: "This is what the Church, the community of God's love, is all about!"

48 What is the sacrament of Reconciliation?

So far in this *Catechism* we have seen how God our Father has created and renewed us. Through the revelation of his Son, Jesus Christ, he has sent us his Holy Spirit so that we can share his life. The sacraments, beginning with Baptism, are "high points" of our sharing by which we are truly made one with Christ.

But this, of course, is not the whole story. Our attempts to deepen our union with God are spoiled by sin. Like Saint Paul, we cannot understand our own behavior. We fail to carry out the things we want to do; we find ourselves doing the very things we hate (see Romans 7:15-16). God offers to raise us up to his own level by the gift of his grace. But our human nature, weakened by original sin, lets us down.

We need, literally, a complete change of heart. And, in the Old Testament, this is what God promised to give. Through one of his prophets, he promised: "I will remove the heart of stone from their bodies and give them a heart of flesh instead. . . . Shake off all the sins you have committed against me, and make yourselves a new heart and a new spirit" (Ezekiel 11:19, 18:31).

A famous professor once revealed that he had discovered a new sin. But he refused to say immediately what it was. "The world," he said, "must wait." And, indeed, the whole world waited with mounting excitement for his announcement. As the day drew nearer, reporters from all corners of the earth fought for tickets into the lecture hall where the professor was due to speak. The newspapers and TV dealt with nothing else. Experts in all fields of learning and radio commentators were called upon to discuss what this new sin might be. Every politician realized the importance of making a statement on the matter.

At last, the day came for the professor to reveal the new sin. He began his lecture by condemning the world for its obsessive curiosity. "You are all so foolish," he said, "that you will not understand what I have to say." And he promptly left the lecture hall, refusing to utter another word.

The author of this story, Monsignor Ronald Knox, was, of course, poking fun at the curiosity of his readers which carried them on to the end of his tale. It was a tale of fiction.

Yet our interest in sin can be no fiction. It is too much part of our nature to be disregarded. Sometimes, we think of sin — falsely — as like a contagious disease, a disease which principally affects other people. Sometimes, too, we expect a glossy catalog of sins to be supplied by the Church as an aid to better living. Looking through the catalog perhaps we expect, even occasionally, to discover a new sin!

But sin is not like that at all. A catalog can be a helpful guide to a smarter home interior or an improved garden. But it doesn't provide one penny of the cash required for the improvement. Nor is sin something which is waiting to be discovered. There is not a single person who has been free from the temptation to sin. And there is not a single person — outside the grace of Christ — who has not sinned. With the exception of the Blessed Virgin, sin is in each of us.

Sin is in each of us. In this *Catechism* we have already seen something of the origin and effects of original sin (Lessons 7-8). The origin is in our rejection of God. The effect is the continued loss of familiarity between God and ourselves.

Sin is in each of us. Our true nature is fractured. Sin cannot be overcome, then, by the healing efforts of the counselor or the soothing words of the psychoanalyst.

Sin is in each of us. We find that by ourselves we are "incapable of battling the assaults of evil successfully" so that we all feel we are bound by chains (see *The Church Today*, #13). The mending of our nature can only be the work of our Creator.

This gift — a change of heart — must be accepted by us before we can celebrate the sacrament of Reconciliation which Christ instituted when he said to his disciples: "Receive the Holy Spirit. For those whose sins you forgive, they are forgiven; for those whose sins you retain, they are retained" (John 20:23).

49 What is meant by change of heart?

Our "change of heart" by which we allow God to "convert" us to himself can never be an overnight experience. The life of God within us, which we call grace, begins to change us when we begin to believe in the Gospel of Jesus Christ. This is the moment of faith. For most Christians today this is the moment of Baptism. Because we were infants at the time, the belief of our parents or godparents supplied the faith that was necessary.

Occasionally, the beginnings of our "change of heart" come later in life, as it did for Saint Paul. On his way to persecute the Christians in Damascus "there came a light from heaven all round him. He fell to the ground, and then he heard a voice saying, 'Saul, Saul, why are you persecuting me? . . . I am Jesus, and you are persecuting me'" (Acts 9:3-5).

But for Saint Paul this was only the beginning. He discovered that "every single time I want to do good, it is something evil that comes to hand" (Romans 7:21). And for all Christians the deepening of God's grace within us is a gradual one. "God gives most of us a whole lifetime in which to turn to him completely, and we need the whole of this time, every moment of it" (Brian Newns). The constant rediscovery of corners of our lives which Christ has still not reached, areas of our existence where we are still selfish or self-indulgent, leads us to contrition. We are sorry for our sin.

Did you ever have a bad quarrel with someone you know well? The tension has built up over several days, perhaps even months or years. The reasons for the tension can sometimes be quite serious. There is ignorance, prejudice, misunderstanding, awkwardness. But then some event occurs which brings the tension to breaking point. Something explodes inside you. You flare up. And there is a monumental quarrel.

If you have had such an argument, you will have noticed, perhaps, how the incident which brought the quarrel to a head was often quite trivial. It was, simply, the "last straw" in the buildup to the explosion. And this is why, when we witness an argument between other people, the dispute often seems so pathetically petty and even funny. The violence of the quarrel seems totally out of proportion with the immediate subject of the dispute.

We have seen that our human nature has been fractured by original sin. There is a tension between ourselves and God. And this tension builds up until we commit sin. This we call personal or "actual" sin.

It is these "personal" sins which we confess in the sacrament of Reconciliation. But most of us find confession very difficult. And the reason, often, is that even though we tell our sins (usually the same ones!) we realize that we haven't really gotten to the root of the trouble between ourselves and God. We are vaguely aware that an outsider listening in might find our confession "pathetically petty and even funny." It seems so inadequate to express what we feel and know to be the situation: that there has been a buildup of ignorance, prejudice, misunderstanding, and awkwardness which has led to the serious quarrel — to sin.

This is partly why the Church emphasizes that our confession should truly reflect the relationship between ourselves and God. Our sorrow cannot always be expressed adequately in a whispered "shopping list" of sins. The Church encourages us, rather, to sit down occasionally with the priest to take a searching look at the *root* of the problem between ourselves and God.

In this *Catechism* we hope to do this over the next few lessons. For the present, we ask you to take part in a short test. As a first step we ask you to answer this question: "When you confess your sins to the priest in the sacrament of Reconciliation, what is the most important thing to remember?"

Perhaps your answer is something like "I must remember what my sins are . . . or the act of contrition . . . I must remember that I am speaking to Christ . . . I must be sorry for my sins."

All these things are important. But they are all concerned with *ourselves*. The correct answer, simply, is: "I must remember that what *God* does is infinitely more important than anything *I* do."

50 What is sin?

All sin is an offense or rebellion against God. (We will leave till later the distinction between mortal and venial sin.) Every sin spoils the relationship between ourselves and God. And so we must ask two questions:
1. What does God ask of me? That is, what is God's law for me?
2. How do I respond to what God asks of me? In other words, how do I fulfill God's law?

The Bible emphasizes these two sides of our relationship with God. The Old Testament word for sin is *hata*: which means *to miss the mark.* Sin, in other words, is our failure to reach the goal set for us by God. Our failure is like the arrow which fails to reach its target or like the stone thrown from the sling which has been badly aimed.

In the New Testament, Jesus explains the kind of relationship between God and ourselves: it is the most intimate possible. We sin when we separate ourselves from God like the prodigal son (in Luke 15:11-32) separating himself from the intimacy of his father's home. Sin is like leaving our loving Father.

Its true malice is to be judged not primarily from the action itself but from the evil in the heart. "It is what comes out of a man that makes him unclean. For it is from within, from men's hearts, that evil intentions emerge: fornication, theft, murder..." (Mark 7:21-22).

Very few people actually enjoy going to the sacrament of Reconciliation. At first, this might seem strange. For in this sacrament our sin is forgiven. We receive the Holy Spirit. We enjoy the peace purchased by the death and Resurrection of Jesus Christ.

The truth is that confession is like the first meeting between the apostles and their risen Lord. Their initial reaction was fear and embarrassment. They thought they were seeing a ghost, and they only too clearly remembered how they had failed their Lord. Only after he had spoken to them did their agitation turn to joy.

Most of *us* approach confession anxiously. We are concerned with our failure and sin. We can think only about our past and what we are going to say to the priest. It is only after Christ has spoken to us, through the priest, that our agitation turns to joy. We are forgiven. With God's help we can start again. At last, the peace of Christ is ours.

This is why, in the previous lesson, it was emphasized that what *God* does in the sacrament is infinitely more important than anything *we* do. Nonetheless, we must express our need of God's help and prepare ourselves to receive it if the sacrament is to transform our weakness into joy. This process by which God so transforms us may be better understood if we look at the four parts into which the Rite of Reconciliation is divided:
1. *Contrition.* Here the Lord prepares us to listen to his word by reviving our sorrow for sin and our intention of sinning no more.
2. *Confession.* Here the Lord leads us to open our heart to his minister.
3. *Satisfaction.* Here the Lord leads us to make up for the damage caused by our sin.
4. *Absolution.* Here the Lord gives us his pardon by breathing the Holy Spirit into us to strengthen us in his love.

In order to deepen our understanding of the sacrament, we will spend some time in looking at these four parts in turn. For the present we will continue our examination of the question, "What is meant by change of heart?"

Most Catholics, of course, are familiar with the distinction between imperfect contrition (sorrow for sins because by them we have lost heaven) and perfect contrition (sorrow for sin arising purely from the love of God). This distinction can be helpful. But its very simplicity can mislead and confuse us. For as God calls us to make the embarrassing approach to him in confession, he is constantly purifying our understanding and motives. How he does this will be our concern as we deal with "change of heart."

51 What is God's law?

Every sin spoils the relationship between ourselves and God. But what does God ask of us? What is God's law for us?

God has revealed his law in nature. Even though totally ignorant of God, all people "can point to the substance of the Law engraved on their hearts" which is recognized by conscience (Romans 2:15).

This natural law was to be uniquely expressed in the Old Law or Law of Moses. The giving of the Law of Moses, issuing from the Ten Commandments, was the formative event of the Old Testament by which the Jews were separated from other nations to become God's own. The Commandments sum up the fundamental demands of the human conscience with an accuracy and sureness rarely attained by the pagan philosophers. For the Jews the fulfillment of the Law meant salvation.

The Ten Commandments are:
1. I, the Lord, am your God. You shall not have other gods besides me.
2. You shall not take the name of the Lord, your God, in vain.
3. Remember to keep holy the Sabbath day.
4. Honor your father and your mother.
5. You shall not kill.
6. You shall not commit adultery.
7. You shall not steal.
8. You shall not bear false witness against your neighbor.
9. You shall not covet your neighbor's wife.
10. You shall not covet anything that belongs to your neighbor.
(See Supplement pp. S13-S14 for an examination of conscience based on the Commandments.)

Jesus did not come to abolish the Old Law but to complete it. The Old Law was written on tablets of stone, but the New Law is written in our hearts. The Old Law led to confusion and self-righteousness, but the New Law is ordered and leads to intimacy with God. On several occasions Jesus reaffirmed the Ten Commandments (see Matthew 19:17ff; Mark 10:17ff; Luke 18:18ff). But he also gave us the Sermon on the Mount, his discourse at the Last Supper, and numerous other indications, in word and example, of how he expects us to live.

What, then, is the New Law?

The Ten Commandments, many believe, are the most useful guide we have to the Christian life. If we keep them in mind, we can judge whether our behavior is "up to standard." They are a kind of thermometer measuring the quality of our Christian living.

If you agree with all this, you would have to argue with Saint Paul. He regarded it as nonsense! He wrote his greatest letter precisely to contradict this false way of thinking in the infant Church. His Roman readers wanted to hold on to the Laws based on the Ten Commandments as a support and reassurance of their justification in God's eyes. But Paul wrote to them: "You are living by grace and not by law" (Romans 6:14).

Paul was not saying, of course, that the Ten Commandments are pointless. Christ himself said: "If you wish to enter into life, keep the commandments" (Matthew 19:17). But it is equally clear that Christ transformed them. And Paul's concern was to give them their true value — their value as a kind of map from which, if we strayed, we were clearly losing our way.

Why, then, are the Ten Commandments so inadequate as a "standard" of the Christian life?

First, because they inevitably lead to a type of person whose relations with God are controlled entirely by laws. If something is not commanded in black and white, it can be ignored! If it is commanded, especially under threat of punishment, it must be done. If the punishment is not too severe, well, risk it!

Second, because they inevitably lead to self-righteousness. If our life is founded on the Commandments — on keeping the "rules" — we can end up quite satisfied with ourselves. "I've done my bit," we say. "Now God must keep *his* end of the bargain!"

Third, the Commandments are inadequate because they can only lay down the bare minimum. God requires that we do far more than observe set laws; and he gives us the grace to do it. For example, the love of God within us may inspire us to send a hot meal across the street to a widow who can't cook for herself. There is no law that demands we do so. *But our failure to do so may be sinful.* For we have failed to do what God asks. As Paul tells us, God does not intend us to be observers of the Law, but to become "images of Christ."

Fourth, a life based on the Commandments leads us to judge others harshly by our own standards rather than by God's. God demands more of some than of others. For example, he can demand less of a person who has had little chance in life through family or social circumstances. A child trained to shoplift by the parents will clearly not be judged harshly by God for breaking the Seventh Commandment. People cannot be judged simply by the standards of the Commandments. They can be judged only according to the Law of Christ.

52 What is the New Law?

The New Law is the Law of Christ. This does not contradict the Old Law as summarized in the Ten Commandments, but it sheds a totally new light upon it. It sheds this light in three principal ways:

1. Jesus established order among the various laws that had grown up in the Jewish tradition. He established love of God and of neighbor as the center of his moral code: "You must love the Lord your God with all your heart, with all your soul, with all your strength, and with all your mind, and your neighbor as yourself" (Luke 10:27).

2. Jesus imposed perfection on his followers. Under the Old Law imperfections had been tolerated because "you were so unteachable" (Matthew 19:8). But Jesus told them: "You must therefore be perfect just as your heavenly Father is perfect" (Matthew 5:48). This is the perfection of the Good Samaritan who "loved his enemies" (Luke 10:29-37).

3. Most importantly, Jesus offers us the means by which we can become perfect. He offers us his own life: the life of the Holy Spirit. He gave us the Holy Spirit for the overcoming of sin. After his Resurrection, he breathed on the apostles, saying: "Receive the Holy Spirit. For those whose sins you forgive, they are forgiven. . ." (John 20:23).

"God loves Karel — even more than you do — and if you ask him, he will give you his love for this man, a love nothing can prevent, nothing destroy. Whenever we cannot love in the old human way, Corrie, God can give us the perfect way."

The young girl fought back the tears as her father spoke. It seemed impossible that Karel, simply to please his family, should have asked someone else to be his wife. But, thank God, her father had not said, "There'll be someone else soon." Because she already knew deep down that there would not be — soon or ever — any other man for her.

As Corrie ten Boom listened to her father's footsteps winding back down the stairs, she began to pray that God would help her to see Karel through his divine eyes — that she would love him with his divine love. Later she realized that her father had given her the key not only to this desperate moment but to a thousand other desperate moments she was to endure in the concentration camp and remember so vividly in her book, *The Hiding Place*. This wise old man had introduced her to the *New Law of Christ*.

But what does Corrie's experience tell us about the New Law spoken about by Jesus? A great deal, in fact! Corrie was not the first person in the history of Christianity to be surprised at this strange power within which enabled her to see exactly what she must do, how she must act, if she were to remain free of the bitterness and cramping self-pity which go hand in hand with rejection and suffering. She had merely been granted a privileged insight into the words spoken by Jesus to those who looked only to external laws and instructions for guidance: "If you make my word your home, you will indeed be my disciples, you will learn the truth and the truth will make you free" (John 8:31).

Corrie now knew how the apostles must have felt. Saint Peter, who was probably the least likely candidate to set a worldwide propaganda campaign in motion, found himself making all sorts of decisions with considerable confidence. The highly organized Saint Paul, whose natural bent lay in the direction of detailed instructions and future planning, was amazed at how many times he was "led" to act in a certain way. We remember him as the great apostle who crossed the Bosporus and brought the Gospel to Europe. But he was, in fact, on his way to Asia when the Spirit turned him back!

Saint Paul became convinced that it is the Spirit who imprints the Law of Christ in our hearts when he pours the love of God into our hearts (see Romans 5:5). We are able then to see as God sees, love as God loves. As Corrie's father put it, "God can give us the perfect way."

53 How do we fulfill God's Law?

We have seen what is meant by God's law. There is the law of nature, observed by the pagans who follow the voice of conscience.
There is the Law of Moses, observed by the Jews who follow the voice of God as revealed to them in the Bible. But God's law truly means the law of Christ. This is the Holy Spirit within the Christian moving him or her to follow a conscience matured in the love of Christ.

Our growth in observing God's law progresses through these stages. In each of us there is the pagan. Like the child, we act instinctively in accordance with outside pressures. We act because we fear punishment or disapproval.

In each of us, too, there is the Pharisee. We act in accordance with the Law because we realize that society, good order and, indeed, our own self-satisfaction require it. Here, sorrow for sin is based on the fact that we have really let ourselves down.

In every Christian there is the Holy Spirit, the life of God, who is the source of true morality. Now, it is not the laws, but the values of the law, which are accepted as calling toward God. Here, sorrow for sin is not based on fear or the fact that we have let ourselves down, but on the love of God who invites us, even in our sin, to share his love ever more deeply.

"The simplest and best means to unite ourselves to Christ is to act, speak, and think, always and in all things as he did, remaining in his presence and imitating him. . . . In all that we do, say, or think, we should ask ourselves, how did he do it, say it, think it."

Charles de Foucauld, the founder of the Little Brothers of Jesus, was always very simple and direct when it came to speaking of the imitation of Christ. His is the ease and familiarity of the saint. But it is an ease which is not entirely shared by many of us today. While we recognize, along with the psychologists and sociologists, that imitation is an important part of growing in maturity, we worry that too much stress on a too slavish imitation of Christ runs the danger of reducing him to a great moral guide or holy man.

We will have a great deal more to say on this subject later on. For the moment, we suggest you turn to the New Testament and take note of how the first followers of Christ discovered, in their day-to-day contact with him, a whole new set of values in their lives. Read chapter 8 of Saint Luke, for example, and you will certainly find yourself wondering why the woman who had been cured, Mary Magdalene, and the wife of Herod's steward took to the road with Christ. Their action, and it must have caused a big upheaval in their lives, certainly seems to point to a strong *personal* attachment to Christ, which should in some way be reflected in our lives.

It would also be extremely valuable to notice how Saint Matthew seems to lay a great deal of stress on the importance of being "with Jesus." He is the only evangelist who describes Jesus as Emmanuel, a name which he tells us means "God-is-with-us" (Matthew 1:23). And it is he who ends his Gospel with the words: "And know that I am with you always; yes, to the end of time."

It is this "being with Christ" which is at the heart of our daily fulfillment of his law. We, in a mysterious way, follow him on the road to Jerusalem and death along with the women and his disciples. We are with him when he is *filled with the Spirit* in the Jordan, when he allows himself to be *led by the Spirit* into the desert, and when he preaches, dies, and rises from the dead in the *power of the Spirit*.

How, then, do we fulfill the Law of Christ? First, we must allow ourselves to be *filled* with the Spirit and so *led* by the Spirit. Then we will "be with" Christ, share his life, and live in the *power* of the Spirit.

54 What Christian value is expressed by the first Beatitude?

We have seen how it is from the heart that good or evil intentions emerge.
Good or evil is in our attitudes. Sin is a false attitude of mind and heart.
The Law of Christ to love God and neighbor is expressed in the Beatitudes (see
Matthew 5). We will look at each of the eight Beatitudes in turn; for they uniquely
contain the attitudes of the Christian whose following of Christ
means happiness.

The first Beatitude is: Blessed are the poor in spirit; for
theirs is the kingdom of heaven.

This attitude (that of the poor) is one of total
dependence upon God our Father. It is an attitude of
constantly turning toward God in prayer, in worship.
This worship begins in our hearts and in our homes; its
climax is the Sunday Eucharist.

When Saint Paul instructs us to
"pray constantly" (1 Thessalonians
5:17), he means us to take this
attitude of dependence on God into
every moment of our everyday life.
This means recognizing that the
world and all it contains has
been entrusted to us to build
up into an acceptable offering
to God.

In this way the Christian builds up
and possesses the kingdom
of God on earth.

The Christian law is summarized in the Beatitudes. Many, perhaps, find this disappointing. After all, if we want to know whether a particular action is sinful, it's a great deal easier to refer to, say, the Sixth Commandment, "Thou shalt not commit adultery," than to the sixth Beatitude which refers to the "blessedness of the pure in heart." The Commandments are clear. They tell us what's right and what's wrong. For many, the Beatitudes are a little vague. They don't seem to tell us exactly where we stand with God!

The truth is that the Commandments only deal with our *actions*. The Beatitudes go deeper. They deal with our *attitudes*. They go to the *heart* of our Christian belief. Right *attitudes* will always produce right *actions*. Right actions, on the other hand, do not always mean right attitudes; and, in fact, self-satisfaction with our "good behavior" can result in the most fatal disease of our Christian faith — self-righteousness.

If we want to know where we stand with God, then the Commandments are not in themselves a reliable guide. Jesus sat down to eat with tax collectors and sinners. These were "the poor in spirit." They needed help; and they knew it! And so they were the ones to receive help. They were the ones closest to God.

It is the Beatitudes which tell us where we stand with God. And they are far from vague. They are very clear! In them, Jesus shows us that we are not to live according to a set of laws but by an inner revolution of attitude and outlook. In a startling reversal of the world's standards, Jesus proposes poverty, meekness, even tears of sadness and repentance as the only path to happiness in this life. Only these will create a "heaven on earth."

This contradiction needs an explanation. How, for example, can one be poor but possess all things? How can one mourn and, at the same time, be comforted?

Christ realized that it is only when we are destitute, with no pride or self-satisfaction left in us, that we will turn to him. And only he can give true happiness. This isn't easy to understand or to follow.

Archbishop Bloom gives an illustration that may help us. If we say, "I have this watch, it is mine," and then close our hand over it, we have gained a watch. But we have lost the use of a hand! We become so intent to keep the watch that we barely notice the high price paid for it.

While we clutch at earthly values we barely notice the high price paid for them. For they prevent us from approaching Christ; they give us the feeling that we are secure without him.

The Beatitudes powerfully express the principal message of the Gospel. For they are a promise to us that if we free ourselves from our human ambitions and attachments, true happiness will be ours.

55 What Christian value is expressed by the second Beatitude?

The second Beatitude is: Blessed
are the meek; for they shall
possess the land.

This attitude (that of gentleness and humility) is one of patience.
Following Christ, who patiently accepted suffering, the Christian is
called to "love your enemies and pray for those who persecute you"
(Matthew 5:44). If there has been anger or hatred, it means that "If you
are bringing your offering to the altar and there remember that your
brother has something against you, leave your offering there before the
altar, go and be reconciled with your brother first, and then come
back and present your offering" (Matthew 5:24).

The word *humility* derives from the word *humus* which is
defined as an organic part of the soil. It is the decomposing
and decaying of useless plant materials from
which issues rich and luxuriant growth. In the same way,
from humility, which is self-dying, comes a fruitful
and abundant growth.

In this way the meek
"shall possess the land."

A recent survey among Catholics put this question, with the following results:

Question: Many people do not like going to the sacrament of Reconciliation. If you find it difficult, indicate whichever of the following comes closest to expressing your difficulty.

Results: (a) I don't like telling my sins to someone else — 9%; (b) I find myself confessing the same old sins every time, and it seems so pointless — 39%; (c) I never know what to say — 10%; (d) I get embarrassed and tongue-tied — 14%; (e) I'm afraid of what the priest will say — 5%; (f) I do not find it difficult — 23%.

It is clear that the greatest difficulty is the apparent "pointlessness" of confession. We find ourselves confessing "the same old sins." The reason is obvious, but perhaps it is worth stating. We *confess* "the same old sins" because we *commit* "the same old sins."

We are not breaking the seal of the sacrament in revealing that, at the top of this list, are the sins of impatience, bad temper, anger. These are the sins that *everyone* commits. They are the sins that we almost take for granted as part and parcel of our everyday life.

And this is frequently the difficulty. We take the evil of impatience for granted — even to regarding it as a virtue! We can be proud of the fact that we "don't suffer fools gladly." And we regard the "meek" or "gentle" person as really spineless!

The truly gentle person is quite the opposite, of course. Nothing takes so much out of us or demands such strength of character as patience. And it is always hardest with those we know best — with our families. Certainly, there are times when a good fight helps to clear the air. But how much unnecessary friction and unhappiness is caused by plain bad temper? The normal human respect, which acts as a brake on our anger with outsiders, we ignore in our family relationships; and we let fly!

Yet Christ's teaching does not allow contradiction. "Anyone who is angry with his brother will answer for it before the court" (Matthew 5:22). We are to go even beyond normal human respect to a respect and reverence for others founded on God's love. We are to respect others in the same way as God respects them. This is the source of patience.

This Beatitude, then, is not calling us to a "grin-and-bear-it" attitude. Our Christian life is not an endurance test with the reward of "blessedness" or happiness for the toughest contestants. Rather, it demands from us a profound change of attitude by which we recognize the real presence of Christ in all people — even those we find most difficult. We cannot take any person for granted. Each one *deserves* our patience.

56 What Christian value is expressed by the third Beatitude?

The third Beatitude is: Blessed are they who mourn; for they shall be comforted.

This attitude (that of grief) is one of recognizing what really matters in life. For in grief we come to recognize our sin, which leads to repentance; and we learn to recognize the sufferings of others, which leads to compassion. In this way, we follow Christ who identified himself with a sinful and suffering world. This led Jesus to "mourn" over the spiritual condition of Israel, the root cause of her troubles: "Jerusalem, Jerusalem, you that kill the prophets and stone those who are sent to you! How often have I longed to gather your children as a hen gathers her chicks under her wings, and you refused!" (Matthew 23:37)

Such grief leads to prudent action. Prudence is the grace to know what to do in a given situation. Confronted by sinners, for example, Jesus often showed compassion; yet when the situation demanded it, he was ruthless. And so Jesus, "making a whip out of some cord, drove the money-changers and the people selling cattle and sheep and pigeons out of the Temple saying, 'Take all this out of here and stop turning my Father's house into a market'" (John 2:16).

In this way, those who mourn and so act rightly, will be comforted.

"When I suffer a lot or have to go through difficult and painful things, instead of feeling sorry for myself, I smile. At first I did not succeed very well, but now I'm so happy that it has become a habit with me."

With such simplicity did Terese of the Child Jesus become a saint. She lived just 24 years, hidden in a Carmelite convent. But her "little way" of doing even the smallest thing with love has helped millions to come close to God.

Her "little way" is no "easy way," however. It means facing the daily difficulties head on — and beating them with a smile! We are to be like the commuter who always greeted the train conductor with a friendliness and pleasantness which was only matched by rudeness and unpleasantness. When asked why he was polite when the conductor was so unfriendly in return, he replied: "Because I don't want *him* to decide how *I'm* going to act."

Who, then, does decide how *I'm* going to act? Some people, of course, grow old without ever growing up. Like the child, they change dramatically from smiles to whimpers — and back to smiles again. Their actions are determined by outside forces. But for mature Christians there is a deeper inner resource who determines how they act. This is the Holy Spirit — the Comforter. He overcomes our mourning. As Jesus told Saint Paul, who pleaded three times for the removal of a "thorn in the flesh," "My grace is enough for you; my power is at its best in weakness" (2 Corinthians 12:9).

And in the life of Saint Paul we see the result of the comfort he received from God. With unparalleled success he was able to *win* people to Christ. He was able to choose just the right words and adopt just the right manner to win people over. We can only describe this as prudence: a value of Christ's law about which most of us seldom think.

Like each of us, Paul had to deal with all kinds of different people in a variety of sensitive situations. He made no pretense of the fact that he adapted his way of acting to his audience: "I made myself all things to all men in order to save some at any cost" (1 Corinthians 9:22). His knowledge of human nature made him realize that people couldn't be changed overnight. But his knowledge of God's power made him realize that people *could* be drawn from their false attitudes to God's attitudes if he worked patiently and prudently.

We do not win people to Christ, in other words, by silence. But, equally, we do not approach people like a bull in a china shop, insensitive to their real needs. Prudence is that essential value of Christ's law by which we learn to distinguish. It is a gift of God. And its sign is the winning smile.

57 What Christian value is expressed by the fourth Beatitude?

The fourth Beatitude is: Blessed are they who hunger and thirst after justice; for they shall have their fill.

This attitude of the Christian (that of "good relations" with God) is one of giving God and his creatures what is due to them. We recognize that we can stand with dignity in God's presence — because of God's gift of grace we are "justified" — and our gratitude for this gift leads us to share it with others. Justice, then, means treating and respecting others with the same grace as God treats and respects them. We are to "hunger and thirst" for justice. "Do not say, 'What are we to eat? What are we to drink? . . .' It is the pagans who set their hearts on all these things. Your heavenly Father knows you need them all. Set your hearts on his kingdom first, and on his righteousness [justice], and all these things will be given you as well" (Matthew 6:31-33). In this way, those who hunger and thirst for justice shall have their fill.

If we take or steal another's life or property or good name or anything that is his or hers, we are obliged, as far as possible, to restore it and to make restitution. A person's good name, for example, is more valuable than his or her property, and, if we take it away by rash (unjust) judgment, we are bound to make every effort to give it back.

There is a legend from the East that tells of a brave warrior who died, came before the gates of eternity, and was given the option of choosing to go to heaven or hell. First, he decided to visit hell; and, upon entering, he discovered a large table laden with exotic dishes. But those seated at the table looked miserable. On asking why they were sad, he was told that the only rule in hell was that all food had to be eaten with ten-foot-long chopsticks. Those at the table could not get the food into their mouths — hence the suffering.

The warrior, unhappy at the prospect of hell, then went to heaven. Here, he discovered a similar banquet. But this time the people were happy. Asking whether the rule of eating was different, he was told that people in heaven have to eat with the similar long sticks, but they have learned to feed one another across the table, instead of attempting the impossible task of trying to feed themselves.

The legend is crudely expressed. But the lesson is clear. It is the message of the fourth Beatitude: Those who are unselfish in fighting for justice will have their fill. Justice means having the interests of others at heart.

What does this mean in today's world — a world in which salaries and wages within a nation and within an industry are so finely weighed against each other, and the balance of payments between countries is so critical? The answer is not an easy one; but it lies in recognizing where the *greatest* injustices lie.

For the truth is that injustice is as inevitable as selfishness. From our infancy — when we try to match up to the different expectations of our parents through to old age when our own children fail to give us the respect we would like — injustice confronts us at every corner. These injustices are real.

But to a certain extent we have to learn to live with them. In our fight against injustice, our struggle should be directed primarily against the *extreme* inequalities in the enjoyment of individual and social rights, material goods, and spiritual freedom.

Time and time again Jesus reminds us of our obligations toward the poor and that it is no excuse to say we didn't notice them. We are not deliberately cruel. We don't kick them in the teeth. We don't do *anything*. And that was the sin condemned by Christ.

In more modern times the Church has continued Christ's warnings. In the encyclical *Development of Peoples*, 1967, quoting St. Ambrose, she reminds us that when we give to the poor "we are not making a gift of our possessions. We are only handing over to him what is his. The world is given to all, and not only to the rich."

58 What Christian value is expressed by the fifth Beatitude?

The fifth Beatitude is: Blessed are the merciful; for they shall obtain mercy.

This attitude of the Christian (that of loyal compassion) is one of forgiveness and outgoing love. We give to others what we ourselves have received from God. In this we follow Christ who came "not to condemn the world, but so that through him the world might be saved" (John 3:17). Jesus' parable of the unforgiving debtor (see Matthew 18:23-35), who was excused payment of a fortune by his master but enforced payment of a few pennies from a fellow servant, illustrates the horror of our reluctance to forgive.

God will judge us on the way we share his mercy with others: "If you forgive others their failings, your heavenly Father will forgive you yours; but if you do not forgive others, your Father will not forgive your failings either" (Matthew 6:14-15). Our forgiveness must go so far as to win back those who have strayed — as Christ, the Good Shepherd, seeks out the lost sheep, joyfully takes it on his shoulders, and invites all to rejoice.

In this way, those who show mercy will have mercy shown them.

We are told that on one occasion the great Italian artist, Michelangelo, was spending a quiet evening with some friends. The conversation turned, as it so often does, to the faults and failings of absent friends. The personality of each was closely analyzed; and none emerged from the scrutiny completely unscathed. As the evening wore on, the group noticed that Michelangelo was quiet and not joining in the fun. They turned to the great artist and asked him why.

"I'm thinking of a painting," Michelangelo explained. At this, the friends' interest was roused; they knew that a painting from Michelangelo would be great indeed and asked him what it was. The artist offered to paint it for them, then and there. He covered a canvas with white paint and in the middle painted a small black circle, filling it with black paint.

"What do you see?" asked Michelangelo. The friends looked puzzled. "We can see a black spot," they replied. Michelangelo paused for a moment. "I thought you would see that," he said. "What I see is a large area of white."

The story portrays the attitude of most of us. In each of us there is a great deal of goodness — a large area of "white." And yet the first thing we see in another's character is the blemish — the "little black spot." And by our words, we magnify that spot out of all proportion, destroying the character of another.

Of course, we all have our faults. And so, like Peter (in Matthew 18:21-22), we wonder what limits we are to place on our mercy: "Lord, how often must I forgive my brother if he wrongs me?" Christ's answer is clear. There is no one whom he did not consider worth dying for. The love of Jesus for all people has made them all lovable. There is to be *no* limit to the mercy we offer others.

But we cannot show mercy if we have not learned to experience God's mercy with ourselves. So often, we allow the memory of past sins to weigh us down. We are like the old woman climbing a steep hill carrying two heavy buckets of water. A farmer driving a wagon stopped to ask if she wanted a lift. Gratefully, she climbed into the cart, still carrying the buckets of water. After a while, the farmer suggested she put the buckets down, but the woman refused. "No," she said, "I would prefer to take some of the weight off the poor horse by carrying them myself!"

Jesus took the weight of our sins upon himself on Calvary. It would be the worst form of ingratitude to allow past sins to come between ourselves and God. God forgives us. And, in the same measure, we are to show mercy to others.

59 What Christian value is expressed by the sixth Beatitude?

The sixth Beatitude is: Blessed are the pure in heart; for they shall see God.

This attitude of the Christian is one of purity of intention. The gift of God's Spirit frees our actions from motives of pride or self-interest. The disciples once complained to Jesus that the Pharisees had been "shocked" by his statement: "What goes into the mouth does not make a man unclean; it is what comes out of the man that makes him unclean." And Jesus later explained: "The things that come out of the mouth come from the heart, and it is these that make a man unclean. For from the heart come evil intentions: murder, adultery, fornication, theft, perjury, slander" (Matthew 15:11,18-19).

Purity of intention is evidenced in the chaste heart, free from lust. For such an attitude means love for the other person's sake rather than one's own. "You have learnt how it was said: 'you must not commit adultery.' But I say this to you: 'If a man looks at a woman lustfully, he has already committed adultery with her in his heart'" (Matthew 5:27-28).

In this way, those whose hearts are set on God will enter into his presence.

Sex and sin are so often placed side by side — so often, in fact, that many find it hard to separate them. Two commandments deal with the sin side of sex: "Thou shalt not commit adultery . . . Thou shalt not covet thy neighbor's wife."

Jesus' words express the Christian attitude to sex in quite different terms: "Blessed are the pure in heart; for they shall see God." In all his moral teaching, Jesus' primary concern was with the heart. This Beatitude clearly expresses the Christian's fundamental attitude. If our heart is set in the right direction — if it is a "pure" heart — there will be no sexual sin.

The point, quite simply, is that our sexuality is an essential part of our personality. In her recent *Declaration on Sexual Ethics* (1975), the Church began by stating that "the human person is so profoundly affected by sexuality that it must be considered as one of the factors which give to each individual's life the principal traits that distinguish it." This is why the Church has always been so concerned with sexual morality. Our attitude to sex is a sensitive thermometer which measures the quality and direction of the heart. Sexual sin is a sign that the heart is sick.

What, then, is the right attitude to sex? What is the right direction for the heart? What is "purity" of heart?

The answer is not easily stated. After all, we are penetrating our innermost nature — our very dignity and destiny. Briefly, however, the answer is that the "pure in heart" are concerned for "wholeness." They want "holiness." In a word, they are people who love.

The truth is that sex can be understood only in the context of love. Sex becomes sinful when it is removed from this context — when it is displayed and exalted as anything less than a part of our innermost personality. Sex is part of our "holiness" by which we express our deepest union with the one we love. This is the union of marriage — a sign of the union between Christ and his Church.

Any divorce between sex and the "holiness" of marriage is a sign of a disordered heart — a heart turned in on itself. And a disordered heart is as powerful a force for destruction as is the ordered heart a power for building up. The Church is almost alone in placing the sexual side of our nature in its right context, giving it the importance it deserves.

It is the greatest tragedy, then, if we can only place sex side by side with sin. It means that we have totally failed to understand the wonderful mystery of the human personality: we have failed to see God.

60 What Christian value is expressed by the seventh Beatitude?

The seventh Beatitude is: Blessed are the peacemakers; for they shall be called the children of God.

In this attitude (one of establishing right relations between all people) the Christian does God's work of reconciliation. Peacemaking (as opposed to troublemaking) is the most practical fruit of love. Christ's "program" for peacemaking is first to approach the person who does something wrong and "have it out with him alone, between your two selves. . . . If he does not listen, take one or two others along with you. . . . But if he refuses to listen to the community, treat him like a pagan or a tax collector [outcasts]" (Matthew 18:15-17).

Christ's gift of peace is the greatest fruit of his Resurrection. He died that we "all may be one." The Christians' greatest task is to find peace among themselves so that God's gift of peace may be offered to the whole world.

The sixth and seventh Beatitudes, concerned with purity and peacemaking, deal with the two instincts most troublesome in society, namely, sexuality and aggression. They are only overcome by the gift of the Holy Spirit who makes us "children of God."

The feats of skilled "skateboarders" are quite spectacular. They can spin around an almost vertical wall; and, as long as their speed is kept up, centrifugal force prevents them from toppling over. The vital secret in retaining balance, of course, lies in keeping up the high speed. Trouble starts when they begin to slow down.

Many people manage to keep their balance in life in a similar way. They keep busy, rushing from one job to the next. And while they keep up their speed they manage to survive. It is only when they slow down that they panic and topple over.

In the whirl of modern life it's not easy to stay still and keep a sense of balance. For this requires the ability to discover in oneself the inner resources to carry on living. We are afraid of ourselves and of what we might discover if we turn our attention to the kind of persons we really are. We seek peace of mind by looking in all directions except one; we are scared to look into our own hearts.

"Blessed are the peacemakers," Jesus tells us. The "peacemaker" who is not at peace with himself is a hypocrite — an ineffective hypocrite. This is why the priest must be a man of genuine peace; only such a man can make true peace between Christ and the sinner. And all of us, at one time or another, are called upon to bring peace into the lives of others.

But how do we discover such peace? Is it a matter, simply, of pausing occasionally to examine the quality of our lives? Is it just a question of stopping to take a genuine look into ourselves?

Yes it is! It is as simple as that! For every Christian has been given the gift of the Holy Spirit, the source of peace. After his Resurrection, Christ appeared to his disciples with the words, "Peace be with you." And he breathed on them, saying: "Receive the Holy Spirit." And Christ breathed the same Spirit into our own hearts.

All the time the Spirit is closer to us than we dream; he is within our heart and soul which we search so very seldom. The Holy Spirit is closer to us than we are to ourselves, drawing us deeper into the personal and intimate love of Father, Son, and himself — bringing us peace.

Even the busiest of us can allow the Holy Spirit within us to cry out, "Abba, Father." "Abba" is a Hebrew word that the child uses to address his father in the intimacy of home. It is the word Jesus used to address his heavenly Father in Gethsemane as he approached the climax of his life. It is our perfect prayer, proving that we are children of God.

When we recognize the Spirit of peace who makes us cry out, "Abba, Father," we can follow Christ in his work of bringing peace to the world.

61 What Christian value is expressed by the eighth Beatitude?

The final Beatitude is: Blessed are they who suffer persecution for justice' sake; for theirs is the kingdom of heaven.

This attitude is one of penance. It is comprised of the joyful following of Christ in his suffering and death. When we ourselves are the victims we are to offer the wicked person no resistance. "On the contrary, if anyone hits you on the right cheek, offer him the other as well" (Matthew 5:39). And, at his trial, guards standing by gave Jesus a slap in the face (see John 18:22).

Following Christ's own practice in the desert we are to deny ourselves. Our sharing in Christ's death, celebrated in the Eucharist, is to be extended into our everyday life through voluntary penance in the form of prayer, fasting, and works of charity. The Church commends fasting for those who are materially prosperous and the acceptance of suffering (while still seeking to promote better social justice) for those who are poor.

A small boy was carrying his little brother up a steep hill. Moved by the sight of the boy obviously struggling under the weight of his burden, a passerby called out, "Isn't that a very heavy load you are carrying?" "No," the boy replied, "it isn't a load; it's my brother."

Saint Paul once described the burden of his sufferings in a similar way. "The only thing I can boast about is the cross of our Lord Jesus Christ . . . the marks on my body are those of Jesus" (Galatians 6:14,17), he wrote. Everywhere he traveled Paul took the burden of persecution upon his shoulders for the sake of the Gospel. But his sufferings were not too heavy to bear; for in them he carried Christ his Brother.

It is easy to accept God's will when it coincides with our own. The trouble is that it so often doesn't! In carrying Christ we will *always* be asked to carry, too, some of the weight of the Cross.

Nothing calls for a more complete change of attitude than that of accepting suffering for Christ's sake. Every fiber of our flesh, every human conviction of our mind cries out against pain and rejection. In all the world there is no question asked more often than, "Why suffering?"

We try to think it out. Maybe we start with the Old Testament idea that we are being punished for our sins. From there we go on to think of offering up our sufferings in payment of our sins. We are making some progress, but we have a long way to go yet. We only realize how far when we are faced with suffering in the innocent — maybe in a child who is dear to us. Then we are really left with a big question, *why?* We look to heaven, somewhat reproachfully, for the answer.

There is no need to look too high, no higher than the crucifix on our wall. The moment of suffering can be the moment we look on the crucified Christ for the millionth time, and see him for the first time. For there is the most innocent One who has suffered the most.

There is an alternative to the burden of the Cross. But the alternative is heavier still. It is the burden of hate. A short while before being struck down by the assassin's bullet, Martin Luther King spoke the following words: "I've seen too much hate to want to hate, myself . . . and every time I see it, I say to myself, hate is too great a burden to bear. . . ."

"In your minds you must be the same as Christ Jesus: His state was divine, yet he did not cling to his equality with God but emptied himself to assume the condition of a slave, and became as men are; and being as all men are, he was humbler yet, even to accepting death, death on a cross" (Philippians 2:5-8).

"Happy are you when people abuse you and persecute you and speak all kinds of calumny against you on my account. Rejoice and be glad, for your reward will be great in heaven" (Matthew 5:11-12).

62 How do we use the Beatitudes to examine our conscience?

The values of the Law of Christ are contained in the Beatitudes. These values are concerned with our relationship with God and with our fellow human beings. They are expressed in our "attitudes."

The right attitude to God is that of worship and of attachment to him in suffering and penance (*1st and 8th Beatitudes*).

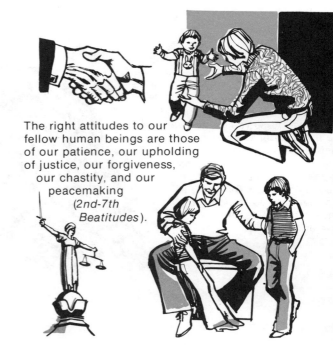

The right attitudes to our fellow human beings are those of our patience, our upholding of justice, our forgiveness, our chastity, and our peacemaking (*2nd-7th Beatitudes*).

Sin is a false attitude. We are judged by God on the attitudes we adopt. It is upon these attitudes, then, that we are to examine our conscience regularly and in the sacrament of Reconciliation. And it is in these attitudes that our conscience is to be formed, for they are always binding and are absolute.

When we began to summarize God's law through the Beatitudes we pointed out that "for many, the Beatitudes are a little vague. They don't seem to tell us exactly where we stand with God." So far, we have tried to show that the Beatitudes are far from vague; and they tell us *exactly* where we stand with God.

Of course, we have not been able to cover even a fraction of the material on the moral law written in the New Testament and over the centuries. We have not mentioned by name such sins as idolatry, blasphemy, masturbation, drunkenness, and so forth. But, primarily, it is because we considered it more important to provide the reasons *why* such sins are wrong.

A wrong attitude to suffering will *always* lead to bitterness and anger; a wrong attitude to sex will *always* lead to sexual sin. To overcome such sins our minds must be informed with the attitudes of Christ. Then, there will be no question of sin. Sin will disappear.

What are *my* attitudes in my everyday living? We suggest an examination of conscience, based on Christ's eight Beatitudes:

1. Blessed are the poor in spirit:
Do I recognize that the world is God's — not mine? Do I thank him for it? Do I express my thanks in my weekly worship? Does the world center around me?

2. Blessed are the meek:
Do I recognize that every person is created by God and equally loved by him? Does my behavior reflect this realization? Do I resent criticism? Do I take out my impatience on those who are weak and least likely to fight back?

3. Blessed are they who mourn:
Do I recognize that every person is created as frail as myself and is as much in need of help and encouragement? Am I sensitive to the real needs of others? Do I realize the power of my words and actions to heal or to harm? Am I indifferent to the misfortune of others?

4. Blessed are they who hunger and thirst after justice:
Do I recognize that all creation is for the good of every person and equally to be enjoyed by all? Do I steal from others the goods or the good name which belong to them? Am I lazy?

5. Blessed are the merciful:
Do I recognize that I am myself in need of mercy? Do I ever see goodness in others? Do I make hasty judgments? Am I grateful for the forgiveness I receive from others?

6. Blessed are the pure in heart:
Do I recognize that the heart will only rest when it is centered on God? Do I use others or try to possess them for my own satisfaction? Do I abuse the gift of sex to satisfy my own ego?

7. Blessed are the peacemakers:
Do I recognize the source of peace: the dignity God has given me in making me one of his adopted children? Do I enjoy making trouble for others? Am I the kind of person who needs to be humored?

8. Blessed are they who suffer persecution for justice' sake:
Do I recognize that it is in suffering that I enter most deeply into the mind of Christ? Do I ever do penance to make up for the damage caused by my sins? Do I resent suffering so that it becomes a barrier between myself and God?

63 What is conscience?

Conscience is a person's ability to make a moral judgment. "Always summoning him to love good and avoid evil, the voice of conscience can when necessary speak to his heart more specifically: do this, shun that." By conscience we reason to what we ought to do; it is our consciousness of God's will for us. "Conscience is the most secret core and sanctuary of a man. There he is alone with God, whose voice echoes in his depths" (*The Church Today,* #16).

We are obliged, therefore:
1. To follow the demands of conscience. "Obedience to one's conscience, even if the conscience is in error, is the best way to the light" (Cardinal Newman). Saint Paul demanded respect for people whose conscience was in error. He instructed Christians in Corinth not to eat meat offered to idols and then sold in butcher shops — even though this was permissible — for fear of upsetting those who wrongly considered eating such meat to be sinful (see I Corinthians 10:25-30).

2. To inform our conscience correctly. This means drawing on the wisdom of the past and consulting others. Above all, the "voice of conscience" can only be true if it echoes God's voice. By prayer and listening to the Word of God our conscience is informed with the attitudes of Christ. Conscience is not a teacher of doctrine. Doctrine is taught by the Church, and we have a serious obligation to know what the Church teaches and adhere to it loyally.

The size of the world depends on your conscience. Conscience can make the world bigger or smaller.

This may seem a very strange thing to say. But it was our Lord himself who told us this. Two men can look at the "lily in the field" and the one sees more than the other. The first sees the stem and petals of the flower. The second sees all this and something beyond: the Providence of the Father who clothes it more magnificently than "Solomon in all his regalia."

For the second man, the Christian conscience is something more than a "still, small voice" at the back of the head. His world is bigger, and he is too big a person to be crippled by a chilling fear of punishment when he does wrong or a feeling of guilt when he dares to be unconventional. Such a man can see the whole stage and not just part of the scenery. He recognizes the Christian conscience to be a very special spiritual gift for which all must pray. Father Gerald Vann, O.P., calls this gift "the Vision of the Whole."

The modern Catholic rarely prays for this gift — the Vision of the Whole. Ours is a specialist world. The tremendous growth of our knowledge means no individual can become expert in the whole of any subject. To stay sane, we must specialize in a small area of knowledge.

We moderns, then, are forced to be "small-minded." And this — because we are people of the time — can constitute a real danger to the quality of our Christian life. When we begin to look at the world through a microscope, we soon become prey to childish fears and anxieties. We become too scared to step out of line, to stand up and be counted, because we imagine ourselves to be alone. Like the Athenians Saint Paul engaged in discussion, we soon forget that God is a real Person who loves us, cares for us, and speaks to us in the depths of our hearts.

Saint Paul reminded the Athenians that God "is not far from any of us, since it is in him that we live, and move, and exist" (Acts 17:28). Catholics talk much too little about God in this way. Too often he is a distant God who lacks any real vitality. Is it at all surprising, then, that for many in the world today God and his Church are merely odd relics from a bygone era?

We must constantly pray for the Vision of the Whole. Speaking one day to his disciples, our Lord described those without such a vision as people who "look without seeing, and listen without hearing or understanding." But then he added: "Happy the eyes that see what you see . . . and hear what you hear" (Luke 10:23,24).

Our Lord obviously wants to be involved in the world around us. Conscience is all a question of seeing and hearing. It is the power, a gift of God, to see and hear correctly — to see Christ involved in every human situation; to see Christ involved in our own everyday lives; to listen to him who called himself the Way, the Truth, the Life.

64 What is confession?

The sacrament of Reconciliation is divided into four parts: contrition, confession, satisfaction, and absolution. We have examined contrition in detail; it is a change of heart and attitude by which one begins to consider, judge, and arrange one's life according to the mind of Christ.

Confession is the opening of one's heart to the minister of God. The confession of sin has taken many forms throughout the centuries. The early Church followed the example of Paul in excommunicating the person guilty of serious public sin (as Paul — in I Corinthians 5:5 — excommunicated the incestuous Corinthian); then, of course, she brought back the sinner to the community after public penance.

The form of the sacrament in the first centuries of the Church is not known for certain, and customs varied widely. Generally, only the grave sins of apostasy, murder, and adultery were confessed; only the bishop could forgive these sins, and he received back the penitent publicly, usually on Holy Thursday, after rigorous penance. Such confession followed by reconciliation was accepted as a "once in a lifetime" practice.

There is a truth we must never lose sight of. We need to confess our sins because we need forgiveness. Sin makes us very lonely people. It withdraws us from those around us. The more isolated we become, the more destructive is the power of sin over us, and the more deeply do we feel the need to confess.

"Sin," wrote Dietrich Bonhoeffer, "wants to remain unknown. It shuns the light. In the darkness of the unexpressed it poisons the whole being of a person. This can happen even in the midst of a pious community. In confession the light of the Gospel breaks into the darkness and seclusion of the heart." We all know from experience that this is true, that we need the light of forgiveness in our lives. Nevertheless, we find confessing to a priest, especially today when the priest's human weaknesses have been exposed as never before, extremely difficult. "Why should I confess to a man? If my sins are against God, why can't I simply confess privately to him? Anyhow, it is God who forgives me."

It is a fact of history, however, that the need to confess to another person generally overrides such difficulties. It is God who forgives our sin. There is no doubt about that. But, he forgives and saves and sanctifies through his Church. And that is why we find the practice of confession in the Church is a very ancient one indeed.

Saint Clement, who was pope in the last decade of the first century, attached great importance to the confession of sins. And in the *Didache,* an early Christian work, we read: "On the Lord's day break bread after you have confessed your sins. . . ."

The practice of confession in the Church arises from the basic belief that Jesus Christ founded a community of goodness, his Church, where people would help and be helped by each other, in and through Christ himself. Now just as personal goodness affects the whole community, so does personal sin affect it. This is a teaching deeply rooted in the Scriptures. The Book of Genesis, in fact, is a long account of how the initial selfishness of Adam and Eve led to evil spreading in ever-widening circles over the earth — murder and lust and competitive greed — until finally came the flood.

Christians recognize that their own personal sins harm the community. But they also recognize that sin will never totally destroy it, because it is the Body of Christ. But sin can and does destroy them. And so Christians turn to Christ in their brother, and confess their sins. Once they repent, God forgives their sins; and the priest, acting on behalf of the community and God, welcomes them back to the family table. The branch is grafted back onto the vine, which is the Body of Christ — his Church.

65 How do we confess and what sins are to be confessed?

Today, we confess our sins privately to the minister (bishop or priest) who, acting in the person of Christ, exercises a spiritual judgment and pronounces his decision of forgiveness or retention of sins in accord with the power of the keys (see John 20:21-23).

This practice of total privacy began in the monastic communities of the Celtic Church in the sixth century. Absolution was given by priests (not solemnly, by the bishop) and on any day (not just on Holy Thursday). And so confession became much more frequent, absolution was given before the period of penance began, and penances were far less rigorous than formerly.

The confession of sin took its pre-Vatican II form after the Council of Trent in 1551. The Council taught that all mortal sins must be confessed and that the sacrament (at least implicitly desired) is necessary for the forgiveness of sin.

Those guilty of mortal sin should confess as soon as possible; they should never defer confession beyond a year. Perfect contrition (see Reconciliation #50), accompanied by at least the implicit desire for the sacrament of Reconciliation, is sufficient for the forgiveness of mortal sin.

Mortal sin is the attitude of wanting to break with God as he is encountered through our fellow human beings and in our conscience. The punishment of unforgiven mortal sin is the eternal continuation in hell of that break freely chosen in life (see Matthew 26:24).

There is no obligation to confess venial sins, for they can be forgiven by prayer and good works and by our sharing in the Eucharist. However, the habit of venial sin can lead to mortal sin. And so the Church recommends that venial sin be confessed so that "the conscience is purified and the will strengthened" in the grace of God.

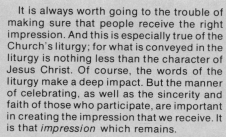

It is always worth going to the trouble of making sure that people receive the right impression. And this is especially true of the Church's liturgy; for what is conveyed in the liturgy is nothing less than the character of Jesus Christ. Of course, the words of the liturgy make a deep impact. But the manner of celebrating, as well as the sincerity and faith of those who participate, are important in creating the impression that we receive. It is that *impression* which remains.

This is why the forms of the liturgy are constantly being renewed. The Church is concerned that the liturgy remains *alive* — that we receive the impression of Christ and so become images of Christ.

One of the characteristics of the revised Rite of Reconciliation is the flexibility it allows both to priest and penitent. For example, various forms and prayers are offered, and the penitent may choose to confess either behind the traditional screen or face-to-face with the priest.

This sacrament allows the character of those who take part — priest and penitent — to emerge. Nonetheless, the form of the sacrament emphasizes throughout the most important character — Jesus Christ. Everything is ordered so that he can "take over." (*For a description of how to confess, see Supplement, p. S14.*)

Christ makes a deep impression on us. Sometimes, perhaps, we wonder and worry about what impression we make on Christ. But there is no need to worry. It is only the impression made by Christ that matters. We are required only to confess all mortal sin; and it is usually helpful, of course, to confess our main faults besides. Forgiveness does not depend upon what *we* say, but on what *God* says.

But how do we recognize mortal sin? In his first letter, Saint John reminds us that "every kind of wrongdoing is sin, but not all sin is deadly" (1 John 5:17). What is "deadly" or "mortal" sin? What kind of sin results in eternal separation, hell?

Traditionally, three criteria for determining mortal sin have been proposed. First, of course, the transgression of God's law must be grave. Second, there must be full awareness or knowledge of its gravity. Third, there must be full freedom of will or consent to the transgression.

There is a difference, then, between sins. Mortal sin is a total break with God, by which we willfully reject God's law as recognized in our conscience. Venial sin is not that at all — the matter is less serious and there is less advertence to what we are doing. When we commit a mortal sin, *we know it*. We cannot commit a mortal sin by accident, nor commit a mortal sin when our attitude toward God in our everyday life is to love him. As Saint Alphonsus writes: "It is morally impossible that the will, confirmed in her good purposes for a considerable lapse of time, should on a sudden undergo such a total change as at once to consent to a mortal sin without clearly knowing it; for mortal sin is so horrible a monster that it cannot possibly enter a soul by which it has long been held in abhorrence, without her being fully aware of it."

Of course, we can deceive ourselves. But Saint Paul writes that we should avoid "people living immoral lives" — idolaters, adulterers, sodomites, thieves, usurers, drunkards, slanderers, and swindlers (see 1 Corinthians 6:9-13). If we find ourselves committing such sins, we have to ask ourselves seriously about our attitude to God's love.

We have emphasized the infinite difference between mortal and venial sin. But we know that venial sin can lead to mortal sin. Every sin is like each blow of the ax which takes the cutting of a tree one step further until the final blow brings it crashing down.

This truth reminds us that, ultimately, sin is a false attitude to the values of God's law.

66 What is meant by satisfaction for sin?

After opening our hearts to true sorrow and confessing our sins to God's minister, true conversion is completed by acts of penance or satisfaction for sins committed. There are three principal forms of penance — prayer, almsgiving, and fasting — by which we share in Christ's satisfaction for sin:

Prayer repairs the damage caused by our sin in our relationship with God.

Almsgiving repairs the damage caused by our sin in our relationship with our neighbor.

Fasting repairs the damage in our own nature caused by our sin.

This satisfaction (penance) will correspond to the seriousness and nature of the sins confessed. It may take the form of prayer, self-denial, service of neighbor, and works of mercy. These will emphasize the fact that sin and its forgiveness have a social aspect.

The penance given by the priest is not sufficient to make full satisfaction for sin. For, although the sin is forgiven, the damage caused by the sin remains; and this damage can only be repaired by further penance.

We can never fully repair the damage caused by sin; we need to depend, in the end, on the mercy or "indulgence" of God. An "indulgence" (either partial or plenary) is a remission (partial or full) of the punishment or penance due to sin after its guilt has been forgiven. This remission is obtained by some "token" gesture of goodwill on our part. Indulgences have often been misunderstood and their abuse was the occasion of the Reformation.

The Church recognizes that we do not always fully repair the damage caused by our sin in this life. Our final purification begins with death and is completed by what lies beyond death. This purification is known as purgatory. It has been the constant tradition of the Church to pray for the dead, especially in the Sacrifice of the Mass.

There is strong evidence that the Celtic monks, referred to in Lesson 65, were of the opinion that the priest who forgives sins on behalf of Christ must himself take steps to help sinners make restitution for their sins and avoid sin in the future. Their life of penance was their only way of showing sinners that they were not left entirely on their own. And it is in this example that we are provided with an insight into the notion of satisfaction which can enrich our own spiritual lives.

The monks were well aware of the Church's teaching that when we sin our actions have repercussions in every area of life. The penances they imposed emphasized their belief that we must make restitution for the damage we have done in the temporal order — to the world around us. But their life of penance reveals an even deeper understanding of the notion of satisfaction; they wanted to shoulder the sinners' cross with Christ, to help them restore the world they had injured, to build Christ's kingdom on earth.

The story of history is very largely the story of the family. The Old Testament, the story of creature continually rejecting Creator, tells the story of Adam and Eve and their children. It is the turbulent story of a family breakup so violent that brotherly love gives way to hate, jealousy, and eventual murder.

The New Testament, the story of God's love for humankind, introduces us to a very different family. This is the family of the Father who wants all men and women to share his own life. We believe that we are one Body in Christ, that we are united to each other. "If one part is hurt, all parts are hurt with it. If one part is given special honor, all parts enjoy it" (1 Corinthians 12:26).

It is here, in the vision of the Church as a family, that we find the basis of the doctrine of indulgences. This teaching brings to our attention two separate but related beliefs. First, that our own personal sin harms the rest of the Body of Christ and that, even after we have been forgiven, we need to make restitution and reparation to the community for the damage we have caused. Second, the doctrine proclaims the magnificent belief that all God's gifts are for giving away, for sharing. Within the family of the Church, we can benefit not only from our own personal gift of forgiveness and reconciliation but from gifts given by God to others.

The following story helps to explain this. A boy goes out into the street and heaves a brick through the sitting room window. Not surprisingly, his father is very angry; but when the boy says he is sorry, his father forgives him. Friendship and reconciliation are established. But the father goes on to say: "To repair the costly damage you must give me ten cents a week out of your pocket money until the new pane of glass is paid for." When this has been agreed and the first payment made and goodwill is apparent, the father puts his hand in his pocket and says, "I am pleased with the effort you are making. Here is an extra twenty cents to help pay off the debt more speedily."

An indulgence is concerned with the debt which remains to be paid for the damage done by our sins. Like the boy in the story, we can turn to our family for help. We can share in the treasury which the saints already have in Jesus Christ.

67 What is absolution and what are its effects?

Through the sign of absolution God grants pardon to sinners who in sacramental confession reveal their change of heart to the Church's minister. In this way, the sacrament of Reconciliation is completed. The forgiveness of sin is through the gift of the Holy Spirit who lifts us up to share in the life of God, just as he raised up Jesus Christ at Easter.

God's re-creation in the sacrament of Reconciliation parallels God's creation in the beginning: "The Lord God fashioned man of dust from the soil. Then he breathed into his nostrils a breath of life, and thus man became a living being" (Genesis 2:7).

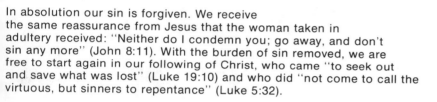

Jesus instituted the sacrament after his Resurrection. He breathed on the apostles and said:
"Receive the Holy Spirit.
For those whose sins you forgive,
they are forgiven;
for those whose sins you retain,
they are retained" (John 20:23).

In absolution our sin is forgiven. We receive the same reassurance from Jesus that the woman taken in adultery received: "Neither do I condemn you; go away, and don't sin any more" (John 8:11). With the burden of sin removed, we are free to start again in our following of Christ, who came "to seek out and save what was lost" (Luke 19:10) and who did "not come to call the virtuous, but sinners to repentance" (Luke 5:32).

Absolution enables us to return fully to the life of the Church. We can share at the table of the Lord's Supper and the final table of the kingdom of God in heaven. Our sharing in the Eucharist reflects the banquet which Jesus often shared with those whose sins he had forgiven.

Jesus Christ spent over 30 years in his earthly life trying to lift people up to his own level.

His touch, accompanied by the right word, gave new life. And today in his Church the sacraments are those crucial moments when Jesus touches us and lifts us up so that we can look him in the face. They raise us up to his level. The words of Jesus give us new life; they are the breath of life, by which we are given the life of the Holy Spirit. *They change us*.

This *change*, of course, is a gradual process. Many of us feel depressed sometimes because celebrating the sacrament of Reconciliation seems to make so little difference to our lives. We receive Christ's forgiveness but the effect soon seems to wear off. But we must understand that God can raise us up only when we experience our own weakness. It is precisely our falling down which brings our heavenly Father to our aid in raising us up.

That God has the power to *change* us is the core of our Christian belief. Of course, the "worldly wise" explain that "a leopard cannot change its spots," and the cynic tells us that there is no hope of changing our

nature. God's forgiveness in the sacrament of Reconciliation, however, tells us that he is always there — lifting us up to his own level.

This change in us is secured by the priest's obligation to treat as absolutely secret everything revealed by the penitent in the sacrament of Reconciliation. The seal of confession can never be broken, even when the safety of individuals or the state is at risk.

Forgiveness, therefore, means that we are totally free to start again. As we have seen in this *Catechism* (Lesson 66), some of the effects of sin remain, of course. We cannot undo the damage already caused by our sins to other people and to our own nature. But God's forgiveness is complete. He totally wipes out the memory and burden of past sin.

It is here that our experience of human relationships is so unhelpful. For, with the best will in the world, it is almost impossible when we claim to "forgive" the offenses of others to also totally forget. In our minds, the sins of others remain very far from a secret! Only time can wipe out the burden of guilt which remains. But our relationship with God is different. God doesn't need

time. In his mind the forgiveness is complete. The sin is forgotten.

The "seal of confession," then, reminds us that the sacrament is a most intimate meeting between the individual and God. And it reassures us that our sin, once confessed, is blotted out.

Nonetheless, we can never forget that the sin of one member of Christ's Body damages the Body as a whole. The early Church recognized that public sins demanded public penances; the sin had to be confessed to all those to whom it was a source of scandal. But even those sins which lie in the secrecy of our conscience weaken the strength of the Church. And so they must be confessed to the Church's minister.

(For further information, see Supplement page S13.)
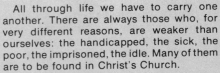

68 What do the words of absolution teach us?

Absolution by the priest brings the whole of God's saving work into the life of the sinner. The words of absolution (revised in 1973) reflect this truth:

"God, the Father of mercies, through the death and resurrection of his Son has reconciled the world to himself

and sent the Holy Spirit among us for the forgiveness of sins;

through the ministry of the Church may God give you pardon and peace, and I absolve you from your sins in the name of the Father, and of the Son, and of the Holy Spirit. Amen."

All through life we have to carry one another. There are always those who, for very different reasons, are weaker than ourselves: the handicapped, the sick, the poor, the imprisoned, the idle. Many of them are to be found in Christ's Church.

That such people can find a home in Christ's Church can only be a source of pride. It was a sign of Christ's strength that he could carry such people and still rise victorious. His Church enjoys the same power; and this is why Saint Paul instructed his converts to "carry each other's troubles and fulfill the law of Christ" (Galatians 6:2).

To "carry each other's troubles" means relieving the weaknesses of others; it means forgiving one another. If our celebration of the sacrament of Reconciliation in which we experience God's forgiveness fails to make us more forgiving toward others, the sacrament has clearly been totally ineffective; we have misunderstood the purpose of the sacrament. We have resisted God's gift of the Holy Spirit given at Easter precisely for the forgiveness of sins.

This is no exaggeration! As Saint Paul reminds us, "Everyone has his own burden to carry" (Galatians 6:5). We are *all* weak. We *all* should be grateful to have found a home in Christ's Church. Our refusal to share with others the forgiveness we ourselves have enjoyed is to cut ourselves off from the Church.

As we conclude our look at the sacrament of Reconciliation in this *Catechism,* we are forced to reflect on its effect in our own lives. Perhaps our growth in the following of Christ has been slow or nonexistent. We have celebrated the sacrament very infrequently, not at all, or simply as a routine gesture.

How often, then, should we confess our sins? The simple answer is that we should do so when we need God's forgiveness. This means, of course, that we must confess every mortal sin (see Lesson 65). But this is hardly sufficient normally. If we find the years slipping by without realizing the need for God's forgiveness of our own weakness, we have to seriously examine whether or not we are relieving others in their weakness by sharing God's forgiveness with them. Rather than allow the years to slip by without celebrating the sacrament, it is clearly better to confess once every month or so.

On the other hand, if we have celebrated the sacrament well, our growth in our following of Christ, although seemingly slow, will nonetheless be real. We always find ourselves confessing the same sins! But what undoubtedly will also have come about is a growth in our humility and willingness to forgive, almost imperceptible to ourselves, but recognized by God as truly his own work.

Our hearts have been transformed. Almost unconsciously, we have grown in our own love and knowledge of God. And by our willingness to forgive we have carried others, too, into the arms of our forgiving Father.

69 What is the sacrament of Anointing?

The sacrament of Anointing is the sacrament of spiritual comfort for the gravely ill whose illness entails danger of death. "It is not a sacrament for those only who are at the point of death. Therefore, as soon as any one of the faithful begins to be in danger of death from sickness or old age, the appropriate time for him to receive this sacrament has certainly arrived" (*Liturgy, #73*).

Christ's disciples followed Jesus in setting off to preach repentance, "and they cast out devils, and anointed many sick people with oil and cured them" (Mark 6:13). This practice was continued in the early Church: "If one of you is ill, he should send for the elders of the church, and they must anoint him with oil in the name of the Lord and pray over him. The prayer of faith will save the sick man and the Lord will raise him up again; and if he has committed any sins, he will be forgiven" (James 5:14-15).

In the Middle Ages the Rite of Anointing became closely associated with the sacrament of Reconciliation and the rigorous penances which accompanied it. The resulting practice of delaying the confession of sin to the deathbed led also, therefore, to the "sacrament for the sick" becoming the "sacrament for the dying." It became too closely identified with impending death.

Make no mistake about it: sickness and death are a curse. And that is how the Bible views them. The author of the Book of Genesis clearly identifies suffering and death as the cursed consequence of our first parents' sin. We hear God speaking to Adam and Eve. To the woman he says: ". . . you shall give birth to your children in pain . . .," and to Adam, "accursed be the soil because of you. With suffering shall you get your food from it . . . until you return to the soil as you were taken from it" (Genesis 3).

And so, when Christ came on earth, he described his mission like this: "The blind see again, the lame walk, lepers are cleansed and the deaf hear, and the dead are raised to life. . ." (Matthew 11:5). His victory over sickness and death was a sign of his victory over Satan. "He cast out the spirits with a word and cured all who were sick. This was to fulfill the prophecy of Isaiah: 'He took our sicknesses away and carried our diseases for us'" (Matthew

8:17). As someone put it: "Every time you meet Jesus in the Gospels he is either actually healing someone, or has just come from healing someone, or is on his way to it."

And it did not end with Christ. On the contrary, he gave that very same mission to his Church assuring his disciples that "they will lay their hands on the sick, who will recover" (Mark 16:18). There is here, perhaps, only a hint of his future intentions. But it is quite clear from the Gospel as a whole that Christ intended his disciples to exercise a special ministry to the sick.

The final instruction of the Lord to his apostles regarding the sick is made known to us in a well-known passage in the letter of Saint James (*see illustrations*). The Council of Trent declared that this passage teaches us that Christ left his Church a special sacrament for the sick — an anointing with oil accompanied by prayers, to be adminis-

tered by the priests of the Church for the healing of the sick.

For the first 12 centuries of the Church's history, the emphasis in this sacrament was on healing — of body as much as of soul. Around about the 12th century, however, some theologians in the Western Church began describing the sacrament of Anointing as the Last, or Extreme, Anointing — a preparation for death and final glory.

The Second Vatican Council, in its document on the liturgy, quite deliberately reversed this trend: "Extreme Unction, which may also and more fittingly be called Anointing of the Sick, is *not for those only who are on the point of death. . . .*" For centuries this sacrament has been considered as a sacrament for the dying only. Certainly, the Lord comes in this sacrament to those who are awaiting the final and total healing in the heavenly kingdom. But we once again have a sacrament for the sick in which Christ reaches out to bring comfort and relief to all.

70 What are the effects of the sacrament of Anointing?

The sacrament of Anointing prolongs the concern which the Lord himself showed for the bodily and spiritual welfare of the sick. By the gift of the Holy Spirit the sick person is enabled not only to bear suffering bravely but also to fight against it.

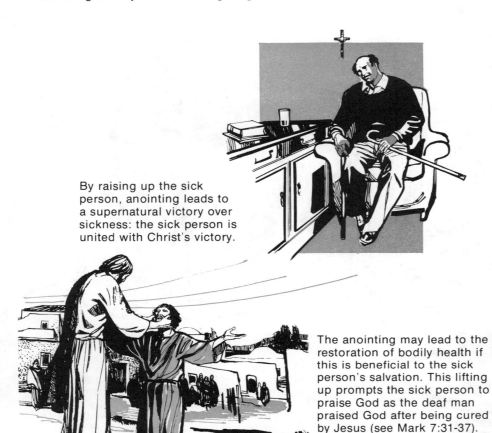

By raising up the sick person, anointing leads to a supernatural victory over sickness: the sick person is united with Christ's victory.

The anointing may lead to the restoration of bodily health if this is beneficial to the sick person's salvation. This lifting up prompts the sick person to praise God as the deaf man praised God after being cured by Jesus (see Mark 7:31-37).

If necessary, the anointing also forgives sin. This forgiveness is part of the spiritual healing produced by the sacrament — just as Christ's work of healing was accompanied by the forgiveness of sins (see Mark 2:1-12).

What does the sacrament of Anointing do for a person? The revised Rite, published in 1972, gives us the answer: "The sacrament provides the sick person with the grace of the Holy Spirit by which the whole person is brought back to health, trust in God is encouraged, and strength is given to resist the temptations of the Evil One and anxiety about death. Thus the sick person is able not only to bear his/her suffering bravely, but also to fight against it. A return to physical health may even follow the reception of this sacrament if it will be beneficial for the sick person's salvation. If necessary, the sacrament also provides the sick person with the forgiveness of sins and the completion of Christian penance" (Section 6).

When we are ill we send for the doctor. Why? Because we hope that he will be able to restore us quickly to health. We hope that he will be able to give us something which will either take the pain away, or at least give us some relief from it. Catholics are now encouraged to treat the priest in the same way. The sacrament of Anointing will relieve those temptations which come to us when we are ill; and how much easier it will be if we give God a chance! We need help to carry out our apostolate as a sick person. This, the sacrament gives us. By it, our sins are forgiven, our faith is renewed, we enter into that phase of life (as a sick person) which offers us the opportunity of exercising another form of service to God which, perhaps, we have not experienced before.

The frailty of old age is recognized too. Old persons may not be desperately ill, but their years do impose burdens that differ from the ones they had when they were younger. Again, the sacrament helps and strengthens them to carry out the apostolate of old age.

Sick children have also special difficulties to overcome. The exuberance of youth is often curtailed to a considerable extent through illness, and some children find this hard to understand and hard to bear. They want to be up and active. Instead, they are confined to bed and a life of boredom. How fitting, then, that the sacrament of Anointing should be administered to them!

What, then, are the grace-filled effects of this sacrament? The best answer is that it brings a strengthening of the whole person. It is a fact that sickness brings with it a marked lack of enthusiasm for the gifts of the Spirit. There is a weariness and lack of vigor which gradually wears us down and can even destroy us. But in this sacrament the Lord grants us the support needed to live the life of the Spirit to the full; he, as it were, puts us together again. And that may mean both a physical and spiritual healing.

71 How is the sacrament of Anointing celebrated?

For the celebration the family should prepare a table, or the corner of a table, in the sickroom, covered with a white cloth on which there should be a crucifix and two lighted candles. There should also be a little bowl of water. The priest will bring the rest.

All those who share in the work of caring for the sick and dying — family, nurses, and others — share, too, in the celebration of the sacrament, in which the sick person is given victory over suffering.

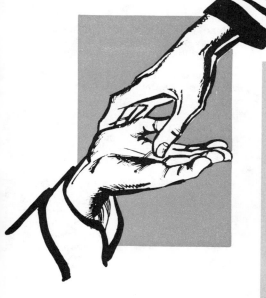

The sacrament of Anointing is administered by anointing the sick person or persons on the forehead and hands with blessed olive oil (or vegetable oil if olive oil is unavailable) and saying once only these words:

**Through this holy anointing
may the Lord in his love and mercy help you
with the grace of the Holy Spirit. Amen.
May the Lord who frees you from sin
save you and raise you up. Amen.**

The simple statement made by the sister of Lazarus — "Lord, he whom you love is sick" — expresses, surely, the absolute trust we should have in our Savior. In the case of serious sickness, he is ready with his healing oil, to comfort us, to bring us strength, to be fit to share with him his Passion and, ultimately, the triumph of his glorious Resurrection.

The sacrament can be administered at home, when the sick person is in bed; and a home Mass — according to diocesan regulations — may be celebrated during which the sacrament is given. It can also be administered in church during Holy Mass, so that the sick persons or those who are aged can — in the presence of their brothers and sisters in the parish — share the Church's sacramental life with those assembled.

Let us suppose that the sacrament is given at home — the more usual way. When the priest enters, he asks a blessing on the house, by invoking the peace of Christ. He then sprinkles the room with holy water saying: "Let this water call to mind your baptismal sharing in Christ's redeeming Passion and Resurrection."

The priest explains, briefly, the significance of the sacrament and then asks all present to prepare themselves for its reception, by calling to mind their sins. The "I confess" is recited by all and absolution given by the priest. A passage from Sacred Scripture is read, dealing with sickness and the Christian attitude toward it. Then a litany is recited which asks for God's blessing on the sick in general and the person receiving the sacrament in particular.

Our Lord said, "They will lay their hands on the sick who will recover" (Mark 16:18). In imitation of our Lord, the priest does just this, without saying anything; a symbol of the spiritual recovery given by the sacrament. (If the sick person wishes to confess privately, he or she does so at this time.)

The sick person is anointed on the forehead and the hands, the priest meanwhile praying that God will grant forgiveness of sins and eternal salvation.

A beautiful prayer follows, asking God to restore health, spiritual and physical, to the sick person, to heal any anguish of mind or body and restore him or her to the Lord's service in the Church.

The Rite ends with the recitation of the Lord's Prayer by all who are assembled. Then the priest gives Holy Communion, if it is then to be received. Finally the following lovely blessing is given: May God the Father bless you. May God the Son heal you. May God the Holy Spirit enlighten you. May God protect you from harm and grant you salvation. May he shine on your heart and lead you to eternal life.

72 Why must we suffer and die?

Sickness and suffering are the result of original sin. The final suffering is death, which completes the process of pain and the deterioration of the body.

Christ overcame these consequences of original sin by identifying himself with suffering and death, but then rising above them. He was lifted up by the Father to a life of resurrection. By faith and the celebration of the sacraments Christians identify themselves with Christ's glorious death.

At the moment of physical death, then, Christians are recognized by the Father as his children; he lifts them up as he raised up Jesus. Death becomes our final achievement in our ascent to God. Like the repentant thief crucified by Christ's side, the dying person is acknowledged in the words: ''Indeed, I promise you . . . today you will be with me in paradise'' (Luke 23:43).

The Jews, like most people in the ancient world, regarded sickness and suffering as God's punishment for sin. This attitude is crude and primitive. But it is also an attitude which has changed remarkably little!

For the fact is that a surprising number of people regard sickness in others as an intolerable nuisance. If you are ill, most people just don't want to know you. You may not be explicitly excluded from normal society; but it is made clear, nonetheless, that you must expect to take the full consequences of suffering on your own shoulders. The implicit suggestion, even, is that your sickness is probably your own fault.

The fallacy of such an attitude is only fully exposed, of course, when sickness strikes oneself. But by then it is too late. The attitude of society, which each one of us has helped to form, has matured into a rigid intolerance of suffering.

The Christian conviction, on the other hand, is that Christ took the full consequences of suffering on his own shoulders. He carried the Cross. As his followers, we can only make every effort to reduce the weight of that Cross — to make up by our suffering, as Saint Paul tells us, ''all that still to be undergone by Christ for the sake of his body, the Church'' (Colossians 1:24).

By our suffering, in other words, we share in the central mystery of our faith, the death and Resurrection of Christ. This truth does not ease the physical pain of suffering. Indeed, it makes the problem of suffering even more difficult to unravel. Suffering forces us to enter more deeply into a mystery which we can never fully penetrate.

This *Catechism,* however, in bringing up the question frequently, has reflected Christ's own preoccupation with suffering. The truth is that there is no easy answer that makes strong faith and deep reflection unnecessary. As the Church reminds us, for the Christian, as for the atheist, ''It is in the face of death that the riddle of human existence becomes most acute'' (*The Church Today, #*18).

There is a wonderful prayer by Teilhard de Chardin which will help us to face the experience of suffering in a Christian way:

''When the signs of age begin to mark my body (and still more, when they touch my mind); when the ill that is to diminish me or carry me off strikes from without or is born within me; when the painful moment comes in which I suddenly awaken to the fact that I am ill or growing old; and above all, at that last moment when I feel I am losing hold of myself and am absolutely passive within the hands of the great unknown forces that have formed me; in all those dark moments, O God, grant that I may understand that it is you (provided my faith is strong enough) who are painfully parting the fibers of my being, in order to penetrate to the very marrow of my substance and bear me away within yourself. . . .''

73 What is meant by the resurrection of the body?

By the resurrection of the body is meant that "man with his entire being is joined to God in an eternal sharing of a divine life beyond all corruption" *The Church Today,* #18). After passing through death as Jesus Christ passed through death, we will rise again in the same manner as he rose again. Our Lord Jesus Christ "will transfigure these wretched bodies of ours into copies of his glorious body" Philippians 3:21).

We suggest, before you read this section of the *Catechism,* that you try and find a place where you can be alone. In this brief introduction to the Catholic teaching on the resurrection of the body, we want to stress again the need for stillness and quiet in our approach to God's mysteries. To quote Saint Paul, we are considering here "the things that no eye has seen and no ear has heard, things beyond the mind of man, all that God has prepared for those who love him" (1 Corinthians 2:9). And that is a very tall order!

When you have found yourself a place away from the noise and rush of everyday life, ask yourself this question: If someone mentions the resurrection of the body, what thoughts does it bring to mind? You may find that the mechanics of it all interest you. Your mind searches for some image of a glorified body and speculates on powers such as passing through walls and walking on water. But these questions, real as they are, do not concern us here. We would like you to put them to one side and simply call to mind four different scenes.

First, imagine a little child being consoled by her or his mother after being frightened by a nightmare. Second, imagine a group of children playing without a care in the world in a very busy street. Now try and think of someone you know who refused to give up

hope in spite of great odds stacked against him or her. And finally, try and recall the sensation of the last time you laughed heartily at a marvelous joke.

In his book, *Rumors of Angels,* Peter Berger suggests that we can find in these four scenes not only intimations of our own personal resurrection but a hint of what resurrection will be like.

The four scenes bring before us four important elements in our makeup: trust, play, hope, and laughter. Berger suggests that we think of each one of these traits of our character as angels because, like angels, they each remind us of the possibility of a life beyond this one.

It is good to try and think in a different light about age-old questions. Do you feel an angel of trust at work in you that stubbornly rejects the possibility that the love in your life, a reflection of God's love, will end? Is there not in the joy of play a hint of an everlasting joy? And what of that angel of stubbornness which refuses to believe that our personality can be wiped out? And can anyone really laugh if life is going to be snuffed out forever?

It is hard for us to think on things "beyond the mind of man." But in these moments of trust, play, hope, and laughter, we Catholics often gain a real insight into the wonder of the doctrine of the resurrection.

he form in which our bodies will rise gain is beyond our imagining. Someone may ask, 'How are the ead people raised, and what sort of ody do they have when they come ack?' They are stupid questions" Corinthians 15:35). And Jesus, in ontroversy with the Pharisees xplained: "For at the resurrection en and women do not marry; no, they re like the angels in heaven" Matthew 22:31).

The traditional distinction between body and soul emphasizes our physical and spiritual nature — the "soul" being directly created by God. But human beings are "one" in body and soul, and they are inseparable in this life and in eternal life. The faculties of the soul are intelligence and will.

74 What is judgment?

Judgment is the process by which God reveals each of us as we really are. Judgment begins with our acceptance or rejection of God's Word; for the Word of God is the light which shows up what is in a person. "He who rejects me and refuses my words has his judge already; the word itself that I have spoken will be his judge on the last day" (John 12:48).

The "last day" for each of us is the day of Particular Judgment — when, at the moment of death, the light of Christ reveals the way in which we have used the talents given us by God. "For those who sought renown and honor and immortality by always doing good there will be eternal life; for the unsubmissive who refused to take truth for their guide and took depravity instead, there will be anger and fury" (Romans 2:7-8).

"Judgment" sometimes conveys images of a balancing act on the heavenly scales of justice — with the good actions of our lifetime on the one side and the bad ones on the other. Or we think of the judgment as a trial in which God sums up — while we listen in agonized suspense — and then passes a decision which could have us dragged away screaming for mercy or protesting our innocence. But judgment is not like that at all.

The truth is that we will be our own judge. And we save or condemn ourselves according to the way we judge Christ. Such is the power of Christ's words that our salvation or condemnation depends on our reaction to them! If we believe in Christ's words and accept them, they will fill us with eternal life. But if we reject his words, they will destroy us.

Go into a room on a summer evening when the sun is streaming through the window. The rays of the sun light up the room in a way that no artificial light can; everything seems transformed. But as every housewife knows, each speck of dust and every little stain is shown up also, and exposed for all to see. And so the curtains are discreetly drawn to keep out the bright sun.

The words of Christ have the power of light. They show up what is in us. But some cannot accept this. They try to "draw a curtain" to shut out the light that is Christ.

"You want to kill me," says Jesus, "because nothing I say has penetrated into you" (John 8:37).

It is a sad truth that so often we resent the goodness in other people. Their virtue shows up our own faults and failings; and so we try to bring them down to size! We behave, indeed, as Christ's accusers did. We judge. And by our judgment we are condemned with our own lips.

It would be wrong, therefore, to fear the judgment as we fear the unknown. Judgment — and heaven or hell which follows — is known to us only too well. If our present life is one of hatred, of vengeance, walled up from the care of others, we are already experiencing something of the agony of hell. Our rejection of God and goodness because we prefer selfishness and sin can only lead to a continuation of the world we have built up for ourselves in eternity. We are not cast into hell; we ourselves do the casting.

On the other hand, if our present life is one of trying to receive Christ's words by accepting his brethren, even to the extent of "giving a cup of cold water in his name," we need have no fear of what follows judgment. Christ's words of welcome will show us up for what we are: "Come, you whom my Father has blessed, take for your heritage the kingdom prepared for you since the foundation of the world" (Matthew 25:34).

The General Judgment is the day when Christ comes in glory at the end of time. On that day of the Lord, God's revelation will be complete and all people "will see the Son of Man coming in the clouds with great power and glory; then too he will send the angels to gather his chosen from the four winds, from the ends of the world to the ends of heaven" (Mark 13:26-27).

The kingdom of heaven is the rule of God among men and women. Jesus sowed the seed of his kingdom by his preaching and miracles. His word is like a seed sown in a field; those who hear the word with faith and become part of the little flock of Christ receive the kingdom itself. Thus by its own power the seed sprouts and ripens until harvest time.

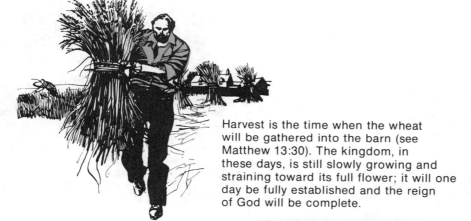

Harvest is the time when the wheat will be gathered into the barn (see Matthew 13:30). The kingdom, in these days, is still slowly growing and straining toward its full flower; it will one day be fully established and the reign of God will be complete.

Jesus emphasized the total commitment required to enter the kingdom of heaven. The nature of that commitment is evidenced in the climax to Jesus' earthly life immediately before he entered into his inheritance. "At Passover Preparation Day, about the sixth hour" Jesus was brought out to the crowd and Pilate announced: "Here is your king" (John 19:14)

Why doesn't God simply "take over" his creation and reveal his power for all to see? If he is really all-powerful, wouldn't it save so many problems if God were to take this torn world and do exactly what was needed to put it back on its feet? These are the kinds of questions, especially when things go badly, that most of us ask at some time or another.

These are also somewhat like the questions that Jesus' disciples asked. Sensitive to his power, they perpetually wondered why he didn't reveal it in magnificent majesty. On one occasion, indeed, when a Samaritan village refused to receive Jesus they asked point-blank: "Lord, do you want to call down fire from heaven to burn them up?" (Luke 9:54)

Jesus' answer remains a secret. He divulged the secret to his closest disciples, of course, but even to them full disclosure was a life's work. And only at the end of Jesus' earthly ministry was the secret publicly revealed. It was "Passover Preparation Day, about the sixth hour" when Jesus was brought before Pilate. "Here is your king," said Pilate to the Jews.

The "secret" was out! Jesus had come to establish a kingdom — his own kingdom. But this wasn't the kind of kingdom which involved an immediate "take-over" of the world and would solve all its problems. It wasn't the kind of secret which Jesus could shout from the housetops. In Jerusalem, its publication had only led to the crowd shouting, "Crucify him!" Jesus could only share the secret with those who joined his intimate circle of friends.

This kingdom was to be the kind that grows slowly, like the seed in the earth. It was to grow within us, but in a way that would hardly be perceptible. Yet once it had taken root, it would be so powerful that, in the end, every purely human value and, indeed, creation itself would be turned upside down in a universal upheaval — beginning with our death and completed at the end of time when Jesus Christ will come "in the clouds with great power and glory."

On that day, the Lord's "secret" will be revealed to all people. The kingdom will be established. We will see God face-to-face. Only our glimpses of love, joy, peace, and security in this life can provide a shadowy foretaste of what is to come. As Saint Paul tells us: "No eye has seen and no ear has heard, things beyond the mind of man, all that God has prepared for those who love him" (1 Corinthians 2:9).

To the question, "Why doesn't God take over his creation?" we can only answer, then, that he is taking it over. He is conquering it in secret — in our hearts. This is why Saint Ignatius could say: "He who carries God in his heart carries heaven with him wherever he goes."

All the members of God's kingdom on earth, in heaven, and in purgatory are in communion with one another, for they enjoy the life of Christ and so form one Body. This is what is meant by the communion of saints. The faithful on earth are in communion with one another by professing the same faith under the one visible shepherd, the Bishop of Rome, assisting one another by prayer and works of charity.

The faithful on earth are in communion with the saints in heaven by honoring them as the glorified members of the Church. We can turn to them for assistance and intercession before God.

The faithful on earth are in communion with the faithful in purgatory by prayer and works which help to repair the damage caused by sin.
"If one part is hurt,
all parts are hurt with it.
If one part is given special honor,
all parts enjoy it.
Now you together are Christ's body . . ."
(1 Corinthians 12:26-27). And Judas Maccabaeus had "atonement sacrifice offered for the dead, so that they might be released from their sin."
(See 2 Maccabees 12:43-46.)

A few years ago a family was being evicted from their house. They were loading all their possessions onto a handcart so that they could move it to temporary accommodation. The whole operation was watched from across the street by a neighbor who noticed that the family seemed strangely unconcerned about the difficulties that awaited them.

At last, he spoke to one of the children, almost without realizing that he was uttering his thoughts aloud: "You poor child! You are so young and you have no home!" The neighbor never forgot how a look of fright came into her face and tears into her eyes, as she said, "Oh, but we do have a home! We do! It's just that we've nowhere to put it."

A home is not made out of bricks and mortar, nor luxury carpets and kitchen gadgets. These things are important, of course; but if we seek them first, we will quickly discover that the happiness of the home cannot be bought by accumulating comforts. The home is built on a deeper foundation — the foundation of love. As Jesus pointed out — in an observation often repeated by parents today — it is often the child alone who reminds us of this truth. It is the children who bring love into God's kingdom; it is the children who bring love into the home.

As Christians, we cannot afford to "settle down" to a life of ease and security. One day we are going to be "evicted" from the earthly home we have built up for ourselves with its comforts. If what we have built has not been founded on the only true foundation — the foundation of love — we will simply go to pieces. Our "eviction" will mean that we simply wander around, totally lost. That is hell.

But the bond of love is too strong to be broken by physical discomfort — even the ultimate discomfort of death. Love unites us with every member of our family — of God's family. It unites us in this life; it unites us in the next. Family ties unite us, whatever our physical circumstances.

The members of God's family, whether on earth, in heaven, or in purgatory, are intimately united with one another — because among them all there is love. It is God's love. Our union is never more evidently shown than at Mass when, around the altar, is grouped the whole of humanity, living and dead. Our celebration draws us to embrace the whole world: the pope, the bishops, searching people everywhere, the departed brothers and sisters of all centuries, including the first disciples.

If our enjoyment of the fellowship of those so distant from us in time and space is founded on true love, one very positive and even surprising effect will become evident. Our love will be deepened, too, for the person sitting next to us. Ours will become a true home.

A saint (from the Latin *sanctus*, meaning holy) is one who shares in the divine life of Christ. The New Testament refers to the "poor saints in Jerusalem"; and in Acts, Saint Luke refers to Peter visiting the "saints in Lydda," one of whom he cured from paralysis (Acts 9:32).

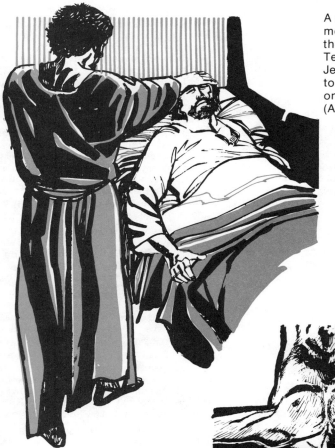

Saints are the sort of people who are never satisfied with a "doing what we've always done" approach to life. There is never the slightest chance of them falling into a rut, because saints are men and women who want to do what Jesus wants. And that can lead to a very exciting life! "They are led," writes Father John Dalrymple, "into mad escapades of folly and scandal like Franz Jagerstatter refusing to serve in the German Army when everyone else did or, like Charles de Foucauld, going off to live with the Saharan Tuaregs as one of them."

Now this tendency to approach life in completely novel and fresh ways makes it very difficult to say exactly what a saint is. There is no ready-made mold into which we can pour the required virtues needed to make a saint.

We sometimes think we have the gift of recognizing true sanctity; but if it were possible to choose any saint from the Church's calendar and invite him or her to dinner, we would probably get quite a shock. Plaster statues of very calm and quiet-looking saints serve to remind us that the saints are always ready to help and keep their memory before us. But they rarely capture the energy and enthusiasm of men and women who are always ready to turn the world on its head!

The truth, of course, is that many biographies of the saints down the years have made them out to be solemn-faced fanatics. Good fanatics, holy fanatics, but fanatics nonetheless. And that's a great pity, for it has left us with a stereotype image of the saint that not many of us fancy imitating. After all, who wants to be a fanatic?

To understand the true greatness of the saint, we have always to remember that saints are men and women of flesh and blood. The canonized saints were people with limitations just like the rest of us — people who allowed God's grace to work in them and, even after they had attained great holiness, kept their own distinctive personalities. First and foremost a saint is a human being. What makes the saint different from the rest of us is his or her complete openness to the promptings of the Spirit.

There is a saint and a sinner in all of us. But if we do choose to be a saint, to follow the promptings of the Spirit, we will be an entirely unique kind of saint. For as Evelyn Waugh once wrote: "There is only one saint that Bridget Hogan can actually become, Saint Bridget Hogan. She cannot slip into heaven in fancy dress, made up as Joan of Arc."

The early Church quickly began to honor her first saints in heaven — the martyrs who had witnessed to their faith by the shedding of blood. Saint Peter himself witnessed to the life of Christ by his close association with Jesus — completed by the manner of his death. According to legend he was crucified upside down. The anniversary of these saints' death was observed as their feast day, altars were placed over their tombs, and churches were dedicated to their memory.

The names of holy men and women recognized by general acclamation were entered in a list or "canon" controlled by the bishop. Since the first formal canonization by Pope John XV in 993 the process of "canonization" has become progressively more exacting. It is for the pope to declare a person a saint and to propose him or her as a positive example and help to the Church on earth.

"The perfect example of . . . spiritual and apostolic life is the most Blessed Virgin Mary" (*Apostolate of the Laity,* #4).

Mary's role as Mother of God is unique. "Adorned from the first instant of her conception with the splendor of an entirely unique holiness (see *Feast of Immaculate Conception,* December 8), the Virgin of Nazareth was, on God's command, greeted by an angel as 'full of grace'" (see *Feast of Annunciation,* March 25).

Full of faith, Mary brought forth on earth the Father's Son (see Luke 2:1-20). Saint Joseph was "guardian" or "foster father" (see Matthew 1:18-25).

"Mary, having completed the course of her earthly life, was assumed body and soul into heavenly glory" (see *Feast of Assumption,* August 15).

The special honor we show Mary differs essentially from the adoration which is offered to God. "The Church has endorsed many forms of piety toward the Mother of God, provided that they were within the limits of sound and orthodox doctrine" (*The Church,* #66). Two examples are the Angelus and the Rosary (see Supplement pp. S6-S7) — devotions which particularly help to sanctify the day.

As we pay honor to Mary, our worship of God deepens. For Mary shows us the true meaning of worship by the way in which she leads God's creatures in prayer, just as she led the apostles in the upper room after our Lord's Ascension when they awaited the coming of the Holy Spirit at Pentecost.

In Old Testament times, the situation between God and humankind may be compared to a very unsatisfactory experience between ourselves and a poor listener. God tried to speak to the people, but they didn't want to listen. The result was that, quite literally, God could not fully reveal himself. The relationship between God and his people broke down.

It broke down, that is, until someone became an attentive listener. At last, God enjoyed the perfect response to his attempts to make himself known. He could reveal himself fully in the flesh. God found himself an attentive listener in Mary; and the relationship between God and humankind totally changed.

Mary received the word — listened to it attentively — so that in her the word was made flesh. Mary is the greatest of God's saints. Her faith sets the pattern for our growth in maturity in our own Christian life.

Mary sought no fame, but her name is praised wherever Christ's name is known. Her listening to God's word and her fidelity in doing his will make her the greatest woman that ever lived.

Mary is part of a divine mystery which is totally beyond our grasp. We hardly need to be told that. But do we remind ourselves enough that an essential part of the divine mystery is that the Mother of Christ is the mother also of all those who share his life?

For a moment think of your own relationship with your natural mother. Most will agree that it has so many different sides to it that we would find it impossible to define or explain fully to anyone. And there is nothing unusual in this. It is simply a fact that the most intimate of all relationships, the bond of mother and child, defies human discussion.

It is because the mother and child relationship is concerned with an area of experience far beyond our rational understanding that when our thoughts turn to Mary we find ourselves turning simultaneously to prayer. Prayer is the language of the Spirit; and when the Spirit reveals to us the power of Mary's supplication on *our* behalf, her intimate relationship to *us,* then our closest friend will never understand or will we be able to explain just why we feel as we do.

But the Spirit does. And, indeed, in leading men and women down the centuries to meditate on the mysteries of the Rosary, to pray the Angelus, to turn to Mary in countless devotions, the Spirit has led us even deeper into the life of the Trinity.

At the Wedding Feast of Cana, Mary found out what the needs of the young couple were and simply brought them to the attention of her Son: "They have no wine!" The Church believes that Mary speaks to her Son in the same way about us all. And the Church further believes that the greatest honor we can give to Mary is to listen to her when she says to us, as she did to the waiters, "Do whatever he tells you" (John 2:5).

Jesus extended Mary's motherhood to all his disciples when, from the Cross, he gave her as mother to his beloved disciple, John (see John 19:26-27).

Very little of Mary's life is recorded in the Gospels. John, on the two significant moments of Christ's life, reminds us, simply, that "the mother of Jesus was there." At Cana in Galilee Jesus worked his first sign or miracle. On Calvary he worked his last sign that won life for all people. In the first, Mary brought those in need to Jesus: "Do whatever he tells you" (John 2:5). In the last, Jesus brought those in need to Mary: "This is your mother" (John 19:26).

For us, as for Jesus, Mary is there as our mother. She helped Jesus to walk his first steps in life and, in a similar way, she helps us. She stood by him in his suffering and, in a similar way, she stands by us. She is always there.

When we fall, by accident or our own foolishness, she comforts and she cares. She guides us until we are restored to full life by the healing grace of her divine Son. Her loving attention enables God's grace to restore us to health.

Everything that the Church means may be discovered in a right understanding of Mary. And so if we think about the Church and Mary together, we will not fall into the trap of thinking about the Church solely as an institution. It is easy to criticize an institution; but it is hard to show bitterness toward one's mother. If we love Mary we will love the Church, and vice versa. For the Church is the Body of Christ, to whom Mary gave birth when she consented to be the mother of Jesus at the Annunciation.

We need the help of the saints; and we need the help of others who, like ourselves, are struggling members of the Church on earth. How much more, then, do we need the help of Mary! To those who ask her help Mary is always there.

Mary's life most accurately reflects that of her divine Son. We do well, then, to follow

Mary. But what does this mean? Clearly, the concrete situations of everyday life that we meet are very different from hers. But the Church reminds us that we are to imitate the attitude of Mary in our daily life and especially in our worship.

Perhaps we can understand this more fully by realizing what is meant by Mary's virginity. Quite simply, this means that Jesus had no earthly father. The Gospels are very clear about it and the first teachers of Christianity included the doctrine of Mary's virginity as part of the faith. But all Christians are not called to physical virginity. What, then, does Mary's virginity mean to us?

In trying to answer this question we cannot simply presume that virginity is superior to marriage and that therefore it was the "way" chosen for Mary. We have only to recall the dignity given to marriage by Jesus to realize that this is not the answer.

Jesus was born of a virgin so that no one could be confused about where he had come from. The Son of God was born because God in his goodness and love chose to give him. He was not born because creatures willed it.

The human nature of Jesus was a pure gift of God. But it was achieved through the Virgin Mary. And so Mary teaches us what it means completely to abandon ourselves to God's will.

We learn from Mary's attitude. She was ready to receive God's grace. She responded joyfully to God's word. She emptied herself, realizing her complete dependence on God. Mary shows us in her virginity that whatever we give for the sake of the kingdom of God is repaid a hundredfold in the end.

er title "Mother of the Church" is losely linked to her more ancient tle "Mother of God," which goes ack to the Council of Ephesus, .D. 431. This Council, faced with he difficulty of stating that Jesus was both God and man, but not wo persons, expressed the truth by tating that Mary, the Mother of esus, is Mother of God.

evotion to the Blessed Virgin can bring about reestablishment of Christian nity. "Just as at Cana Mary's intervention resulted in Christ's performing is first miracle, so today her intercession can help to bring to realization he time when the disciples of Christ will again find full communion in aith" (see Devotion to the Blessed Virgin Mary, Paul VI, 1974.)

Mary, while completely devoted to the will of God, was far from eing a timidly submissive woman; on the contrary, she was a woman who did not hesitate to roclaim that God vindicates the humble nd the oppressed. . . . She was a woman f strength who experienced poverty and uffering, flight and exile . . . and her ction helped to strengthen the apostolic ommunity's faith in Christ" same reference as above).

The Blessed Virgin Mary offers a calm vision and a eassuring word to people of today. . . . She shows forth he victory of hope over anguish, of peace over anxiety, f eternal visions over earthly ones, of life over death" same reference as above).

All people are modeled in Christ's image; for all people are created in God's image and likeness. And so, as Pope John Paul II reminds us in his first encyclical, we recognize that "in the creative restlessness of every person there beats and pulsates what is most deeply human — the search for truth, the insatiable need for the good, hunger for freedom, nostalgia for the beautiful, and the voice of conscience" (*Redeemer of the World*).

By his birth into the world as a human being, Jesus Christ, the Son of God, "in a certain way united himself with all people. . . . Every person, without any exception whatever, has been redeemed by Christ; and with each person, without any exception whatever, Christ is in a way united, even when people are unaware of it" (*Redeemer of the World*). Christians, then, are to accord to all persons the dignity given them by Christ.

The Church's task is Christ's task: to reveal the "Good News" of the dignity people enjoy as God's children, which has been obscured by sin. Those who grasp this truth are overcome by a deep amazement; they will not only turn to God in adoration, but also be struck by "deep wonder at themselves" and at "how precious people must be in the eyes of the Creator" (*Redeemer of the World*).

There is no magical significance in the year 2000. Nevertheless, as Pope John Paul II pointed out at the very beginning of his first papal encyclical, "for the Church it will be a year of great jubilee." Of course, it cannot have escaped the Pope that the health of the Church in the year 2000 will greatly depend upon him.

This is why the quotations in the illustrations are so important. They illustrate the Pope's vision of the future. When the encyclical *Redeemer of the World* was published on March 4, 1979, it did not create the kind of explosion caused by earlier encyclicals — for example, Pope Paul's on birth regulation. Nor does it provide easy reading! But it will have an even more profound effect on the Church's life.

If you read the short quotations opposite, one fact becomes immediately evident. The encyclical *couldn't* have been written three centuries ago. Pope John Paul's words just do not belong to an age in which Christians are savagely putting one another to death for their faith. But more, the encyclical *couldn't* have been written even 30 years ago. For even in that short period of time a fresh consciousness of every person's dignity has penetrated the mind of the Church.

What this means in practice cannot be discovered in a textbook. It can only be revealed by looking at the personality of Jesus Christ himself. He never forced himself on people. He never merely "tolerated" them. He never condemned outright a single individual — even when that individual was wrong!

Simply, Jesus offered every person a share in his own life. He possessed the fullness of truth — the truth that "makes us free." And not once did he contradict our freedom. Jesus treated every person with respect; we might almost say "reverence."

And that is the truth that the Church must reveal in her attitude toward all people: an attitude, as Pope John Paul comments, "which seems to fit the special needs of our times." Pope John Paul has developed his teaching from the truth which he himself helped to formulate at the Second Vatican Council: "The human person has a right to religious freedom, so that in matters religious no one is to be forced to act in a manner contrary to his/her own beliefs" (*Religious Freedom*, # 2). As one bishop explained: "This teaching is a genuine development of doctrine, perhaps the greatest progress of the Council."

Pope John Paul tells us that in spreading the Catholic faith we are to respect what those who are not Catholic or Christian have "already worked on in the depths of their spirit concerning the most profound and important problems." This is not a contradiction of Catholic principles; nor is it a "watering down" of the truth. Quite the contrary! It places new demands on us; it requires a deeper understanding of the truth Christ revealed in his life and death. Such an understanding can only lead to a happier Church in the year 2000.

81 How are Christians to work for the dignity of all people?

ur full dignity as human beings will be
evealed only when we are in union
ith Christ achieved in the completion of
od's heavenly kingdom. But on earth,
here that kingdom is being
stablished, Christians reveal their
ignity by upholding their freedom:
reserving each person from becoming
he slave of things, the slave of
conomic systems, the slave of production,
he slave of his/her own products. . .''
Redeemer of the World). Such forms of
avery lead to injustice and
ppression.

rue freedom springs from serving the
Holy Spirit of God, the Spirit of truth
romised by Jesus Christ (see John 16:13).

his means that in spreading the
ospel, like Christ himself, Christians
re to proclaim the truth ''with full
orce of spirit while preserving a deep
steem for all people, their intellect, their
ill, their conscience, and their freedom''
Redeemer of the World).

Karl Barth was minister of a church in
Switzerland. He was a great theologian and
also a great preacher. One day, someone
asked him the secret of his carefully
prepared sermons. He replied: ''I take the
Gospel in one hand and the morning
newspaper in the other, and I try to see what
the light of the Gospel is telling me about the
deeds of the day.''

Ideally, of course, all preachers should do
the same! And not only all preachers. It is
every Christian's task to shed the light of the
Gospel on the events of the day and to
arrange the day accordingly.

The trouble is that when we pick up the
morning newspaper our task isn't so easy.
Faced with the world's major issues, beginning with tyranny and torture, there seems
so little we can *do.* Even the local newspaper, with its stories of the elderly dying alone
and a father being sentenced to jail for
cruelty to his children, can seem remote
from our own concerns. Christians know
they are to raise the world to a higher
standard of existence. But how?

The worst mistake, almost, that Christians
can make is to presume they know all the
answers. The statement in a British national
newspaper, *The Guardian,* that ''Roman
Catholics often do not know where they
stand; but when in doubt, they have a pope
to tell them,'' is a falsehood made all the
more dangerous by the fact that many —
including Catholics — think it to be true.

Under the guidance of the Holy Spirit the
Church has outlined many of the solutions
to the problems in the world; but it is for
each one of us, under the guidance of the
same Holy Spirit, to discover how the
Church's ''outline'' can be given concrete
shape.

This is why the *worst* mistake that Christians can make is to presume that they have
been given *no* answers to the problems of
the world. The consequence of such an
attitude is disastrous: the feeling of being
totally overwhelmed by the sheer weight of
suffering — from which one can only escape
by hiding away in a quiet corner.

Jesus Christ told his followers that ''in the
world you will have trouble.'' ''But,'' he
added, ''be brave: I have conquered the
world'' (John 16:33). In the end, only God
within us can confront the world and win.
Or, as Cardinal Suenens reminds us, finding
God ''is the number one social service that
Christians can and must perform in society.''

The only solution to the problems of the
day is to find God. But finding God is the
most demanding solution: not because God
is difficult to find but because, when we
have found him, he is a demanding God. He
demands love. He demands our heart so
that he can change it. The human heart is
the root cause of so many problems in the
world. The human heart transformed by
God's grace is their only solution.

''The best use of freedom is charity,
which takes concrete form in self-giving
and in service. . . . The Church truly serves
all people when she guards the truth with
untiring attention and when in the whole
of her own community she transmits it
and gives it concrete form in human life
through each Christian's fidelity to his/her
vocation'' (*Redeemer of the World*).

82 Do all Christians enjoy an equal dignity?

"All the faithful of Christ of whatever rank or status are called to the fullness of the Christian life and to the perfection of charity" (*The Church*, # 40). However, the dignity of the Christian enjoys different expressions. While those in Holy Orders are ordained to the sacred ministry, the laity, on the other hand, "seek the kingdom of God by engaging in temporal affairs and by ordering them according to the plan of God" (*The Church*, #31).

By their work Christians "perfect themselves, aid their fellow citizens, and raise all of society, and even creation itself, to a better mode of existence. . . . Let them truly imitate Christ, who roughened his hands with carpenter's tools, and who in union with his Father is always at work for the salvation of all" (*The Church*, # 41).

"If Christians are to imbue civilization with right ideals, they must involve themselves in the work of institutions and strive to influence them from within. But in a culture like our own, no one can do so unless he or she is scientifically competent, technically capable and skilled in the practice of his or her own profession" (*Peace on Earth,* John XXIII).

The laity can also be called in various ways to a more direct form of cooperation in the apostolate of bishops and priests; for example, they can be deputed to exercise certain church functions for a spiritual purpose, such as the distributing of the Eucharist as ministers of Communion.

Slave, *noun,* person who is legal property of another or others and is bound to absolute obedience, human chattel; helpless victim *to* or *of* some dominating influence. . . .

Definitions in dictionaries have a way of obscuring the true horror of our inhumanity to others which lies behind a perfectly harmless-looking word. History testifies to the fact, however, that the word *slavery* carries within it countless stories of personal tragedy, heartbreak, and suffering.

It has been the constant teaching of Christianity that all men and women are equal. But in the rough and tumble of life we seem to find it very difficult to believe that our neighbor is a unique person in the eyes of God and in some ways unlike any other person alive.

"A thing has a price," wrote the German philosopher Immanuel Kant, "if any substitute or equivalent can be found for it. It has *dignity* or *worthiness* if it admits of no equivalent." If you think that some men and women can be easily replaced, it is a short step to placing some limit on their rights as individuals. This sort of thinking led in the civilizations of Greece and Rome to the creation of two classes of men and women. There was the slave-owning class with full rights and a slave class with hardly any rights at all. But such thinking does not belong to the dim and distant past. Even today in some totalitarian countries there are men and women who are accorded only limited rights because of their religion, race, or color. They are judged to be half-people, cogs in a machine who can so easily be replaced.

When we come to consider the Church's teaching on the equal dignity of every Christian, it is good to remember that any society is made up of a group of individuals who share something in common. That "something" may be made up of such things as land, possessions, color, religion, or anything at all. The important thing is that all persons within the group recognize the right of their neighbor to a share of what they hold in common. Once this right is withheld from anyone, that person is no longer a full member of the society. Limits have been set on his or her individuality. So when we talk of a society being *totalitarian* we are really saying that the total rights of an individual have been taken over by the state.

Catholic teaching on the equal dignity of every member of the Church is based on the belief that each one of us is given a full share in the life of Christ. To each member of the community Christ says, "Follow me." And to each he gives that transforming power which is the life of God himself. Only at our peril do we stop others from exercising that power in their own individual way. Such is their call, such is their right, and in such a way do we form together Christ himself.

Apart from the clerical and lay states the religious state also expresses the dignity of the Christian. Certain of Christ's faithful are called by God from among the clergy and laity to live a life of chastity, poverty, and obedience and so remind all people that seeking the kingdom of God is to be valued above all earthly considerations.

Throughout the Church's history, various forms of solitary and community life as well as different religious families have developed. In the earlier centuries, monastic communities dedicated to the worship of God and to contemplation played a vital role in reminding the Church of its primary function and in civilizing society.

In the Middle Ages, as the Church grew remote from the common people, Orders of Friars emerged to preach the Gospel throughout Europe. These Orders, notably the Franciscans and Dominicans, served to remind the Church of her duty to reflect the life of her divine Master.

In more recent centuries many religious congregations and secular institutes (composed of men and women who make a religious consecration but live in the world) have grown up to perform such essential tasks as teaching, nursing, and so forth within the Church. But all base their apostolic activity on a life of prayer and contemplation.

"The glory of God," wrote Saint Irenaeus, "is man fully alive." It seems a harmless sort of thing to say really until one realizes that the life of Christians is not limited to their own resources. They are persons who bear the imprint of Christ deep within them — persons who have been struck by the Word of God which is "something alive and active: it cuts like any double-edged sword but more finely; it can slip through the place where the soul is divided from the spirit, or joints from the marrow; it can judge the secret emotions and thoughts."

In his encyclical, *Redeemer of the World,* Pope John Paul II reminded us that the Church is made up of individuals who have received a special and particular call. If we wish to understand the People of God, which is so vast and so extremely differentiated, we must see Christ saying to each member of the community: "Follow me."

Here is no charter for a Church which has been lulled to sleep by a sterile uniformity.

Think of the bluff Peter, the headstrong Paul, and the quiet, philosophical John each inwardly transformed by the power of the Word, each determined to do his "own thing." On the face of it, one would seem to have a recipe for disaster!

Jesus said that he came not to bring peace but a sword (see Matthew 10:34). In his choice of apostles, in everything he said and did, he made it quite clear that the building of his Body on earth, the Church, would not be the result of an indifferent, cut-and-dried relationship with God. "I would rather have blood on my hands than water — like Pilate," says one of Graham Greene's characters. Being indifferent to certain people is worse than hating them.

Christ did not choose such followers. He chose men of a vital, robust faith who were sometimes riddled with doubt, aware of the conflicts of love and hate to such an extent that one of them betrayed him.

The true life of faith inevitably involves a man or woman in the real conflicts of life. And this is true of two quite different groups we meet in the Gospel. The first group of people is made of those who followed Christ wholeheartedly but did not change their everyday occupations. Think of Martha, Mary, and Joseph of Arimathea and their own particular stories. The second group is made up of those who follow Jesus along the way and leave their settled life-style. This group is made of persons like Peter, James, John, and the others.

Both these groups are to be found in the Church today. None is better than the other; each is called to live life to the full. But those who "follow Christ along the way," the religious who are described in the illustrations, face a special challenge. They must declare themselves *publicly* for Jesus and so they must follow him publicly. That means they cannot hide from life. They must give glory to God by being fully alive.

84 Why is prayer necessary?

Prayer is the foundation of the Christian life; for prayer is communication, or communion, with God. Through prayer we are drawn deeper into the life of Father, Son, and Holy Spirit: "The proof that you are sons is that God has sent the Spirit of his Son into your hearts: the Spirit that cries, 'Abba, Father'" (Galatians 4:6).

Christ himself taught us the need for prayer. In Gethsemane, as he prepared himself for the climax of his life, Jesus received the strength he needed in prayer to his Father: "Abba (Father)! ... Take this cup away from me. But let it be as you, not I, would have it" (Mark 14:36).

And, at moments of his public ministry when those in need were pressing around him, Jesus "went off to a lonely place and prayed there." Peter and his companions were then forced to set out in search of him; and when they found him they complained, "Everybody is looking for you" (Mark 1:35-37).

Many people believe that it is difficult to lead a good Christian life. This, of course, is nonsense. The Christian life isn't difficult at all. The Christian life is *impossible*. It is *impossible,* that is, without prayer.

The message of this *Catechism* has been that our Christian faith is a *personal* friendship with Jesus Christ, and that it is a friendship which lifts us up to Christ's level. We cannot live such a life by our own power. We need the grace, the help, of God. And to obtain this help we must first ask for it.

All the Church's saints have said the same thing. Saint Alphonsus, for example, puts it simply: "If you pray, you will be saved; if you do not pray, you will be lost." But Jesus himself expressed the same truth even more simply: "Cut off from me, you can do nothing" (John 15:5).

The trouble is that everyone is so busy! We don't have much *time* for prayer! It's not easy to put aside a set period every day to be with our Lord. To his apostles before his arrest, Jesus complained: "Could you not watch one hour with me?" Few of us, certainly, could devote an hour a day to prayer. But ten minutes? . . . Two minutes? Would honesty demand some of us to admit that if we spent even two minutes a day in prayer it would be two minutes longer than we spend at present? And is there anyone who cannot give a few minutes of every day to God? The plain fact is that if we are too busy to pray, we are too busy!

There are two main reasons, possibly, why we find prayer difficult. First, we are worried by distractions. In the very same instant that we begin our prayer our minds are flooded by all kinds of anxieties and petty concerns. Most of us are perpetual daydreamers!

In fact, we feel that when God our Father hears us trying to pray it must be rather similar to when we hear tiny children trying to hold a conversation — to us it seems almost totally incoherent. That's prayer! We don't criticize tiny children for not speaking clearly; and surely our heavenly Father takes the same pleasure as we do when tiny children speak to us.

The second reason is that we feel our prayer isn't answered. Of course, simply to ask God for something isn't prayer. There was once a man who, as a child, used to pray for the ability possessed by an elderly uncle of being able to take his teeth out every night and put them in a glass of water!

No, prayer is not concerned with *our* will. It is concerned with *God's* will. He may not answer our prayer in the way *we* want. But he has promised that he will answer our prayer in the way *he* wants. And isn't that an infinitely better way?

When visiting the two sisters, Martha and Mary, Mary was content to let her sister look after the guests while she "sat down at the Lord's feet and listened to him speaking." Martha's complaint to Jesus brought the retort: "It is Mary who has chosen the better part" (see Luke 10:38-42). There are moments when the Lord is speaking and we cannot allow distractions to prevent us from listening!

We can pray anywhere and at any time. We must pray as we can and not try to pray as we can't. We must take ourselves as we find ourselves and start from that. And so the first step in prayer is to place ourselves — as sinful creatures with sorrow in our hearts — in the presence of God.

The second step in prayer is to pray. This means speaking to the Lord, asking him for our needs and thanking him for his gifts. This prayer leads to adoration and praise. If our thoughts wander (and they usually do), it may be helpful to pray a well-known prayer or reflect on an episode from the Gospel, to guide the direction of our mind and heart.

The third step in prayer is to be silent, so that the Lord himself who "is nearer to us than we are to ourselves" can guide the direction of our hearts. To be effective, prayer must be honest. And it must be persevering — like the man knocking on his friend's door for bread. For Christ assures us that such persistence will be rewarded: "The one who knocks will always have the door opened to him" (Luke 11:10).

There are five essential points to remember when we pray:

1. Prayer is a meeting with God. We cannot forget this. It is not some magic formula for disciplining the mind. Neither is it a soothing way of escaping from the pressures of life.

If it is to be a real meeting with God, there is a second step we must be prepared to take.

2. Be ourselves! We have all heard of the sad clown who hides behind the smiling mask. All of us have a wardrobe full of masks.

The tragedy is that as long as we have our mask on, others never meet us. They meet the highly professional businessman, the capable teacher, the home-loving mother; but they never see the insecure, anxious, sad clown we really are. What a relief it is when we can reveal our true self to someone who loves us!

God does love us. It is easy to be ourselves with him. But if the meeting is to be a success, there is something else we must do.

3. Let God be himself! Notice how arrogant many of us are. We are like the child who told his mother he was about to draw a picture of God. "But no one knows what God looks like," he was told. "Not at the moment," he agreed, "but they will when I've finished."

We think we know God and understand him. But there is a truth we cannot avoid. No man or woman can fully understand the Creator of all things. He is completely beyond our grasp or understanding. We must throw away all our preconceived notions about him, and let God come to us as he really is, not as we would have him be. Then we will be ready to take one more step forward.

4. Give him our worries! "Come to me all you who labor and are overburdened and I will give you rest" (Matthew 11:28). As long as we hang on to our worries, we will have to carry a burden which is so unwieldy that it obscures our vision of God.

We should take God at his word and give him all our worries. If we trust him, we will be amazed how relieved we feel.

Once the barrier has gone, we are ready to talk to God. We may use set prayers if we wish. We may just talk to him if we are able. Or we may sit in silence, if that is what we prefer. Then we prepare for the next and final step.

5. Listen! A child's saying of long ago comes straight to the point: "God has given you two ears and one mouth that you may listen to him twice as much as you speak to him."

A conversation is not only talking but listening. It is so easy to ignore the obvious. We must be silent and listen to our God speaking to us.

More than that, we must let Jesus Christ speak through us. He will, if only we give him the chance. And when he does, we will gain the strength of the saints who grasped the breadth and the length, the height and the depth of the Lord. Then, knowing the love of Christ, which is beyond all knowledge, we will be filled with the utter fullness of God.

OUR FATHER

Our Father, who art in heaven, hallowed be thy name. Thy kingdom come. Thy will be done on earth, as it is in heaven. Give us this day our daily bread. Forgive us our trespasses, as we forgive those who trespass against us. And lead us not into temptation, but deliver us from evil. Amen.

HAIL, MARY

Hail, Mary, full of grace; the Lord is with thee. Blessed art thou among women and blessed is the fruit of thy womb, Jesus. Holy Mary, Mother of God, pray for us sinners, now, and at the hour of our death. Amen.

GLORY BE

Glory to the Father, and to the Son, and to the Holy Spirit: as it was in the beginning, is now, and will be for ever. Amen.

ACT OF FAITH

My God, I believe in thee, and all that the Church teaches because thou has said it and thy word is true.

ACT OF HOPE

My God, I hope in thee for grace and for glory, because of thy promises, thy mercy, and thy power.

ACT OF CHARITY

My God, because thou art so good, I love thee with all my heart, and for thy sake I love my neighbor as myself.

ACT OF CONTRITION

O my God, because thou art so good, I am very sorry that I have sinned against thee, and I will not sin again.

HAIL, HOLY QUEEN

Hail, holy Queen, mother of mercy, hail, our life, our sweetness and our hope! To you do we cry, poor banished children of Eve, to you do we send up our sighs, mourning and weeping in this valley of tears. Turn, then, most gracious advocate, your eyes of mercy toward us; and after this, our exile, show unto us the blessed fruit of your womb, Jesus. O clement, O loving, O sweet Virgin Mary!

The best prayers are those which come from the heart. But there are times when we find it almost "impossible" to pray; and it is then that we need the help of prayer books and the prayers that we have learned "by heart." We include some prayers that we should learn, and also suggestions for Morning and Evening Prayers.

APOSTLES' CREED

I believe in God, the Father almighty, creator of heaven and earth; and in Jesus Christ, his only Son, our Lord. He was conceived by the power of the Holy Spirit and born of the Virgin Mary, suffered under Pontius Pilate, was crucified, died, and was buried. He descended to the dead; on the third day he arose again; he ascended into heaven, and is seated at the right hand of the Father; he will come again to judge the living and the dead. I believe in the Holy Spirit, the Holy Catholic Church, the communion of saints, the forgiveness of sins, the resurrection of the body, and life everlasting. Amen.

COME, HOLY SPIRIT

Come, Holy Spirit.
Fill the hearts of your faithful and make the fire of your love burn within them.
Send forth your Spirit and there shall be another creation.
And you shall renew the face of the earth.
Let us pray: O God, you have instructed the hearts of the faithful by the light of the Holy Spirit. Grant that through the same Holy Spirit we may be always truly wise, and rejoice in his consolation. Through Jesus Christ our Lord. Amen.

GRACE BEFORE MEALS

Bless us, O Lord, and these your gifts, which we are about to receive from your bounty, through Christ our Lord. Amen.

GRACE AFTER MEALS

We give thanks for all your benefits, almighty God who lives and reigns forever. May the souls of the faithful departed, through the mercy of God, rest in peace. Amen.

PRAYER BEFORE A CRUCIFIX

My good and dearest Jesus, I kneel before you, beseeching and praying with all the ardor of my soul to engrave deep and vivid impressions of faith, hope, and charity upon my heart, with true repentance for my sins, and a very firm resolve to make amends. Meanwhile I ponder over your five wounds, dwelling upon them with deep compassion and grief, and recalling the words that the prophet David long ago put into your mouth, good Jesus, concerning yourself: They have pierced my hands and my feet; they have counted all my bones!

MORNING PRAYERS

In the name of the Father, and of the Son, and of the Holy Spirit. Amen.

O my Jesus, thank you for keeping me safe through the night. Please give me the grace necessary to go through this day with patience and a firm will to do all that is good in your name. I ask you this because I know that I can do nothing without your help. Please, Lord, help me always and make my weakness your strength.

Remember, O most gracious Virgin Mary, that never was it known that anyone who fled to your protection, implored your help or sought your intercession was left unaided. Inspired with this confidence, I fly to you, O virgin of virgins, my Mother. To you I come, before you I stand, sinful and sorrowful. O Mother of the Word Incarnate, despise not my petitions, but in your mercy, hear and answer me. Amen.

EVENING PRAYERS

Jesus Christ, my God, I adore you and thank you for all the graces you have given me this day. I offer you my sleep and all the moments of this night, and I ask you to keep me free from sin. Therefore I place myself in your hands and under the mantle of my Mother, our Lady. May your holy angels surround me and keep me in peace; and may your blessing be upon me. Amen.

(Saint Alphonsus)

Soul of Christ, sanctify me.
Body of Christ, save me.
Blood of Christ, inebriate me.
Water from the side of Christ, wash me.
Passion of Christ, strengthen me.
O good Jesus, hear me.
Never permit me to be separated from you.
From the evil one protect me.
At the hour of death call me.
And bid me come to you that with your saints I may praise you forever. Amen.

Jesus, Mary, and Joseph, I give you my heart and my soul.
Jesus, Mary, and Joseph, stand by me in my last agony.
Jesus, Mary, and Joseph, let me draw my last breath at peace with you.

The most effective prayer is the prayer of the Church's liturgy. For in this prayer we unite ourselves in a special way with the Body of Christ in the worship of the Father and in interceding for the salvation of the world. This we do "not only by celebrating the Eucharist, but also in other ways, especially by praying the divine Office" (*Liturgy,* # 83). The praying of the divine Office is a primary duty of priests; but all are encouraged to pray the Office. It is most suitable, too, for those who are shut-ins.

A hand held before the eyes hides from view even the tallest mountain. In much the same way this earthly life hides from our gaze the boundless splendor and the amazing mysteries contained in this world of ours. If we can take life from before our eyes, as one takes away one's hand, we will see the rich brilliance within the world.

There is a sense in which it is the task of the liturgy of the Church to unite the everyday life of the world and the mystery of God's kingdom which lies below the surface of even the most trivial. We all know what it is like to wake up of a morning and feel that the day ahead, life itself, seems so dull as to obscure the real beauty of the world. Faith, knowledge, and prayer all involve us in the art of seeing below the surface of things. And that is precisely what Jesus Christ enables us to do in the liturgy.

When we use the word *liturgy*, we are usually referring to the official prayer of the Church found in the Mass and other sacraments together with the divine Office. In the Church's teaching, each one of these moments of prayer or liturgical actions is seen as the work of Christ the High Priest and his Body which is the Church. And because they are the work of Christ and his whole Church they are such sacred actions that nothing else that the Church does can compare with the liturgy's effectiveness.

Christ promised that "where two or three meet in my name, I shall be there with them" (Matthew 18:20). All prayer leads us to a closer communion with God and also with one another. Family prayer expresses this union in a special way.

Reading this last statement, some people — especially those with young children — may well wonder about its real truth. The young often complain that the liturgy is boring. And even we in our efforts to combat their protests have to concede that it very often does not fit our mood or hold our interest.

We may feel terribly guilty about talking of the liturgy in terms of boredom and lack of interest. But when we remember what Saint Paul told the Corinthians when writing to them about the Eucharist, we can begin to see some meaning in this conflict which the liturgy so often inspires in us.

"For this is what I received," wrote Paul, "and in turn passed on to you" (I Corinthians 11:23). Paul is underlining the fact that he did not make up the liturgy of the Eucharist; it was *given* by the Lord. That the liturgy is something that is given to us is a very deep truth and, as Father Simon Tugwell, O.P., remarks: "It is a forcible reminder that when we come to God, it is not to force our moods or interests onto him, but to receive his interests and to let him, in a sense, share his moods with us."

The first step in understanding liturgical prayer is to understand it is a gift. It is like a doorway to the life of eternity. In the liturgy Christ comes to us exactly where we are. We should not try to hide behind an event we ourselves have "made up," but let Christ do things his way, take the scales from our eyes, and reveal the true beauty hidden beneath the pots and pans and the everyday round of events.

Our celebration of the liturgy and prayer shared with others helps — and is helped by — our own individual prayer. Jesus told his disciples: "When you pray, go to your private room and, when you have shut your door, pray to your Father who is in that secret place" (Matthew 6:6). The putting aside of such moments for private prayer is within the capacity of even the busiest of people.

Prayer (which includes the celebration of the sacraments) is the only means of uniting ourselves more closely with Christ. There is no other way. And so Christians are obliged to use the various forms of prayer which they find most valuable in helping them to identify with Christ in the worship of his Father.

A particularly helpful way of doing so is in living through the liturgical year in which Christ's life is unfolded and "in some way made present at all times" (*Liturgy*, #102). The liturgical year starts with Advent, which prepares us for Christ's coming at Christmas and for his Second Coming at the end of time. And so Advent helps us to be ready.

The center of the liturgical year is Easter, prepared for by the 40 days of Lent. Lent recalls Baptism and it stresses a penitential spirit. In this way the feast of the Lord's Resurrection may be celebrated by hearts suitably prepared.

During the Sundays of the Year (Ordinary Time) the events of Christ's public ministry are recalled and celebrated so that the Holy Spirit who led Jesus Christ through the course of his earthly life may lead us, in a similar way, through ours.

Travelers usually return home with heavier luggage than they traveled out with. As they journey from city to city, or country to country, the accumulation of souvenirs increases. There is an infinite variety of them; and there is never any shortage of shops and merchants to supply the tourists' needs. Some souvenirs are valuable for their own sake; some are valuable for the memories they conjure up; some are trash.

In this *Catechism*, we have made a journey together in the Christian life. As we come to its conclusion we can look back over our life so far and realize that we have accumulated many facts about the Catholic faith. More importantly, we have been able to put the faith into practice — to enrich it with the experiences of everyday life. But such knowledge of Christ and, indeed, such practice of the faith are no substitutes for the love for Jesus Christ. If, along the way, this *Catechism* has failed to deepen our love, it has been so much trash.

Saint Paul expressed this truth with customary bluntness: "If I have all the eloquence of men or of angels, but speak without love, I am simply a gong booming or a cymbal clashing. If I have the gift of prophecy, understanding all the mysteries there are, and knowing everything, and if I have faith in all its fullness, to move mountains, but without love, then I am nothing at all. If I give away all that I possess, piece by piece, and if I even let them take my body to burn it, but am without love, it will do me no good whatever" (1 Corinthians 13:1-3).

God revealed his love fully to his Son, Jesus Christ. This *Catechism* has attempted to reveal this love as fully as space, time, and the printed word have allowed. Inevitably, we have been unable to include all that would be possible. But in the *Supplement* to the *Catechism* we will cover important areas of the Church's life; such subjects will include the Church in History, the Church at Prayer, and the Law of the Church.

We can never forget, however, that every aspect of the Church's life has one purpose alone: to increase, deepen, and regulate our love of God. And this love of God, like a souvenir, is not only valuable for its own sake, but also for the memories it conjures up. It is as though it produces within us the memories of Christ's life on earth, which we want to reproduce in our own life and in our own individual and unique way.

Monsignor Ronald Knox said that the only luggage we can take to heaven is charity. Let us praise God in this life so that when we return to our heavenly home after life's journey, our luggage will be heavier with the love of God and we may praise him for all eternity.

SUPPLEMENT

NO. 1 THE APOSTOLIC PERIOD

This is the period when the Church of the Apostles, reflecting on the words of the Lord Jesus, expressed her faith in written and spoken form. The writings of some of the apostles make up the New Testament. We include a short glossary of well-known terms associated with the New Testament, which are here listed in alphabetical order:

Apocrypha: Religious books used by both Jews and Christians which were not included in the collection of inspired writings. In the Protestant Church, this term also designates the Old Testament books of Tobit, Judith, I and II Maccabees, Wisdom, Baruch, and Ecclesiastes which are contained in the Catholic Bible. The Protestant Bible follows the Jewish canon; the Catholic Bible follows the Alexandrian Greek translation made by the Jews in the 3rd-2nd centuries B.C.

Apostle: One of the twelve chief disciples appointed by Jesus to be the foundation of his Church. They were: Peter, Andrew, James, John, Philip, Bartholomew, Thomas, Matthew, James the Less, Jude, Simon the Zealot, and Judas, who was replaced by Matthias. The "apostolic succession" means that the college of bishops, with the Bishop of Rome at their head, enjoy direct succession from the apostles.

Canon (meaning *rule*): The term given to the collected books of the Bible recognized by the Church as the inspired Word of God and hence to be taken as the "rule" of faith.

Dead Sea Scrolls: The popular name given to numerous manuscripts discovered on the shores of the Dead Sea by a shepherd boy in 1947. They include most of the Old Testament books and evidence of the life and hopes of a Jewish "monastic" community at Qumran at about the time of Christ. It is thought that John the Baptizer and some of his disciples were members of this community.

Didache (meaning *teaching*): A manuscript of great value because it dates from apostolic times and is evidence of how the liturgy was celebrated in the early Church. It shows that the Mass had the same essential features that it has today.

Evangelist: Originally meant "Preacher of the Good News," but now generally reserved for the authors of the written Gospels: Matthew, Mark, Luke, and John.

Gospel (meaning *god-spel*, that is, *good news*): The Gospel in its written form is often divided between the "Synoptic Gospels" of Matthew, Mark, and Luke, which give a "synopsis" or one view of the life and teaching of Jesus and are clearly dependent upon each other, and the "Gospel of John" which reflects a different tradition in the apostolic Church.

Inspiration: The term given to the "breathing" of the Holy Spirit into a person so that what that person writes is truly the Word of God. "Since everything asserted by the inspired authors or sacred writers must be held to be asserted by the Holy Spirit, it follows that the books of Scripture must be acknowledged as teaching firmly, faithfully, and without error that truth which God wanted put into the sacred writings for the sake of our salvation" (*Revelation*, #11).

Interpretation: Only the Church, under the inspiration of the same Holy Spirit by whose power the sacred books were written, can understand and explain the true meaning of the Scriptures. This means investigating what meaning the sacred writer really intended and what God wanted to reveal by means of the author's words.

Versions of the Bible: The languages in which the Bible was originally written (Hebrew, Aramaic, and Greek) are not generally understood and so need to be translated. Many English language "versions" are approved by the Church. In the United States today *The New American Bible* and the *Jerusalem Bible* versions are the two used in the liturgy.

NO. 2 THE PATRISTIC PERIOD

This is the period (up to about A.D. 800) when the Church reflected on the apostolic tradition to produce outstanding Christian "Fathers" in the faith. These great teachers were often associated with the Councils of the Church to produce a period of profound deepening in the understanding of the faith. We include a short glossary of well-known terms associated with this period, which are here listed in alphabetical order:

Apologist: The name given to one who explains and defends the faith. The first great "apologist" was St. Justin, a layman, who was martyred A.D. 165.

Apostasy: The renouncing of one's Christian faith. Persecution in the early Church resulted in many "apostates" and controversy arose as to how those who wished to return to the faith should

be treated. Some insisted on rebaptism; others refused to pardon altogether. The solution of insisting on suitable penance was taught by Pope St. Stephen in A.D. 255.

Council of the Church: A meeting of all bishops solemnly convened or approved by the pope to regulate matters of doctrine and discipline. After the Council of Jerusalem in A.D. 51 (recorded in Acts 15) there have been 21 such General (or Ecumenical) Councils in the history of the Church, the last being Vatican II in 1962-65. The Orthodox Church recognizes only the first seven Councils — which were particularly important in the growth of the Christian faith.
1. *Nicaea I* (A.D. 325) settled the Arian heresy by affirming that Jesus Christ is "one in substance" with the Father. The "Nicene Creed" proclaimed at Mass has developed from this Council.

2. *Constantinople I* (381) ratified Nicaea I.

3. *Ephesus* (431) affirmed that Jesus Christ is truly God and truly man; and that Mary is the "Mother of God."

4. *Chalcedon* (451) affirmed that in the person of Jesus the two natures are united unconfusedly, unchangeably, indivisibly, and inseparably.

5. *Constantinople II* (553) condemned various heresies.

6. *Constantinople III* (680) affirmed that in Jesus there are "two natural wills and energies, undivided, unseparated, and unmixed. . . ."

7. *Nicaea II* (787) condemned Iconoclasm (a heresy which forbade the use of images of Jesus and the saints).

The decrees of a General Council, having received papal confirmation, bind most solemnly. "What God has spoken through the Council of Nicaea remains forever," said St. Athanasius. These early Councils of the Church were important in explaining, in human terms, the great central mysteries of the Most Blessed Trinity, the divinity of Christ, and the humanity of Christ.

Doctor of the Church: A title of honor given by the Church to outstanding teachers in the faith. There are 30 such Doctors. The women doctors are St. Teresa of Avila and St. Catherine of Sienna.

Father of the Church: A title given to the great Christian writers of the first twelve centuries. Many of them are Doctors of the Church. These include:
St. Athanasius (295-373) who was the "Father of Orthodoxy" and the man most responsible for destroying the Arian heresy (the most dangerous heresy in the Church's history) and for clarifying Catholic belief in the Trinity.
St. Augustine (354-430) who was the most influential of the Fathers and "doctor of grace." In his *Confessions* he wrote: "Thou has made us, O Lord, for thyself, and our heart shall find no rest till it rests in thee."
St. Jerome (342-420) who was the greatest Doctor divinely given to the Church for the understanding of Scripture. He translated the Bible from the original Hebrew into the living Latin of his day. This *Vulgate* (that is, popular) version became the official version of the Church.
St. John Chrysostom (347-407) who was the most prominent Doctor of the Greek Church and "the greatest preacher ever heard in a Christian pulpit."

Father of the Desert: A monk or hermit of the fourth century who lived a life of prayer. The most famous, St. Anthony, laid the foundations of the monastic system.

Tradition: The living teaching of the Church, of which Scripture is the most important part. The teachings of the Fathers of the Church are an important source of the Church's tradition.

NO. 3 THE EASTERN SCHISM

This is the period of developing friction between Christians who recognized the primacy of Rome and Christians who recognized the primacy of Constantinople. The final break came, it is regarded, in 1054; and it endures to this day. We include a short glossary of well-known terms associated with this period, which are here listed in alphabetical order:

Crusades: The series of expeditions, with the aim of recovering the Holy Land from Islam, beginning in 1095 and lasting over two centuries. The crusades helped to strengthen the papacy and also provided a base for a common religious purpose in Western Europe. In time there arose two principal military Orders founded to help pilgrims: the Knights Templar and the Knights Hospitaller (Knights of St. John).

Friar: A member of the mendicant (meaning *begging*) Orders (as opposed to a member of the more ancient monastic Orders). The four Orders of Friars are:
1. *Dominicans:* Founded by St. Dominic in 1216 to fight the Albigensian heresy, which held that Christ was an angel with a phantom body. Dominic realized that the fine education and organizations of the heretics could only be opposed by employing similar techniques.
2. *Franciscans:* Founded by St. Francis of Assisi in 1223 with the ideals of poverty and humility.
3. *Carmelites:* Founded from a group of hermits by St. Simon Stock in 1247.
4. *Augustinians:* Founded from several congregations of hermits, brought together in 1256.

Each of these four Orders has a Second Order (of nuns) and a Third Order (of the laity).

Heresy: The denial of defined doctrine of the Catholic faith (different, therefore, from *schism* — see below). The need to combat heresy has often led to the formulation of revealed doctrine by the Church.

Monk: A member of a monastic Order who takes solemn vows to God and lives under a fixed rule. The monastery is governed by the abbot. In the Eastern Orthodox Church all monks follow the rule of St. Basil drawn up in 356. In the Western Church the principal architect of monasticism was St. Benedict, who drew up his Rule about A.D. 540. The monk's day is taken up with the divine Office (Scripture-related prayers), spiritual reading, and manual work.

Oecumenical (Ecumenical) Patriarch (meaning *universal father*): This is the Patriarch of Constantinople. Since the break with the Bishop of Rome (who has the title "Patriarch of the West"), he has enjoyed honorary primacy in the (Eastern) Orthodox Church. In ordinary use today, the word *ecumenism* has come to mean the attempt to recover the universal unity of Christians.

Orthodox Church: The largest body of Christians after the Catholic Church. Today, it consists of a federation of thirteen members who acknowledge the primacy of the Oecumenical Patriarch. They do not acknowledge the primacy of the Bishop of Rome but "they possess true sacraments, above all — by apostolic succession — the priesthood and the Eucharist, whereby they are still joined to Rome in a very close relationship" (*Ecumenism,* #15). Particular efforts have been made in recent years to heal the schism. Much of the discipline of the Orthodox Church is different from the Roman Church (for example, priests are generally married and Baptism is by total immersion), but such customs would not have to change.

Rite: A form of ritual or worship. Most Catholics in the Western Church follow the Roman or Latin Rite. There are also several Rites in the Eastern Churches: some of these Churches are in communion with Rome; others are not (see *Orthodox Church*). Some of these Eastern Rites are more ancient than the Latin Rite. All Rites enjoy an equal dignity.

Schism: The separation from the unity of the Church. It is not a heresy (see above) but involves the denial of papal supremacy. The Orthodox Church is a schismatic Church. The Western Schism (Great Schism) of 1378-1415 split the Roman Church when rival claimants to the papacy (antipopes) began the process of fragmentation which led into the Reformation period.

Summa Theologiae (or Summa): This was the work of St. Thomas Aquinas. Divided into three sections, it was written in 1266-73 as a handbook for the systematic study of theology, and has served as a basis for such study down to our present day.

NO. 4 THE REFORMATION

This is the period of religious upheaval between the 14th and 17th centuries which gave rise to the growth of Christian Churches separated from communion with the Bishop of Rome and divorced from the traditional teaching of the Church. We include a short glossary of well-known terms associated with this period, which are here listed in alphabetical order:

Anglicanism: The faith and practice of religious bodies in communion with the Archbishop of Canterbury, who enjoys a primacy of honor. These bodies (dating back to Henry VIII and his Act of Supremacy in 1534) are generally found in the British Commonwealth.

Calvinism: A religious body founded by John Calvin as part of the Reformation movement about 1540. It upholds a strong union between Church and State and is noted for its doctrine of predestination.

Counter-Reformation: The term used to summarize the revival of the Catholic Church in response to the Reformation movement — although certain countermeasures against abuses within the Church were already under way in 1517 when Luther began his actions. The movement for reform expressed itself principally in the foundation of new religious Orders and in the convocation of the Council of Trent.

Lutheranism: A religious body founded in the 16th century by Martin Luther. Traditionally, Luther's act of fixing his ninety-five theses to the door of the university church of Wittenburg began the Reformation movement; but the causes and growth of the Reformation are, of course, less capable of simple definition. Lutheranism accepts one order of clergy only and the chief feature of its worship is the sermon.

Missions: The task of spreading the Gospel was the first act of the apostles after Pentecost. In the Reformation period it received fresh impetus with the discovery of "new worlds." In addition to the spreading of the faith to the Americas, the Gospel was carried, principally by the Jesuits, to India, the Far East, Japan, and China.

Society of Jesus (Jesuits): Founded by St. Ignatius Loyola in 1534 "for the greater glory of God," the Jesuits have probably since been the most influential religious Order in the Church. More flexible, but more disciplined, than other Orders it undertook the work of education and missions, the success of the latter personified in the work of St. Francis Xavier, one of St. Ignatius' first companions. Many were martyred. The *Spiritual Exercises* of St. Ignatius remain the foundation of Jesuit spirituality.

Seminary: A college for training priests. The spiritual and intellectual weakness of the parish clergy, which had been a contributory cause of the Reformation, was overcome by the decree of the Council of Trent which ordered the establishing of diocesan seminaries. The seminary remains the principal means of educating future priests.

Trent (ancient name — Tridentum): This is the city where the famous Council was held in 1545-63. It defined Catholic teaching in those areas brought into question by Protestant reformers — especially with regard to justification, the Mass, and the sacraments. Discipline within the Church was strengthened to overcome the efforts of previous laxity. The so-called "Tridentine Mass" dates from 1570. This provided the form of the celebration of Mass in the Latin Rite until 1969 and reflected the need of the Reformation period for care and uniformity in the celebration of the Eucharist.

NO. 5 PERIOD OF SOCIAL UPHEAVAL

This is the period, from the middle of the 17th century to World War I, when profound social and economic upheavals transformed the way of life in Western Europe, Britain, and the U.S.A. from being predominantly agricultural to being predominantly industrial. New concepts of freedom, liberty, and the organization of society brought fresh challenges for the Church in the world of thought, industry, and politics. We include a short glossary of well-known terms associated with this period, which are here listed in alphabetical order:

Atheism (meaning *without God*): Term applied to the belief that the existence of a personal God must be denied. In the middle of the 19th century Karl Marx proposed atheism as "the cornerstone of a brave new edifice of humanity transformed by total revolution."

Encyclical: A formal pastoral letter written by the pope on doctrinal, moral, or disciplinary matters. Such a letter is known by the Latin phrase with which it opens. Among the many encyclicals of this period, the most important was *On the Condition of Labor,* the pastoral

letter of Pope Leo XIII, in 1891, which came to be known as "The Charter of the Working Man."

Modernism: The accelerated developments of this period in the fields of science, philosophy, and historical criticism, together with changed social conditions, led to renewed study within the Church of the challenge of preaching the Gospel in a manner suitable for the times. The Modernist movement, as it came to be called, was initially encouraged by Leo XIII but was condemned for certain errors by Pius X in the decree of 1907. The term "modernism" came to be used by some in the Catholic Church in a derogatory way. This is hardly to our credit as it grew out of a genuine desire to preach the Gospel in a relevant manner.

Papal States: Those territories controlled by the Church from 756 to 1870 when they were annexed by Italian troops. In 1929 the Lateran Treaty recognized the Vatican City as a sovereign state, guaranteeing the political independence of the See of Peter.

Protestant Churches: In the United States there are more than 250 Protestant Church bodies. Among the most prominent are the following denominations: Baptist, Methodist, Lutheran, Presbyterian, Protestant Episcopal, the United Church of Christ, the Christian Church (Disciples of Christ), Holiness Sects.

Religious Orders and Congregations: These institutes were founded during these centuries to face the problems of a changing world. They are societies whose members (called religious because they observe the three vows of religion — obedience, chastity, and poverty), live a community kind of life according to rules and constitutions approved by Church authority. Priests, Brothers, and Sisters dedicate their lives to special fields: contemplative prayer, education, home and foreign missions, retreats, and various social works.

Vatican Council I: This Council (1869-1870), held under Pius IX, concerned itself chiefly with the condemnation of materialism and pantheism, the relation of faith to reason, and the way God reveals himself through the words of Scripture. The Council is best known for its definition on the universal jurisdictional primacy of the pope and his infallibility when pronouncing solemn dogmatic definitions. The work of the Council was left unfinished when Piedmontese troops, intent on forming a unified Italy, occupied Rome.

NO. 6 THE MODERN WORLD

This is the period embracing the tragedy of two World Wars and unparalleled scientific advances which led up to the Second Vatican Council (1962-1965) — the most authoritative general teaching of the 20th-century Church. We include a short glossary of well-known terms associated with this period, which are here listed in alphabetical order:

Apologetics: A term used frequently in the first half of this century to describe those studies concerned with the defense of the Church's teaching and credentials against her critics. Contemporary apologetics (more frequently referred to as "fundamental theology") is concerned more with believers' search for the reasons that make their faith

intellectually honest, morally responsible, and authentic. At the same time, it invites all people to seek the meaning of their life in that same faith.

Code of Canon Law: In 1904 Pius X announced his intention of codifying almost 2,000 years of Church Law in a single volume. This mammoth task was completed by a team under the legendary Cardinal Gasparri in just thirteen years, was published in 1917, and came into effect on Pentecost Sunday 1918.

Communism: A theory of politics based on the assertion of Karl Marx and Friedrich Engels that all human life is determined by economic facts. Under Lenin, the successful leader of the October revolution in Russia, the theory gave rise to the powerful Communist party system and State which has proved in many parts of the world to be a formidable opponent of the Church.

Subsidiarity: A term which first appeared in the encyclical *Forty Years Later* authored by Pius XI in 1931. He asserted as a fundamental Christian principle that "all social activity should be to the help of individual members of the social body but never to destroy or absorb them."

Vatican Council II: The 21st Ecumenical Council of the Church was convoked by John XXIII in November 1962 and closed by Pope Paul VI in December 1965. The Council enacted four constitutions, nine decrees, and three declarations, setting the seal on three of the chief movements of this century in the Church — the biblical movement, the liturgical renewal, the lay apostolate.
Constitutions: These were:
The *Dogmatic Constitution on the Church* which sets forth the Church's understanding of her own nature, taking her cue from the opening words, "Christ is the light of all nations." Its first chapter, "The Mystery of the Church," presents the vision of a Church which is at once divine and human, embracing all people of good will who make up the subject of the second chapter, "The People of God." Dogmatically, the most important chapter is the third in which the bishops of the Church are seen to constitute a "college" collectively responsible for the work of the Church. Other chapters deal with the laity, the call of all to holiness, and the role of the Blessed Virgin Mary.
The *Dogmatic Constitution on Divine Revelation* which sets forth the Church's teaching on how God reveals himself to humankind. The transmission of this revelation is recorded in written form in Scripture; its transmission by word of mouth is part of the tradition of the Church. Both Scripture and tradition spring from the one source.

The *Constitution on the Sacred Liturgy* which sets forth the Church's teaching on worship as the heart of her life. It instructed that "texts and rites should be drawn up so that they express more clearly the holy things which they signify. Christian people, as far as possible, should be able to understand them with ease and to take part in them fully, actively, and as befits a community" (#21).
The *Pastoral Constitution on the Church Today* which sets forth the Church's attempt to "speak to all men in order to shed light on the mystery of man and to cooperate in finding the solution to the outstanding problems of our time" (#10). It is addressed to "the whole of humanity."
Decrees: The nine decrees covered the following subjects: The Pastoral Office of Bishops, Ecumenism, the Oriental Catholic Churches, the Ministry and Life of Priests, Education for the Priesthood, the Renewal of the Religious Life, the Missionary Activity of the Church, The Apostolate of the Laity, and the Media of Social Communication.
Declarations: The Council issued three formal declarations on religious freedom, the Church's attitude to non-Christians, and Christian education.

O. 1 THE MASS

n the sacred liturgy the power of the
oly Spirit acts upon us through sacra-
ental signs. Actions, symbols, words,
othes, music, buildings are the living
aith and flesh of the worship performed
y Jesus Christ the priest and his Body
he Church. We include a short glossary
f well-known terms associated with the
Mass, which are here listed in alphabeti-
al order:

ltar: The table on which the sacrifice of
he Mass is offered is treated with the
tmost respect by the Church (she
noints, incenses, kisses it) as a sign of
hrist. Embedded in the altar is a stone
ontaining some relics of the saints, and
nto the stone are cut five crosses
ecalling our Lord's five wounds.

ltar Linen: Since the 8th century the
ltar has been covered by one or several
vhite linen cloths as a precaution
gainst spillage from the chalice. The
ollowing linens are also used at the
ltar:
orporal: A square of fine linen spread
n the altar on which are placed the
halice and paten. It is so called since it
olds the body (Latin, *corpus*) of Christ.
Vhen not in use it is held in the *Burse*.
urificator: A strip of white linen used to
lean the chalice.
all: A small square of stiff linen used to
over the chalice.

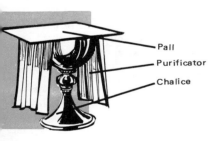

Pall
Purificator
Chalice

andles: Symbols of Christ, the "Light
f the World." There are four kinds of
andles used in the Church:
) The *Paschal Candle,* placed in the
   sanctuary from the Easter Vigil to
   Ascension Day.
) *Altar Candles,* used during the Mass.
) *Blessed Candles,* used in solemn
   processions, for example, the Easter
   Vigil.
) *Votive Candles,* burnt before images
   of the saints in petition or thanksgiving.

halice: The most ancient of all the
acred vessels is this cup in which the

wine at Mass is consecrated. It is
mentioned in all four scriptural accounts
of the institution of the Eucharist and
differs little from the drinking vessels
normally in use at the time.

Ciborium: A vessel shaped like the
chalice but with a cover, in which the
consecrated hosts are reserved in the
tabernacle and from which the minister
distributes Holy Communion.

Concelebration: The celebration of the
Eucharist by two or more ministers.

Liturgical Colors: The Church has long
appreciated that the proper use of color
can help the community to appreciate
the mood and spirit of a particular
season or feast day. Accordingly, Innocent III (1198-1216) introduced a color
sequence which is still followed today.
White is worn on feasts of our Lord, our
Lady, confessors and virgins, and on
Sundays during the Easter Season. *Red*
is used at Pentecost and the feasts of
apostles and martyrs. *Violet* is used
during Advent, Lent, vigils of certain
feasts, and funerals. *Rose* is often used
on the third Sunday in Advent and on the
fourth Sunday in Lent. The use of *black*
for funerals now varies from place to
place.

Paten: A shallow plate usually of gold or
silver on which the large host rests
before and after consecration.

Amice
Stole
Alb
Cincture

Vestments: The Mass vestments origi-
nate from the ordinary secular dress of
the Roman Empire in the first centuries

of Christianity. The principal vestments
are:
Amice: A square or oblong piece of linen
to which two long tapes are attached at
the upper corners. Worn like a scarf, it is
symbolic of "the helmet of salvation."
Alb (Latin, *albus* — meaning white): A
long, white, linen garment; a symbol of
purity, it is a survival of the ancient tunic
or undergarment. It is held neatly in
place by the:
Cincture: A long cord worn around the
waist.
Stole: A long, thin band of silk worn
around the neck and shoulders, sugges-
tive of the "yoke of the Lord." It is worn
by the priest in the solemn celebration of
all the sacraments (the deacon wearing
it over one shoulder only).
Chasuble: The outermost garment worn
by the priest. It is a circular piece of cloth
cut in the center for the head. Over the
centuries the shape has been altered to
allow greater freedom of movement. The
color of the stole and chasuble varies
with the liturgical season (see *Liturgical
Colors*).
In addition to these vestments, the
bishop wears the:
Miter: Originally a soft, low cap, it has
developed into a high, stiff hat consist-
ing of two stiffened pieces of cloth
joined by soft material.
Pectoral Cross (Latin, *pectus* — meaning breast): A cross worn suspended
from the neck by a chain or cord.
Ring: Worn on the right hand as a
symbol that he is wedded to his diocese.

NO. 2 THE SACRAMENTS

The purpose of the sacraments is to
sanctify those who celebrate them, to
build up the Body of Christ, to give
worship to God. As outward signs of
inward grace, they also instruct us, and
by words and objects nourish,
strengthen, and express our faith. We
include a short glossary of well-known
terms associated with the administration
of the sacraments, which are here listed
in alphabetical order:

Baptistery: The room or place set aside
for the celebration of Baptism. The early
Christians referred to it as the *fons*
(pool), and today the central feature — a
large stone vessel containing the baptismal water — is known as the *font*.

Baptismal Name: In the first few centuries of the Church the custom of
changing one's name at Baptism to
express some Christian idea in a name
such as Irene (peace) became common.
The 14th century saw the custom become law and the Ritual of the Council of
Trent (1624) instructed parish priests to
persuade parents to give their children
saints' names and not "strange, laugh-
able, obscene, or idolatrous ones."

Confessional: Place set aside in a church for the celebration of the sacrament of Reconciliation. The traditional confessional, introduced by St. Charles Borromeo in 16th-century Milan, was a simple, boxlike construction with a metal grille between the priest and penitent. Present-day confessionals are variations of the original design, but the introduction of "face-to-face" confession has led to the construction of reconciliation rooms of varying designs around the world.

Homily: The term used to describe the form of preaching that takes place during a liturgical celebration. The homily, based on the Scripture readings and liturgical theme, is regarded as an integral part of the Mass and must always be given at Sunday and feast day Masses. It is also regarded as an essential part of some of the other sacraments.

Oil: Oil is the symbol of strength and has been used from the most ancient times for the consecration of kings. There are three kinds of oil used in the celebration of the sacraments:

A container of holy oil. The initial indicates the type of oil.

Oil of Chrism: Used in the sacraments of Baptism, Confirmation, and Orders. These sacraments give the candidate a share in the priestly "character" of Christ (the title "Christ" meaning "the anointed one"). It is also used in the consecration of churches.
Oil of Catechumens: Used in the celebration of Baptism and so called be-cause it was originally used for anointing those who were about to be baptized.
Oil of the Sick: Used in the sacrament of Anointing of the Sick. Each year, the three holy oils are blessed by the bishop on the morning of Holy Thursday at the Chrism Mass attended by priests representing the entire diocese.

Rubric: The directive in a liturgical book describing how prayers are to be said and ceremonies performed. The Roman Ritual followed the practice of printing such an instruction in red (Latin, *ruber*) — hence the term rubric.

Sponsor (godparent): One who undertakes to foster the faith of a candidate in the sacraments of Baptism and Confirmation. Such a one should be a mature person, living the faith and able to fulfill a spiritual role for the candidate.

Vernacular: The term used to describe the native language of a country as opposed to a language of foreign origin. Following Vatican II the vernacular came to be universally used in the administration of the sacraments.

NO. 3 DEVOTIONS

The heart of the Church's life is the celebration of the liturgy and, above all, the Eucharist. Every liturgical celebration, because it is an action of Christ the priest and of his Body the Church, is a sacred action surpassing all others. But there are many "acts of devotion" which, although not part of the Church's sacred liturgy, are recognized by the Church as especially valuable forms of prayer. We include some of the more important of these devotions.

Benediction of the Blessed Sacrament: The primary purpose for reserving the Eucharist outside the celebration of Mass is for the distribution of Communion to the sick. But from the custom of blessing the sick after Communion arose the practice of blessing the people by making the sign of the cross over them with the sacred Host contained in a monstrance (see illustration) or, in simple form, in a ciborium.

Benediction must always be accompanied by at least a brief period of exposition which allows time for "readings of the word of God, hymns, prayers, and sufficient time for silent prayer." This exposition is intended to acknowledge Christ's marvelous presence in the sacrament and invites us to the spiritual union with him that is completed in sacramental Communion at Mass.

For exposition of the Blessed Sacrament in the monstrance, four to six candles are lighted and incense is used. Incense is a symbol of prayer: a sign of the sweet-smelling offering which rises from a heart glowing with the love of God.

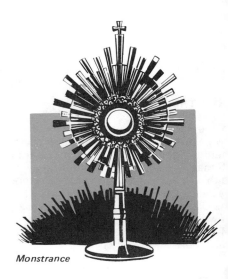

Monstrance

Forty Hours Devotion: Arising from the custom of watching in prayer before the Altar of Repose on Holy Thursday, this devotion is a period of extended exposition of the Blessed Sacrament held with greater solemnity. The Church recommends that solemn exposition of the Blessed Sacrament should take place once a year in every parish, even though the period of exposition is not strictly continuous.

Rosary: A form of prayer which leads us to contemplate the mysteries of salvation. The mysteries are divided into three groups of five as follows:
The Joyful Mysteries
1. The Annunciation
2. The Visitation
3. The Nativity
4. The Presentation
5. The Finding in the Temple
The Sorrowful Mysteries
1. The Agony in the Garden
2. The Scourging
3. The Crowning with Thorns
4. The Carrying of the Cross
5. The Crucifixion
The Glorious Mysteries
1. The Resurrection
2. The Ascension
3. The Coming of the Holy Spirit
4. The Assumption of the Virgin Mary
5. The Coronation of the Virgin Mary

To help the mind and heart attend to the contemplation of these central events of our faith, each mystery is accompanied by the vocal praying of one Our Father, ten Hail Marys, and one Glory Be. Thus "the succession of Hail Marys constitutes the warp on which is woven the contemplation of the mysteries" (Pope Paul VI).

The Church strongly recommends the praying of the family rosary. Although circumstances make such family prayer difficult, it is a characteristic of the Christian not to give in to circumstances but to overcome them. To help the praying of the rosary, beads are generally used.

Angelus: This prayer, said at morning, noon, and evening, provides an opportunity to pause in prayer and to contemplate the coming of God into our midst. It consists in the praying of three Hail Marys together with versicle and response and prayer as follows:

1. The Angel of the Lord declared unto Mary. *And she conceived of the Holy Spirit.* Hail Mary, etc.
2. Behold the handmaid of the Lord. *May it be done unto me according to thy Word.* Hail Mary, etc.
3. And the Word was made flesh. *And dwelt amongst us.* Hail Mary, etc.
V. Pray for us, O holy Mother of God.
R. That we may be made worthy of the promises of Christ.

Let us pray: Pour forth, we beseech you, O Lord, your grace into our hearts, that we to whom the Incarnation of Christ, your Son, was made known by the message of an angel, may by his Passion and Cross be brought to the glory of his Resurrection, through Christ our Lord. Amen.

Stations of the Cross: From the earliest times, pilgrims to Jerusalem have retraced our Lord's steps in his Passion. At those points (stations) where special events took place they stopped to meditate. From this custom sprang the construction of imitations of the "Via Dolorosa" in Jerusalem which are affixed to the inside walls of most parish churches. Each "station" is marked by a wooden cross to which a picture is often added. There are fourteen stations:

1. Jesus is condemned to death.
2. Jesus takes up his Cross.
3. Jesus falls the first time.
4. Jesus meets his Mother.
5. Simon of Cyrene helps Jesus.
6. Veronica wipes the face of Jesus.
7. Jesus falls the second time.
8. Jesus speaks to the women of Jerusalem.
9. Jesus falls the third time.
10. Jesus is stripped of his garments.
11. Jesus is nailed to the Cross.
12. Jesus dies on the Cross.
13. Jesus is taken from the Cross.
14. Jesus is laid in the tomb.

Novenas, Missions, Renewals, Retreats: Every church has a crucifix on, above, or near the altar, and most churches have pictures and statues that remind us of Christ and his holy ones. From time to time special days of prayer are held in their honor. Novenas are nine days of prayer in preparation for a feast day honoring Christ under one of his special titles, Mary under one of her various titles, or one of God's saints. Missions and renewals are of varying lengths. They are preached by missionary priests, for example, Redemptorists, and they are times of prayer, conversion, and renewal of Christian life. Retreats are times of silent meditation on our destiny in life, together with appropriate sermons and time for consultation with a priest.

NO. 3 THE CHURCH BUILDING

From the time that Jesus Christ instructed his disciples to make preparations to eat the Passover in "the large upper room furnished with couches" (Luke 22:12), his followers have set aside a special place for the celebration of the Eucharist. This church building is a sign of the Church, the Body of Christ, united in the worship of the Father. We include a short glossary of terms associated with the church building, which are here listed in alphabetical order:

Bell: At one time the bell tower was an essential feature of every church building and was used to summon the faithful to divine service. In the Mass, a handbell is used to call attention to the principal parts of the Mass.

Chair: The principal "chair" in the church is the celebrant's chair from which he directs the prayer of the assembly. It is normally placed in the center of the sanctuary facing the people.

Consecration Crosses: When a church is solemnly consecrated, the bishop anoints the walls in twelve different places with the oil of chrism. Each place anointed in this way is marked with a cross and a candleholder is placed beneath this cross. The consecration sets the seal on the church, so that it can never afterwards be put to some profane use. The church building is a sign of the Church — with the Twelve Apostles for its foundations, Jesus himself for its cornerstone. By custom, a church is also dedicated either to one of the divine Persons, to the Blessed Virgin, or to a saint; and the church thus becomes known by that title.

Images: In accord with ancient tradition, images of Christ, Mary, and the saints are venerated in churches. The principal image is the cross which must be easily seen by the congregation and be placed either on the altar or near it.

According to legend, the original "image" of Christ was that made by a woman who wiped Jesus' face with a towel as he struggled under the burden of his Cross to Calvary. On the cloth was imprinted Christ's face, which became known as *vera icon,* which translated from the Latin and Greek means "true picture." Over the years, *vera icon* was corrupted to "Veronica," which became the name of the woman who performed this act of charity. The legend is commemorated in the sixth station of the stations of the cross.

Our Lady of Perpetual Help

Lectern: The lectern (or ambo) is the place from which the Scripture readings and the homily are proclaimed.

Sanctuary: This is the area of the church (generally raised slightly) in which the ministers carry out their functions in the celebration of the liturgy. Placed within the sanctuary area is the altar, which should be in a central position which draws the attention of the whole congregation.

Tabernacle: The Blessed Sacrament used to be reserved in a room near the sanctuary or in a cupboard in the wall of the sanctuary. In more recent times it has been reserved in a tabernacle, which must be solid and unbreakable and positioned in the church in a place that is prominent and properly decorated. At all times a sanctuary lamp is to be kept burning as a sign that the Blessed Sacrament is reserved in the church.

NO. 1 NECESSITY OF LAW

"A community without law," wrote Pope Paul VI, "far from being, or ever being able to be, in the world, the community of charity, has never been and will never be anything else than a community of the arbitrary."

Canon Law is the name given to the body of rules (from the Greek *kanon,* a rule) by which the Church provides guidelines for the faithful to help them come closer to Jesus Christ and his Body, the Church.

The laws of the Church are found in a book known as the *Code of Canon Law.* Since its publication in 1917, however, many of the Canons in the Code are now obsolete or have been altered to suit changed times and circumstances. A new and up-to-date Code is now in preparation. The Oriental Churches have their own Code of Law which is also under revision at the present time.

Those who exercise authority in the Church make the laws. The pope, as successor of St. Peter, is obviously an important legislator and issues new laws in documents known as Papal Constitutions or Apostolic Letters. Ecumenical Councils, together with the pope, can draw up new laws in the form of decrees of the Council. Roman Congregations (the Curia), which link the various facets of the Church's life, can also issue laws binding on the faithful. Conferences of bishops may promulgate laws binding on all who live in their territory. A local diocese, acting through the bishop or a local synod, can also draw up legislation on certain matters binding all the faithful living in the territory of the diocese.

The following are bound by the law of the Church: those who are baptized; those who have reached the age of reason; those who have attained seven years of age. A Catholic is only bound by a Church law if it is in force in the place where he or she is resident.

Church law helps us to grasp what under normal circumstances is indispensable for the common good of the Church and for our own individual salvation. But it is important to remember that Church law sets before us the *minimum* demands. The law puts before us in a codified form the minimum efforts of love required to establish order, justice, stability, and freedom. But Christian love will desire to go far beyond the lower limits set by law and will constantly search for what God

requires of us over and above the codified law.

From time to time the Church has listed certain specific duties of Catholics. Among those expected of Catholic Christians today in the United States are the following:

1. To keep holy the day of the Lord's Resurrection; to worship God by participating in Mass every Sunday and holy day of obligation; to avoid those activities that would hinder renewal of soul and body on the Sabbath (for example, needless work and business activities, unnecessary shopping, and so forth).
Note: The precept of Sunday or holy day Mass is satisfied where the local bishop has determined that the celebration may be anticipated the preceding evening. In the United States, the holy days of obligation are the following: New Year's Day — January 1; Ascension Thursday — 40 days after Easter; Mary's Assumption into heaven — August 15; All Saints Day — November 1; Mary's Immaculate Conception — December 8; Christmas — December 25.
2. To lead a sacramental life; to receive Holy Communion frequently and the sacrament of Reconciliation regularly — minimally, to receive the sacrament of Reconciliation at least once a year (annual confession is obligatory only if serious sin is involved); minimally also, to receive Holy Communion at least once a year, between the First Sunday of Lent and Trinity Sunday. (For regulations concerning Communion fast see p. S11.)
3. To study Catholic teaching in preparation for the sacrament of Confirmation, to be confirmed, and then to continue to study and advance the cause of Christ.
4. To observe the marriage laws of the Church; to give religious training, by example and word, to one's children; to use parish schools and catechetical programs.
5. To strengthen and support the Church — one's own parish community and parish priests, the worldwide Church and the pope.
6. To do penance, including abstaining from meat and fasting from food on the appointed days.
Note: In the U.S. the obligation to fast (by eating only one full meal and two lighter meals in the course of the day) and abstain (from flesh meat) holds on Ash Wednesday and Good Friday. All Fridays of Lent are days of abstinence. The law of fasting obliges all Catholics except the sick between the ages of 21 and 59. The law of abstinence obliges all Catholics over the age of 14. At other times (for example, on Fridays), Catholics must

practice self-denial either by continuing to abstain or by any other act of self-denial (for example, by attending Mass, making the stations, saying the rosary, or visiting someone sick or lonely) in union with the death of our Savior on the Cross.
7. To join in the missionary spirit and apostolate of the Church.

NO. 2 RIGHTS AND RESPONSIBILITIES

In recent years the Catholic Church has become more aware of her role as protector and guardian of the rights of the individual and of humankind as a whole. In this section we examine both the rights of the individual in the Church and in the world at large.

The basis of human rights has always fascinated the philosophers and proved to be something of a battleground in the history of human thought.

One group, like the Fascists in recent years, have identified *power* as the source of human rights; they assert that people's rights are those which they can impose on others. Another idea is that the rights of the individual are determined by what the *majority* in society hold them to be. Alternatively, some hold that the *state* alone can decide what a person's rights are. Such a theory is the foundation of all totalitarian states. Christianity, however, always points to the mysteries of creation, incarnation, and the redemption as the source of human rights. As Christians we believe that we share in the life of God himself, and so it follows that our rights, dignity, and responsibilities transcend any one culture, philosophy, or political system. They are part of the mystery of God and as such can never really be fully defined or listed.

Nevertheless there are some basic human rights which belong to us by virtue of our humanity. This notion of fundamental human rights was described by Pope John XXIII in his encyclical *Peace on Earth* (1963) as one of the major issues of our world today.

n the light of the Church's teaching over the last century, the following can be regarded as the most important human rights: the right to life and to housing worthy of human dignity; the right to social security; the right to respect, free inquiry, free expression, and the right to education; the right to full participation in government; the right to free exercise of one's religion and to a free choice of a state in life; the right to a fair share of material goods and full economic rights; the right to free association and assembly; the right to emigrate and immigrate; the right to active sharing in public life and to the legal protection of personal rights, even against the state.

Obviously, every Catholic has certain rights in the Church. It is very important to remember that the divinely established community of the Church is made up of human beings who, because of sin, can sometimes ignore justice and fail to act in charity. We have constantly to remind ourselves that Baptism confers upon the Christian full membership in the Church and all the rights to secure a full share in the life of the community.

Our understanding of these rights and responsibilities in the Church grows as we deepen our common understanding of the mysteries of God. An exhaustive list is for that reason impossible. The American Catholic bishops, however, have recently drawn up the following list: the right to hear the Word of God and share in the sacramental and liturgical life of the Church; freedom to exercise the apostolate and share in the Church's mission; freedom to speak, to be listened to, and to receive objective information on the pastoral needs and affairs of the Church; the right to education, the right to freedom of inquiry and expression in the sacred sciences; freedom to gather and associate together in the Church; the right to protect one's reputation and one's person, to activity in accord with the upright norm of one's conscience, to the protection of privacy; the right not to be deprived arbitrarily of any right or office in the Church.

Recent popes and numerous hierarchies around the world have challenged Catholics to show themselves as protectors of human rights and to speak in defense of those who have been deprived of them. The Church is also a prophet of human rights in that Christians must try to deepen their awareness in a fast changing world of the new responsibilities and rights which change brings. The Church must in every way protect both the rights of the individual and the rights of the community as a whole, whether it be Church or State.

NO. 3 MINISTRIES

"For the nurturing and constant growth of the People of God, Christ the Lord instituted in the Church a variety of ministries, which work for the good of the whole body" (*Constitution on the Church,* #18). In this section we take a closer look at how each person in the Church is called to exercise a particular ministry in the Church.

The word ministry is derived from the Latin word meaning "to render service." It has recently been used in the Church to describe the different ways in which Catholics can exercise functions within the community of the Church. Up until fairly recently the word has been used in Catholic circles almost exclusively of the ordained and hierarchical ministries. The use of the word in a wider context than the activity of priests and bishops reflects a deepening vision in the Church of the service exercised by all in the name of Christ.

In a very real sense there is only one ministry — the ministry of Jesus Christ. It is Jesus Christ who reaches out to serve people through the members of his Body, the Church. To help our understanding of the mystery, however, we speak of three different types of ministry.

Ministries undertaken by baptized Catholics refer to any activity which is undertaken without a formal commission from the Church. One can list here the work of nurses, teachers, social workers. But we must recognize that this type of ministry is not limited to the caring professions. What of those who work in their local parish or go about their everyday work in a spirit of Christian dedication? Obviously, too, the corporal and spiritual works of mercy are types of ministry: *to feed the hungry, give drink to the thirsty, clothe the naked, visit the imprisoned, shelter the homeless, visit the sick, and bury the dead,* as well as *to admonish the sinner, instruct the ignorant, counsel the doubtful, comfort the sorrowful, bear wrongs patiently, forgive all injuries, and pray for the living and the dead.* The

second type of ministry, the instituted ministries, refers to officially recognized forms of service in the Church, such as lector, catechist, and acolyte. The third type, the ordained ministries, refers to the diaconate, priesthood, and episcopate. These ministries are exercised by those who have received the sacrament of Holy Orders.

All forms of ministry, if they are to be true and genuine, must be exercised in the context of the *Church's activity.* If teaching, preaching, and other forms of ministry take place outside the context of the community of those who believe, they run the danger of becoming personal ventures with little real relation to the building up of the kingdom of God. For this reason the Church has always regulated and organized the various forms of ministry.

All ministry has as its ultimate aim the preaching and building up of the kingdom of God. Each baptized person is called to do this. However, different tasks, some officially recognized and others unheralded, are undertaken by individuals to build up the community of believers. They are gifts, Saint Paul tells us, that build up the Body of Christ. Through them we become one in faith and in the knowledge of God's Son, thus forming that perfect man who is Christ come to full stature (see Ephesians 4:11-13). We should search in prayer for the particular ministry that Jesus Christ is calling us to in the Church. Perhaps we are being called by God to the ordained ministry or the religious life. Only in prayer can we discover what God is asking of us, and only in the Church can we truly contribute to the building of the kingdom.

NO. 4 THE SACRAMENT OF BAPTISM

This section supplements Lessons 27-30 of the *Catechism.* The ordinary ministers of Baptism are bishops, priests, and deacons. But in danger of death any member of the faithful (or even any person who has the requisite intention) should baptize, preferably in the presence of a witness or witnesses. Later, a child who survives should be taken to the parish church to be received solemnly into the Catholic community.

Baptism is celebrated by the minister pouring water over the head of the one being baptized and saying at the same time: "I baptize you in the name of the Father, and of the Son, and of the Holy Spirit."

At infant Baptism the parents accept the responsibility of training the child in the practice of the faith and of bringing the child up to keep God's commandments, as Christ taught us, by loving God and our neighbor. This obligation is indicated clearly in the solemn celebration of Baptism, during which the parents publicly ask that their child be baptized; they sign their child with the sign of the cross after the celebrant; they renounce Satan and make their profession of faith; they hold the lighted candle; and they are blessed with the special prayers for mothers and fathers. If one of the parents cannot make the profession of faith (for example, he or she is not Catholic), such a one may keep silent.

In the Baptism of infants the godparents' role is secondary. If necessary, they should be ready to help in the spiritual education of their godchild. The godparent should be: a) sufficiently mature; b) already initiated as a Christian (by Baptism, Confirmation, and the Eucharist); c) a member of the Catholic Church. (A baptized person of a non-Catholic Church may act as a sponsor provided that the other sponsor is a Catholic.)

If the child is in danger of death, he or she should be baptized immediately. Otherwise, the Baptism should take place within the first weeks after birth. Arrangements for Baptism should be made with the parish priest before the birth of the child. For the Baptism of children whose parents are not yet ready to undertake responsibility for the Christian upbringing of the child, it is the parish priest who sets the time.

In 1978 the Church reintroduced the "catechumenate" for adults wishing to be baptized into the Catholic Church. The "catechumen" is prepared for Baptism over a suitable period of time, but he or she enters into a more intense period of preparation at the beginning of Lent in a ceremony of "election" or "enrollment" of names. Then, at Easter, the catechumen receives Baptism, followed by Confirmation and the Eucharist.

A baptized Christian of another denomination is received into full communion with the Catholic Church after suitable doctrinal and spiritual preparation. The baptized Christian is received by the bishop or a priest appointed by him. In the prescribed ceremony he or she makes a profession of faith. The sacrament of Baptism may not be repeated; and only if there is reasonable doubt as to the fact or validity of earlier Baptism is it permissible to confer Baptism conditionally.

NO. 5 THE SACRAMENT OF CONFIRMATION

Through the sacrament of Confirmation, those who have been born anew in Baptism receive the gift of the Holy Spirit. Having received the character of this sacrament, they are "bound more intimately to the Church" and "they are more strictly obliged to spread and defend the faith both by word and by deed as true witnesses of Christ." In this section, which supplements Lessons 31-32 of the *Catechism,* we look at those laws which relate to the sacrament of Confirmation.

The ordinary minister of Confirmation is a bishop. But all priests who baptize an adult or a mature child, or receive them into full communion with the Catholic Church, may administer the sacrament. In addition, if there is danger of death, any priest may confirm. It is the minister's responsibility to ensure that the reception of Confirmation is properly recorded. This is done by notifying the parish where the confirmed person was baptized; there it is entered into the baptismal register. (When a baptized Catholic is married, the record of marriage is similarly entered into the register of Baptisms.)

It is the responsibility of all Christians to prepare the baptized for Confirmation. The initiation of children into the full sacramental life of the Church is, for the most part, the responsibility and concern of Christian parents. The sponsor, too, has a definite obligation to help the candidate to fulfill his or her baptismal promises faithfully under the influence of the Holy Spirit. It is desirable that the godparent at Baptism, if available, also be the sponsor at Confirmation. However, another suitable person may act as sponsor, and even the parents themselves may present their children for Confirmation.

In the early Church, Baptism and Confirmation were usually celebrated at the same time, for most people entering the Church were adults. Today, it remains true that the age for Confirmation is the same as for Baptism. In the Latin

Church, however, the confirming of those baptized in infancy is postponed. "For pastoral reasons ... episcopal conferences may choose an age which seems more appropriate, so that the sacrament is conferred at a more mature age" (*Revised Rite of Confirmation,* #11). The requirements for Confirmation are a state of grace, proper instruction, and the ability to renew one's baptismal promises.

The effect of Confirmation is to draw us more deeply into the life of the Church. This living of the Christian life is expressed in the fulfillment of the twofold love of God and neighbor and in the fulfillment of the commandments of the Church.

NO. 6 THE EUCHARIST

We read in the Acts of the Apostles that the early Christian community "remained faithful to the teaching of the apostles, to the brotherhood, to the breaking of bread, and to the prayers" (Acts 2:42). Since the Eucharist, the Mass, is the focal point of the whole of our Christian life, the Church has been careful to lay down certain regulations to ensure that we also remain faithful "to the breaking of the bread." In this section we examine some of the Church's discipline more closely. This section supplements Lessons 33-38 of the *Catechism.*

The Roman Missal reads: "Every authentic celebration of the Eucharist is directed by the bishop, either in person or through the priests who are his helpers." It is the function of the ordained ministers, therefore, to *direct* our celebration of the Eucharist. But since this mystery stands at the center of the Church's life, all must take their own part according to their place and function in the Church. There is a variety of what are called special ministries which are exercised at any celebration of Mass, such as readers, servers, musicians. The ordained deacon, in particular, exercises a very special ministry in the celebration of the Eucharist.

At the Last Supper Jesus Christ specified bread and wine as the elements of this sacred meal. The Church has therefore been very concerned that the elements used in the celebration of the Mass really are bread and wine. To prevent any confusion in this matter the Church has laid down certain regulations. The bread used must be made of wheat and recent enough to rule out any possibility of corruption. Although leavened bread is valid, the Church prescribes that in the Latin rite unleavened bread be used. In this matter the priest must follow the rules of his own rite. The Church is also strict with regard to the type of wine used. For validity it must be grape wine. The priest must also mix a little water with the wine, in accordance with the Oriental custom that Jesus no doubt followed.

Since the Lateran Council of 1215 every Catholic who has reached the age of discretion has been required to receive Holy Communion at least once a year "at Easter or thereabouts." This obligation, together with the obligation of celebrating the sacrament of Reconciliation, if one has committed mortal sin, make up the "Easter duties" which, in the U.S.A., must be undertaken between the first Sunday of Lent and Trinity Sunday. The precept of Easter Communion lays down the minimum requirement, and frequent Communion (at least once a week) is actively encouraged by the Church. Recent changes in law regarding the Eucharist fast have encouraged frequent Communion.

In 1964 a decree from Rome laid down the following rules which apply at whatever time of day Holy Communion is received: 1. Water may be taken at any time. 2. Solid food may be taken up to one hour before Holy Communion. 3. Alcoholic drinks in moderation and other drinks, with or without food, may be taken up to one hour before Holy Communion. 4. The sick (not necessarily confined to bed) may also take genuine medicines, solid or liquid, as well as nonalcoholic drinks at any time before Holy Communion. A further decree in 1973 laid down that the sick (and those caring for them who wish to receive Communion with them but cannot fast for an hour without inconvenience) may take alcoholic drinks or food up to approximately a quarter of an hour before receiving Holy Communion.

A decree of St. Pius X in 1910 stated that children should be admitted to Communion as soon as they can distinguish between the Bread of the Eucharist and ordinary bread, and they should be instructed at least "in the mysteries of the faith necessary for salvation" according to their capabilities. While the Church is careful that children do not approach the altar unprepared, there has been a constant tradition of not limiting reception to mere knowledge alone. The phrase "according to their capabilities" protects the right of those who may be suffering from some handicap but possess the gift of faith. Such children need very special care and instruction, but a full and perfect knowledge of Christian doctrine is not required of them.

NO. 7 THE SACRAMENT OF ORDERS

We have already seen that within the Church there are "ministries undertaken by the baptized," "instituted ministries," and "ordained ministries" (*The Law of the Church,* p. S9). Now we look at some of the important laws regarding the "ordained ministries" of deacon, priest, and bishop who share in a particular way in Christ's ministry through the sacrament of Holy Orders. This section implements Lesson 39-41 in the *Catechism.*

The minister of the sacrament of Orders is a bishop. He alone can ordain a priest or deacon. For the ordination of a bishop, the principal consecrator must be assisted by at least two other consecrating bishops and his ordination must be approved by the Bishop of Rome.

The ordained minister states his intention to serve the People of God at the time of ordination in response to questions asked by the ordaining minister. In addition, the ordained minister in the Latin Church undertakes to live a life of

celibacy. Celibacy is not demanded by the very nature of the priesthood, but it is a sign of that new humanity which Christ raises up in the world through his Spirit: a humanity "not born of blood, nor of the will of flesh, nor of the will of man, but of God" (John 1:13). Also, it enables the minister to hold fast to Christ with undivided heart and, through him, to the service of God and people.

All ordained ministers in the Latin Church are bound to celibacy except for deacons who are married at the time of ordination. However, in accordance with the traditional discipline of the Church, a married deacon who has lost his wife cannot enter a new marriage.

How do the faithful support the ordained minister? Just as the ordained minister serves the needs of the People of God, so it is a responsibility resting on every Christian to "strengthen and support the Church." This support, in the first instance, is given by serving the Church in love of God and neighbor. It must be expressed, too, by assisting ordained ministers both spiritually and financially. Writing on the subject of priestly virtue, Pope Paul VI explained that "all the faithful should encourage their fathers in Christ to overcome the difficulties of every sort which they meet as they fulfill their duties . . . and by their devoted and warm friendship they can be of great assistance to the Church's ministers" (*Priestly Celibacy*).

One manner of support is the Mass stipend which is the customary offering given to a priest which obliges the priest to apply the fruits of the Mass for the special intention of the donor. The custom has led to abuses in the past, but continues to serve as a reminder of the obligation of supporting the ordained ministers. The stipend also serves as a monetary equivalent of the early offerings of bread and wine. Customary stole fees (for the conducting of Baptisms, marriages, and funerals) are also offered to the minister, but the poor are not expected to make any offering if unable to do so. The minister of a sacrament may not request, directly or indirectly, any compensation for his ministry, no matter what the reason or the occasion. Nonetheless, the minister may expect to be materially supported by those whom he serves.

NO. 8 THE SACRAMENT OF MATRIMONY

We need a deeper understanding of the Church's marriage law — a law which seeks to protect the wonderful relationship of marriage and apply the teachings of Jesus to this human reality which he has raised to the dignity of a sacrament. Supplementing Lessons 42-47 of the *Catechism,* the following will answer some common queries regarding the marriage laws of the Church.

The Church has tried particularly hard in recent years to deepen her understanding of the notion of fidelity in marriage by reflecting on the Scriptures and tradition. Scripture scholars are in general agreement that on the question of fidelity the teaching of Jesus is clear and without qualification. "So then, what God has united, man must not divide. . . . The man who divorces his wife and marries another is guilty of adultery against her" (Mark 10:2-13).

It is divine law that there are two essential properties or characteristics of any marriage — unity and indissolubility. In plain English the term *unity* means that one man has one wife and vice versa. *Indissolubility* is understood by the Church to mean that every valid Christian marriage is permanent and cannot be dissolved.

In 1 Corinthians 7:10-16 St. Paul answers several questions regarding marriage. He asserts the teaching of Jesus on the indissolubility of marriage which he stresses "is not from me but from the Lord." He then goes on to say that in the case of an unbaptized couple, if one of the partners becomes a Christian, and "the unbelieving partner does not consent, they may separate; in these circumstances, the brother or sister is not tied." This teaching, which we refer to as the *Pauline Privilege,* is, he says, "from me and not from the Lord." We can restate Paul's teaching today as follows: two unbaptized marry; one partner becomes a Christian; and the other partner cannot accept this and so departs. If inquiries show that departure really was because of the deserted party's new faith, then by reason of the Pauline Privilege, the bishop can permit remarriage.

It is also the teaching of the Church that a valid marriage between two Christians is indissoluble because it is sacramental. But what about the case of a marriage between a Christian and a non-Christian? Since this marriage is not sacramental in the strict sense, the Church recognizes the power of the Vicar of Christ, the pope, to dissolve such a marriage. This power we call the *Petrine Privilege.* There must, of course, be very serious reasons before such a power is invoked. One example would be if a party of the first marriage which ended in civil divorce now wants to become a Catholic and remarry. Investigations will always be made to prove that the first marriage was nonsacramental. The Petrine Privilege is often referred to as a case of dissolution "in favor of the faith."

In order to preserve the sanctity of marriage, the Church insists that a marriage must be solemnized before a Catholic priest and two witnesses. (This law may be dispensed for a serious reason and under strictly determined conditions.) It may well happen that a couple, for one reason or another, fail to have their marriage solemnized in this way. The term *"convalidation"* refers to the later validation and blessing of the marriage by the Church. The restoration of such a couple to full communion with the Church is always an extremely happy event although, for obvious reasons, it is often done privately.

An *annulment* is an official declaration by the Church that a particular marriage in fact and in law never existed. Annulment cases are handled by special Marriage Tribunals who work under the authority and guidance of the bishops. After intensive investigation into every aspect of the marriage in question, the Marriage Tribunal makes a decision which takes into due account the jurisprudence of the Church.

The one concern of the Church regarding the sacrament of Matrimony is that the couple are enabled to deepen their love relationship. A *Church separation* — the permission to live apart from each other for a time — recognizes the complexities of such a relationship. The saying "Absence makes the heart grow fonder" expresses in a superficial way the sort of pastoral reasons why such a separation may be permitted. The Church recognizes that every relationship is a process of growth and, reflecting on the mystery of the Cross, understands well that true growth can never be achieved by pretending tensions do not exist or by running away from them. This is the solution of the "divorce mentality." Separation, on the other hand, recognizes present difficulties but looks to the future with hope.

"Mixed" marriage is a phrase often used by Catholics of a marriage where one of the partners is not a Catholic. It is not an ideal phrase, as it does not take into account the considerable difference between marriages of Catholics with baptized non-Catholic Christians and those marriages which take place between Catholics and unbaptized persons. Some people prefer to talk of the marriage between a Catholic and a Christian of another Church as an "interfaith marriage."

The Church has always recognized that a "mixed" marriage can prove to be a real obstacle to the unity of the couple. Pope Paul VI (in 1970) stressed this point in his Apostolic Letter on the subject when he reminded Catholics that such a marriage is "by its nature an obstacle to full spiritual communion of the married partners." For this reason the Church requires of both partners to the marriage a very careful preparation. A real ecumenical understanding is vital, and priests are advised to work closely with ministers of other faiths in preparing couples for "mixed" marriages. The Church particularly asks the Catholic party to a marriage to recognize the duty of preserving his or her own faith, and to remember that it is never permitted to expose oneself to the danger of losing it. This is divine law and is absolute.

The Catholic party in a "mixed" marriage is obliged not only to remain steadfast in the faith but also to do all possible to see to it that the children are baptized and brought up in the Catholic Church. The promise to do so must be made orally or in writing (in accord with the regulations of the diocese where the marriage is celebrated) by the Catholic partner before permission will be given by the bishop for the marriage to proceed in the Church. The Church recognizes, of course, that as much respect must be paid to the parental rights of the party who is not Catholic as to those of the Catholic whose conscience must have regard to the teaching of the Church. It is essential, therefore, that a couple contemplating marriage should agree before the wedding about the Baptism and education of any children they might have. The party who is not Catholic is *not* required to make any undertaking in this matter, formally or informally. But it is only right and prudent that he or she be informed prior to the marriage of the obligations of conscience laid by divine law on his or her Catholic partner.

NO. 9 THE SACRAMENT OF RECONCILIATION

It is Catholic belief that because of human weakness the Lord instituted a special sacrament for the pardon of sins after Baptism. Supplementing Lessons 8-68 of the *Catechism,* we look at some of the regulations for the celebration of this sacrament.

Following a decree of the Second Vatican Council that "the rite and formulas of Penance are to be revised in such a way that they may more clearly express the nature and effects of this sacrament," a new ritual for Penance (now called Reconciliation) was issued by Pope Paul VI in 1973. There has, of course, been considerable change in the way this sacrament has been celebrated over the centuries, but the Church has always retained its essential elements.

The essential element which must be present in the sinner who has been moved by the Holy Spirit to approach the sacrament is conversion to God with his or her whole heart. There must be present in him or her an inner conversion of heart (contrition), the marks of which are true sorrow for the sins committed and a firm intention to lead a

new life. This inner conversion of heart brought about by the Holy Spirit is expressed in the following ways: confession made to the Church, due satisfaction, and amendment of life.

It has been the constant teaching of the Church that God grants pardon for sin in and through his Church by the ministry of bishops and priests. In exercise of this ministry of reconciliation, however, the Church requires more of the priest than the power of ordination. A priest who "hears confessions" must have received the faculty or jurisdiction to do so from the proper authorities. But any priest, even though he does not have the required jurisdiction, may validly and lawfully absolve a penitent who is in danger of death.

The revised rite for the reconciliation of sinners — prepared by the Congregation of Divine Worship in 1973 — lays down three ways of celebrating this sacrament. The rite for reconciliation of individual penitents; of several penitents with individual confession and absolution; of several penitents with general confession and absolution. Individual confession and absolution is regarded as the ordinary way for the faithful to reconcile themselves with God and the Church. It is recognized, nevertheless, that "particular, occasional circumstances" may permit or require the use of general absolution for a group of penitents who have not made a previous individual confession. The use of this rite, however, is restricted by Church law and its application is left to the bishop of the diocese and his national episcopal conference.

We have already learned how to examine our consciences for confession in accord with the Beatitudes (see Lesson 62). Here is a further examination based on God's Commandments:

We have certain obligations which flow from our love of God and from our love of neighbor. In preparation for confession, each person should ask himself or herself these or similar questions:
1. Do I sincerely want to enter into a deeper friendship with God through the sacrament of Reconciliation?
2. Did I forget to mention, or deliberately conceal, any grave sins in past confessions?
3. Did I perform the penance given me in my last confession? Did I make reparation for any injury to others? Have I tried to practice my resolution to lead a better life in accord with the Gospel?
Then the examination proceeds by reviewing the duties toward God, toward others, and toward self.

Duties toward God
1. Do I really love God above all, or am I more concerned about the things of this world? Am I guilty of false worship like superstition, spiritism, or other occult practices? Do I know my faith and strive to profess it both in private and public? Do I pray and offer my difficulties, my joys, and my sorrows to God?
2. Do I show proper reverence for God's name by avoiding blasphemy, false swearing, and vain use of his name?
3. Do I observe Sundays and holy days of obligation by participating, with attention and devotion, in the Mass? Have I fulfilled the precept of annual confession and of Communion during the Easter season?

Duties toward others
1. Respecting the dignity of others, do I really love them with the love of Christ? Do I respect all lawfully exercised authority in the home, in civil society, and in the Church? If I have a position of responsibility, do I exercise my authority for the good of others, in a spirit of service?
2. Do I show reverence for human life in all my actions? Do I really believe that only God has absolute mastery over my life and the lives of others? Am I really convinced that murder of the innocent — whether young or old — is morally wrong? What are my attitudes toward abortion, mercy killing, unjust wars? Am I shortening my life by excessive use of tobacco, drink, or other drugs? Am I guilty of extreme anger?
3. Have I, perhaps subconsciously, begun to adopt the values and practices of a sexually permissive society — specifically in the areas of premarital sex, extramarital sex, adultery, homosexual behavior, or other acts of impurity alone or with others? Do I avoid the occasions of sin in these areas?
4. What is my attitude toward justice? Does my greed for material things cause me to cheat, steal, refuse to pay just debts, or deliberately damage the good names or property of others? If I am an employer, do I pay a just and living wage? If I am an employee, do I give a full day's work for each day's pay? Have I made restitution (balanced the scales of justice) for any injustice I have committed in the past? On the positive side, have I shared what I have with others, especially those in real need?
5. Do I realize the importance of being honest — with myself, with God, with others? By lying, have I seriously harmed the reputation of another? Have I revealed, without necessity, a hidden truth about another? If I have damaged the reputation of another,

have I tried all possible means to restore his or her good name?

Duties toward self
1. Do I constantly strive to form my conscience properly through personal prayer, participation in the sacramental life, and loyal adherence to the teaching authority of the Church?
2. Am I humble and patient in the face of my own imperfections, trusting that God will give me the strength to conquer them? Do I resist undue pride in my accomplishments? Am I slothful in resisting temptations? Am I envious of others' success?
3. Am I convinced that the holiness to which God calls me demands self-discipline and self-sacrifice?

The sacramental seal of confession (treated in Lesson 67) refers to the strict obligation laid upon the priest to treat as absolutely secret everything revealed by the penitent in the sacrament with a view to obtaining absolution. Canon 899 states: "The sacramental seal is inviolable. Consequently, the confessor must exercise all diligent care not to betray the penitent in any degree by word, sign, or in any other way or for any cause whatsoever." A priest who violates the seal today incurs an excommunication most specially reserved to the Holy See.

The precept to confess at least once a year is a reminder to receive the sacrament of Reconciliation on a regular basis. If no grave sin has been committed in that time, confession is not necessary. However, frequent confession is of great value; it makes us more deeply conformed to Christ and more submissive to the voice of the Spirit.

Reconciliation is a personal encounter with Jesus Christ represented by the priest in the confessional or reconciliation room. The penitent admits to God that he or she has sinned, makes an act of sorrow, accepts a penance (prayers, acts of self-denial, or works of service to others), and resolves to do better in the future.

After prayer and an examination of conscience to find out what sins you have committed, you enter the confessional.
Father greets you kindly.
You respond and then make and say the sign of the cross.
Father invites you to have confidence in God.
You answer: "Amen."
Father may read or recite some short selection from the Bible.
You introduce yourself (not by name) and tell how long it has been since your last confession. You then tell your sins. (Each mortal sin must be confessed as well as possible.) It is useful to mention your most frequent and most troublesome venial sins.
Father will give you any necessary advice and answer your questions. Then he will impose a penance.
You now make an act of sorrow, using these or similar words:
O my God, I am heartily sorry for having offended you. And I detest all my sins, because of your just punishments, but most of all because they offend you, my God, who are all good and deserving of all my love. I firmly resolve, with the help of your grace, to sin no more and to avoid the near occasions of sin.
Father then places his hands on your head (or extends his right hand toward you) and prays these words of forgiveness:
God, the Father of mercies, through the death and Resurrection of his Son has reconciled the world to himself and sent the Holy Spirit among us for the forgiveness of sins; through the ministry of the Church may God give you pardon and peace, and I absolve you from your sins in the name of the Father, and of the Son, and of the Holy Spirit.
Father then says, "Give thanks to the Lord, for he is good."
You answer, "His mercy endures forever."
Father then dismisses you in these or similar words, "The Lord has freed you from your sins. Go in peace."

NO. 10 THE SACRAMENT OF ANOINTING

In its Introduction to the Rite of Anointing of the Sick, the Church reminds us that this sacrament prolongs the concern which the Lord himself showed for the bodily and spiritual welfare of the sick. Some of the legislation concerning

this sacrament was changed in 1974 and we now include the more importan of these laws relating to Anointing These supplement Lessons 69-72 of the *Catechism.*

The minister of the Anointing of the Sick is a bishop or priest. Viaticum (Holy Communion received in danger o death) may be given by a deacon o another minister who has been ap pointed by the bishop to distribute the Eucharist to the faithful.

All those who help the sick share in the loving ministry of that Christ who wa born to overcome the evil of suffering The family and friends of the sick have a special share in this ministry of comfort If the sickness grows worse, they have the responsibility to inform the pries and by their kind words prudently to dispose the sick person for the reception of the sacraments at the proper time.

The Church regulates the celebration o the sacrament in the following way:
1. The Letter of James states that the anointing should be given to the sick to raise them up and save them. Ther should be special care and concern tha those who are dangerously ill due to sickness or old age receive this sacra ment. (A prudent or probable judgmen about the seriousness of the sickness i sufficient; in such a case there is n reason for scruples, but if necessary doctor may be consulted.)
2. The sacrament may be repeated if th sick person recovers after anointing o if, during the same illness, the dange becomes more serious.
3. A sick person should be anointe before surgery whenever a dangerou illness is the reason for the surgery.
4. Old people may be anointed if the are in weak condition although n dangerous illness is present.
5. Sick children may be anointed if the have sufficient use of reason to b comforted by this sacrament.
6. In public and private instruction, th faithful should be encouraged to ask fo the anointing and, as soon as the time fo the anointing comes, to receive it wit complete faith and devotion, not misus ing this sacrament by putting it off. A who care for the sick should be taugh the meaning and purpose of anointing
7. Anointing may be conferred upo sick people who have lost conscious ness or lost the use of reason, if, a Christian believers, they would hav asked for it were they in control of thei faculties.
8. When a priest has been called t attend a person who is already dead, h should pray for the dead person, askin that God forgive his or her sins an graciously receive him or her into hi kingdom. The priest is not to administe the sacrament of Anointing. But if th

priest is doubtful whether the sick person is dead, he may administer the sacrament conditionally.

The immediate preparation for the celebration of this sacrament consists in providing a small table, covered with a white cloth, on which there should be a crucifix and two lighted candles. As the priest will probably also bring Holy Communion, a small bowl of water should be provided for him to wash his fingers. The family should leave the room if the sick person wishes to confess; but after confession, they should return to join in the prayers.

The remote preparation for the sacrament is prayer, and the sick should be encouraged to pray when they are alone or with their families, friends, or those who care for them. Priests should also be ready to pray with them.

NO. 11 ECUMENISM

The Church's laws reflect her deepest concerns; they express, in human language, her preoccupation for finding the most effective means of preaching the Gospel. Mindful of the Lord's prayer on the night before he died that his followers "may all be one," the Church has, where possible, regulated her life to achieve this aim. We now look at some recent changes in legislation which reflect the Church's concern for ecumenism.

The Decree on Ecumenism of Vatican II began with the words: "Promoting the restoration of unity among all Christians is one of the chief concerns of the Second Sacred Ecumenical Synod of the Vatican." It continued: "Discord among Christians openly contradicts the will of Christ, provides a stumbling block to the world, and inflicts damage on the most holy cause of proclaiming the good news to every creature." Ecumenism is the name given to the Church's "chief concern" to remove the "scandal" of disunity among Christians.

To restore unity among Christians, changes have been made in Church legislation. Several changes have already been mentioned in this *Catechism* (for example, laws regulating "mixed" marriages; laws regulating the reception of baptized Christians into full communion with the Catholic Church). The principal areas of change in legislation relate to common prayer and worship, common study, and cooperation in the field of social and pastoral action. All these changes are founded on the recognition of the life of faith held in common among all Christians and, indeed, the further recognition of the God-given dignity and aspirations held in common by Christians and non-Christians.

As to the principal changes regulating common prayer and worship, the Church distinguishes between "prayer offered in common" and "sharing in liturgical worship." The former (ecumenical or interfaith services) which consist of an assembly for listening to the Scriptures and for prayer are encouraged by the Church as "a very effective means of winning the grace of unity." Such prayer is especially suitable for common concerns, such as Church unity, peace in the world, public mourning. It is often appropriate that ministers of different denominations unite in leading the prayer. However, because "sharing in liturgical worship" ought to express a unity which already exists, such sharing "cannot be applied indiscriminately as a means to the re-union of Christians" (*Ecumenism, #8*). Catholics are permitted to attend the liturgical worship of other denominations for such reasons of family unity, friendship, and courtesy and may join in responses, provided they are not at variance with the Catholic faith; but they may not receive Communion or actively exercise a ministry in such worship.

DOCTRINAL INDEX

(Numbers refer to Lesson; S plus numbers refer to Supplement)